WE LIVE IN A

THEATER OF LIES

Misinformation divides us—with purpose.
How to protect ourselves, and why we must.

TED GRIFFITH

 FriesenPress

One Printers Way
Altona, MB R0G 0B0
Canada

www.friesenpress.com

ISBN
978-1-03-919209-6 (Hardcover)
978-1-03-919208-9 (Paperback)
978-1-03-919210-2 (eBook)

1. PHILOSOPHY, SOCIAL

Distributed to the trade by The Ingram Book Company

For Henry, Oliver, and Nathan

Follow your ABCs: Always Be Curious.

PRAISE FOR
THEATER OF LIES

"Author Ted Griffith expertly portrays the world as a literal *Theater of Lies* populated by villains who not only arise from the stage as producers of lies and misinformation, but also from the audience. These audience members believe the propagandists' lies and repeat them to others. Worse, some members of the audience possess an irresistible need to become part of the actual play's production, which can have deadly results as it did on January 6th, 2021. But fortunately, Griffith perceives a fourth group, the heroes who also emerge from the audience. The heroes are the ones brave enough to not only question the beliefs of the other three groups of actors but also their own beliefs. The real strength of the book is that Griffith explains how we can nurture these heroes, grow their numbers and provide them the tools necessary to defeat these lies and misinformation that threaten society's very existence."

- Tom Johnson, Amon G. Carter Centennial Professor, School of Journalism and Media, University of Texas at Austin.

"Griffith artfully untangles the strings of deception and lies which are twisting media, society, and democracy into a macabre dance of manufactured division. Trust me. You won't believe your eyes."

- Eric Meerkamper, Co-Founder, Centre for Social Innovation

"Ted Griffith is a truth warrior. In *Theater of Lies*, he raises important ideas about how all of us, everywhere, have been drawn into a world where, more and more, facts take a back seat to falsehoods. Relying on his deep and wide experience as a professional communicator, he traces how we have descended into this mirror-world, offering insights into how we can learn to escape and recover. His book is a significant milestone in the slow struggle to rebuild a society where truth still matters."

- David Israelson, writer and journalist

TABLE OF CONTENTS

ACT THREE: HOW WE CAN GET OUT (ME, YOU, AND EVERYONE)

"To live inside a lie is to become a tool is to become the tool of someone else."[1]

– MIKHAIL BAKHTIN, TWENTIETH-CENTURY
RUSSIAN PHILOSOPHER AND LITERARY CRITIC.

....

PREFACE:

WHY I WROTE THIS BOOK.

I grew up in a twentieth-century world threatened by nuclear Armageddon. In the twenty-first century, the new threat is less costly, more efficient, and used by an exponentially larger number of aggressors than the globe's small club of nuclear-armed states. The threat today is lies and misinformation and their ability to weaponize people rather than plutonium.

Of the close to 6.8 million people in the world who have died from COVID-19,[2] how many died because they believed the lies and misinformation of others (forgoing vaccinations, masks, and relying on vitamins and the social media prevention/cure of the moment)?

This much I know: 229,000 people died after the United States dropped two nuclear warheads on Japan[3] (Nagasaki and Hiroshima, August 6 and 9, 1945). That's almost exactly equal to the number of people in the United States who died of COVID-19 between April 19, 2021, and the end of that year.

That April date is a benchmark for misinformation, as it is the day when vaccines became available to all Americans.[4] Every person in the United States was able to be vaccinated, at no cost, if they so chose.

At the time, Francis Collins, National Institute of Health Director (a US institution), said, "Deaths continue . . . most of them unvaccinated, most of the unvaccinated because somebody somewhere fed them information that was categorically wrong and dangerous."[5] Collins was reflecting the data that worldwide, the death rate of vaccinated people was five times lower than that of those who were unvaccinated.[6]

Our belief in lies and misinformation is killing us. So much so that a Pulitzer Prize-winning journalist from Britain, James Ball (and author of *The Other Pandemic: How QAnon Contaminated the World*), has called for misinformation to be treated as a public health issue rather than solely one of media literacy .[7]

This book was born of both frustration and curiosity. Writing it was, at times, like digging a hole with one shovel while the worldwide producers of lies kept refilling it with a backhoe. Finishing it has been an act of hope: that I can add something positive to a world that seems determined to tear itself apart. Lies, misinformation, and the tribalism they've fostered are spreading like an infectious disease. Each of us, both targets and carriers.

During my forty-year career as a communications adviser to governments, corporations, non-profits, and individuals, I had never experienced a time when so many people and organizations were not only lying but were also repeating the lies of others. I understood the reason for lies in general, each born of enlightened self-interest. But I could not understand why so many of us believed these lies, so much so that we allowed them to influence what we put in our bodies (or didn't), how we voted, and perhaps most importantly, how we felt about other people (including friends, family, and foreigners).

In my once-peaceful home country of Canada, thousands of people blocked the nation's capital for weeks (protesting vaccination rules and perceptions of government overreach). In the United States, state governments are banning the books children can read in libraries while doing little to stop anyone from bringing guns into the schools where these libraries are housed. Without evidence, people identifying as transgender, as a group, are being called groomers of children for sexual abuse. Hate crimes—attacks on people because of their race, gender, sexual preference, or religion—are increasing worldwide, each committed with a raised fist of righteousness.

I came to place where I had a desperate need to understand what was driving so many of us to not only believe so many of the liars *but also act upon these beliefs*. Perhaps you've felt the same. As a professional communicator (my profession being persuasion)—I had a driving need to go past my head scratching (and sometimes, head banging) and learn more about the *whys of lies* and how we might be able to limit their ability to manipulate good people to act badly—even against their own interests.

I was finding it was like we were all moths drawn not only to the bright light of lies, misinformation, and hyperbole, but in some cases with flames so hot, they have burned us.

Lies have made so many of us cynical. And that, I have found is one of the bedrock goals of those who create lies the world over. If the producers, as I refer to them, cannot persuade you to believe their messages, they are just as happy to foster enough cynicism to keep you from taking any actions against them. In terms of elections, that means staying home rather than going out to the ballot box. In business, it means purchasing their product or service anyway, because you need it.

For this book, I dove deep into research. I reviewed everything I could about lies and the dozens of other masking words we employ to describe them—misinformation, disinformation, propaganda, falsehood, fiction, hyperbole, and, as my bar-worthy companions would call them out, complete and utter bollocks.

But soon into the process, I discovered it was not enough to find out everything I could about lies. They'd become so ubiquitous; I became compelled to find pathways to how we can better function in a world where truths and lies had become indistinguishable.

What I also found was most people were using one and only one tool to determine the difference; that is, what they *already* believed. The audiences for the most successful liars had become like dogs chasing their tails, cats chasing after laser lights, and the producers of lies were wondering how far they could push the misinformation envelope.

Were we just lazy? Did we just not care? Had the course of our daily lives beaten all the curiosity out of us?

I could not live my life thinking everyone who didn't believe what I believed was fundamentally wrong. They were not bad people, but if some of them knew what I thought about issues of race, gender, or politics, they would not only disagree with me—they'd stop being my friends, ostracize me from my family, and even hate me. I have clients fighting against infrastructure projects being forced into their communities, many of whom have neighbors who support their cause but refuse to speak out. Why? Fear of drawing the ire of those supporting these projects. Fear of being accosted at the grocery store or coffee shops.

Our misinformed opinions and actions have divided us, creating a San Andreas-like series of fault lines through multiple societies around the world. The producers of lies keep pressing upon these cracks, their misinformation a wedge that steadily expands these dangerous fissures—with no thought to the cost of their actions other than their own gain.

Theater of Lies hopes to answer three questions. One, how did we become such a willing audience for the liars? Two, what damage have they already done and can they be expected to cause in the future? And finally, what can we do as individuals, organizations, and societies to defend ourselves? Because to live without hope is not to live at all.

I am not concerned with lies of no consequence (as in, "you look nice in that hat," etc.). My concern is about lies that have been purposefully weaponized to shape the way we think, act, and learn. If we don't act to mitigate their influence, our children will not enjoy the freedoms of thought and action we once enjoyed and are now losing. We will become a world of fools chasing the next charlatans and their contemporary of versions of snake oil. Democracy as we know it may cease to exist.

Writing about lies is like attempting a shot-by-shot commentary of a war in real time. Even with its failings (discussed in Act 2, Chapter 2), this is the role of traditional media. The goal of this book is to help readers identify new and repeated lies in their own real time, appreciate the consequences of how these lies can rot the social infrastructure of our society to the point it may crumble, and understand what we as individuals and societies can do (and must) to protect the rights and freedoms we take for granted being ripped from our lives as easily as a well-worn bandage.

As an unintended consequence of this work, I have also learned more about the art and science of persuasion. As, if lies and misinformation have become so influential in the process of forming our opinions, there must be more influences on how we think than just the facts (or lies) presented to us - and there is.

The expertise I bring to this issue is solely that of a professional communicator. I know the power of words, images, timing, and people to influence opinion. The producers of lies, as you'd expect, know this, too. But their goals are self-serving. They have missions. As individuals and as societies, we must not allow ourselves—unknowingly and without permission—to become cogs in their machines.

We owe this to our children and theirs.

TED GRIFFITH

"A lie is more comfortable than doubt, more useful than love, more lasting than truth."[8]

– GABRIEL GARCÍA MÁRQUEZ, COLOMBIAN NOVELIST.

....

INTRODUCTION:

WELCOME TO THE THEATER OF LIES

As he drove to Washington, DC, Edgar Welch recorded a video message to his daughters. They were at home in Salisbury, North Carolina, a bucolic small town with a history of patriotism and colonial pride, its founding pre-dating the War of Independence. Welch told his daughters his goal was to protect them. "I can't let you grow up in a world that's so corrupt by evil without at least standing up for you, for other children just like you."[9] In the car with him, Welch had a pair of 8-inch hunting knives, a revolver, an AR-15 assault rifle, and a kit filled with ammunition.

Hours later, the twenty-eight-year-old man took those weapons into a pizza parlor in the Friendship Heights neighborhood of Northwest Washington, where he fired the rifle multiple times. He was convinced that leading figures in the United States Democratic Party, notably former US President Bill and his wife, presidential candidate Hillary Clinton, were participating in a worldwide pedophilia and child prostitution cult based out of the Comet Ping Pong restaurant.

According to the arrest warrant, Welch said he "had read online that the restaurant was harboring child sex slaves and that he wanted to see for himself if they were there." He said he was "armed to help rescue them."[10]

On December 4, 2016, Edgar Welch rose from his seat in what I call the Theater of Lies and walked on to its stage. The lies he'd heard moved him so powerfully he wanted to no longer be only a member of the audience but one of the Theater's actors.

Welcome to the Theater of Lies. Here, purpose-driven lies and misinformation are produced, staged, and presented. But rather than for your entertainment (often included at no additional charge), this theater's purpose is to manipulate your mind and influence your behavior, all of which benefit its producers rather than you. Its operations are global, local, and virtual. Its only walls are in your mind; itself a very powerful place (and, easily fooled).

Oxford Professor of Philosophy Nick Bostrom postulated we are all living in a computer simulation—the product of someone else's mind[11] harnessed to a computer with unimaginable processing power. That was in 2003. Since then, his theory has been disputed, promoted, and supported by such celebrity thinkers as Elon Musk (of Tesla, Twitter [now, X], and mission-to-Mars fame) and Neil deGrasse Tyson, science commentator and the director of Hayden Planetarium.

This book doesn't enter that debate because the Theater of Lies isn't a theory. It's real. It's just that we've been living in it so long, we no longer see it. Think of yourself as Jim Carrey in the 1998 science fiction film *The Truman Show*. Without his knowledge, his whole life from birth was staged for him and televised for decades to the world. In our case, messages from the real world are staged for us, with many of those messages false, misleading and/or hyperbolic—each produced to influence our thoughts and actions.

The theater is not a single stage. It is a multiplex with multiple screens and stages, hosting messages from an equally large and diverse number of producers. Unlike the multiverse (a universe for every possible action), our theater is a metaphor. For, as I will demonstrate, the tools used to persuade us of the veracity of the lies and misinformation these producers create and distribute are much the same as the creative tools used in theatrical productions from the early Greeks to modern stages of film and television.

The operation is not a conspiracy. There are no mastermind meetings held across time zones in dark rooms or internet cafes. But they share the same techniques of spectacle, drama, comedy, and raising stakes to draw you into your seat and keep you there.

This book will examine the storytelling process of defining villains and heroes, establishing barriers that seem insurmountable, constantly raising stakes—and how the producers of lies and misinformation have repurposed these tactics, with great success, to manipulate our beliefs.

For simplicity, in the often-binary process of presenting information (this too I will discuss), I often refer to the sum of these producers—political, business, and bureaucratic—as "they." The "we" I refer to are us, the audience, resting comfortably in our seats as the multiplex of productions parade around us. It is a constant presence, as if our lives were lived in a summer theater festival that never ends.

But this theater has become so large, so insidious, and so powerful that believing its fictions has become far easier than any journey to discover truth. Propaganda has become the fast food of information: easily available, deliciously packaged, and satisfying, but devoid of any nutritional value. Its purpose? That emotional hit of confirmation bias and addictive quality of wanting more hits more often.

At one time, this art was the sole practice of kings and clergy. But today, our Theater of Lies has expanded to a group that is much wider and larger, and with a depth of tools available that the monarchs and church leaders of the past would envy. That group is made up of four principal players, each with a unique role.

First, we have the propagandists; they produce the lies and distribute them. This includes government leaders (some), business leaders (some), media leaders (again, some), and their cadres of workers whose livelihoods depend upon their belief in the fictions of their masters.

Second, we have those in the audience, believing the lies of the propagandists and often repeating them to others. The actions of the first don't work without the participation of the second.

The third player in our Theater of Lies is a new role: those whose initiation begins in the audience. They are the Edgar Welches of the world. For them, the propagandists' lies have become so engaging that they morph into an irresistible need to become part of actual production. It's a disturbing kind of audience participation. The magician's playbook gone mad. Moreso, as in the propagation of lies and information, this kind of callout from the stage to the audience to join them can have deadly results (for example, the January 6, 2021, riots on the US Capitol building in Washington, DC, resulted in at least four deaths, perhaps more).[12] At no time in the world's history has running away to join the circus come with such high stakes. Such is the price of becoming an Edgar.

Finally, there is the fourth category, also in the audience. They are the curious. In the search for truth, they are willing to question not only the beliefs of the first three but also their own. They are the heroes, and they are few. Yet, the well-being of every society on the planet depends on them.

We must nurture this rare group. We must grow their numbers. We must provide them with tools and platforms for sharing their questions and insights. We must create safe places for them to challenge the messages coming from the stage. We must protect them from the cancel culture that demonizes their thoughts and casts them aside in the modern version of a biblical shunning or excommunication. Let us not forget Europe once had its own, more deadly version of cancel culture, the centuries-long purge of religious dissidents known as *The Inquisition* (now repeated as criminally political processes in such autocratic countries like China, Russia, and North Korea).

Today, the intensely choreographed productions coming out of the Theater of Lies have eroded society's most precious resource: trust. Without it, international powers risk war, governments risk civil disobedience, and central banks risk defaults. As evidenced during the COVID-19 pandemic and its vaccination process, people will risk their health and even their lives to hold hard their mistrust of authority and science, the power of misinformation fueling their actions.

One of the unforeseen consequences of evolving digital technology is that it has created an enormous buffet of enticing information to consume—and we gobble it like it was popcorn. If this was real food, our bodies could not process it all. We'd self-select. It is the same for information. Yet unlike real food at a real buffet, the information presented in the Theater of Lies is not just in front of us; it constantly surrounds us 24 hours a day. Our only escape is discrimination, a skill that few people truly have. It is a skill of the curious, the critical thinkers, and those that choose to join them.

The process to write this book began during the worldwide COVID-19 pandemic of 2020 and 2021. Though the book is not about this, it certainly informs it. The debates about the virus—its source, its mitigation, and its solutions—thrived in the Theater of Lies. Why? Because the ubiquity and cultural blindness of the COVID-19 virus made each of us a participant, whether we wanted to or not. At some level, each of us became Edgars.

But on a mass scale, we proved we have neither the personal or professional tools to participate in a debate so scientifically nuanced and dynamic as a global pandemic. As an audience, we are conditioned to watch and comment, not participate. To be otherwise would be like watching hours of professional golf or tennis on television and, from that seat on our couch, believing we'd now become better players ourselves. We know how to yell at football players who fumble, at coaches that call the wrong play, but few of us have ever strapped on a helmet and run headfirst into a pile of 300-pound defensive lineman. Yet we feel empowered pointing out their mistakes as much as we do cheering when they win.

This is how our culture has trained us to act as an audience. We comment rather than act. And when a novel situation requires us to get into a game rather than sit on the sidelines, we don't know how to do it. So, we rely on what we believe and want to believe, like football players gazing across the field at the coach—waiting for a signal on what to do from someone whom we trust.

We now approach most every debate—whether it be in science, education, politics, or even in our families—as if it were a contest. We participate to win, not to learn. At worst, we come to be entertained, as if the solutions to the pandemic were a special episode of *America's Got [Medical] Talent.*

But as we have seen, the stakes are much higher than a high school debate. Lives are at stake. At the end of World War II, millions of Japanese people died in defense of the myth of an infallible deity ruling them in human form as their emperor. Hundreds of thousands died in the US Civil War to protect the Confederate lie that slavery was the Christian ideal of saving degenerate Negroes from their base instincts. Thousands more died to protect the Soviet Union's lie that its nuclear technology was infallible while its Chernobyl power plant exploded. For over a century, Canadians justified the stealing of Indigenous children from their parents—with thousands more dying, because (in the words of its first prime minister), "the child [who] lives with his parents who are savages . . . is simply a savage who can read and write."[13]

And through all these times, when we come to understand what we had been long told as truths were actually lies, our most common response is to tell ourselves this self-comforting promise: "We will never let this happen again."

Yet happen again, it does.

Why? Because lies work.

In fact, we've been raised on them.

One of the first lessons we're taught, often by our parents, is that the sun rises in the morning and sets at night. "Good morning," your mother says. "Sun's up and it's time to start the day." Later she tells you the opposite: "The sun's down and it's getting dark. Time to go to bed." Your day, though innocently enough, has been framed in a lie. In all languages. In all cultures.

Compared to the Tooth Fairy and Santa Claus, two other lies so many of us tell our children, the truth about sunrises and sunsets could seem insignificant. But in the former, children soon realize that there is no Santa Claus, and the arrival of the Tooth Fairy, while just as untrue, is a symbolic gesture that takes away the pain of losing baby teeth and rewards an achievement on the road to adulthood. But who among us has ever told our children that the sun is not rising; rather, it is our place on the earth that is turning toward the sun?

None. Because we all live in the same Theater of Lies. The television meteorologist tells us when the sun will rise and set. Its timing arrives daily on our smartphones.

Every year, we create new words to communicate new ideas (Oxford Dictionaries has an award for Word of the Year,[14] like goblin-mode, vax, and youthquake), but no one has yet offered up a word that accurately represents the fact that it's not the sun that actually rises and sets, but our place on the planet.

But surely there is no problem with this, is there?

Except for one. The notion that if you experience something, it must be true. Let's call it the *eyewitness fallacy*. We know, now, that while jurors place great weight on eyewitness testimony, this testimony is often wrong.[15] It is the same for our experience of sunrise and sunset.

Since humankind crawled from the African savanna—and even before that—we've had some inkling of this sunset and sunrise process. It never hurt that we were actually wrong about the whole damn thing.

Except when we see that there remain people on this planet who believe the world is flat, since it's easier to trust their eyes than science. Except when you rank the scientific literacy levels of your country against other countries and find yours woefully inadequate (of

English-speaking countries, the United States ranks last,[16] and of the bottom sixteen countries in the world, each is Christian). When our lives begin with lies, we accept untruths more easily into them.

Moreover, we continue to fill our children's lives with these fictions. Imagine how much more interested a child might be in science if we explained to them that our place on earth actually turns toward the sun, then away.

Our children's first invitation to the Theater of Lies is a party with takeaway gifts. Unfortunately, those can lead many down paths they may never know how to leave. It could lead them to believe that COVID-19 can't affect them, that it was manufactured by pharmaceutical companies conspiring for profit, or maybe that it doesn't even exist at all. They might be easily tricked into believing a fair election was rigged or hold themselves firm in the knowledge their race is superior to every other. Their perspective is being hardened from the beginning—believe what you see.

In my opinion, lies and misinformation have become the most powerful weapons in the world. They are as destructive as nuclear warheads, but their aftermath leaves their victims standing without any memory of the attack or awareness of how their lives and others have been damaged.

It is time for us, both as individuals and a society—to develop the tools to combat them. If we don't, the people who seek to fool us will achieve what is best for them, with little or no care of what is best for us. We must see the Theater of Lies for what it is and address it not merely as a problem but as a clear and present danger. We must defend ourselves against it like the enemy it has become. If not, we risk this 24/7 Theater of Lies evolving into something even worse: the *Rule of Lies*—governance of our lives under laws and controls like those imposed on the citizens of Russia, China, Iran, and other autocratic nations.

Because the Theater of Lies is engaged in a battle for your mind—to influence your beliefs and how you act upon them, it is not just a theater of the mind, but a theater of war. And, in many ways, each of us has been losing these battles for decades.

As he packed his weapons into the trunk of his car, Edgar Welch demonstrated the truth about lies. The most dangerous lie comes not from its source, but from the person who repeats the lie *and* believes it to be true. If this was a real theatrical production, we might refer to them as harmless fanboys (or fangirls). But in the Theater of Lies, these Edgars become fanatics.

If we can't shut down the Theater of Lies, we must at least try to mitigate its overpowering influence. To do so, we must first understand our enemy—for it is an old one, now technologically and socially empowered.

.... ACT ONE: ....

A BRIEF HISTORY
OF LIES

....

1

IN THE BEGINNING, THERE WERE LIES.

Lies are the world's first manmade pollutant. Long before coal fumes darkened the skies of eighteenth-century London, humans produced misinformation by the barrelful to explain the world to themselves and change the opinions of others.

First employed in families, then tribes, then kingdoms, the purposeful use of lies has spread like a virus, embedding itself in all means of communication. The Bible blames the first lie on the devil, embodied in a serpent. That, too, is a lie used to entrench the myth that the knowledge of good and evil brings chaos and retribution (as well as its corollary, "ignorance is bliss"). Moreover, it provides rationale for the world's most powerful lie: women are subservient to men.

Here's how God responded to Adam and Eve, before evicting them from the Garden of Eden after they'd eaten an apple from the *Tree of Knowledge*:

> To the woman He said: "I will greatly multiply your sorrow and your conception; In pain you shall bring forth children; Your desire *shall be* for your husband, And he shall rule over thee."[18]
>
> And unto Adam He said, "Because thou hast hearkened unto the voice of thy wife, and hast eaten of the tree, of which I commanded thee, saying, Thou shalt not eat of it: cursed *is* the ground for thy sake; in sorrow shalt thou eat *of* it all the days of thy life;[19]
>
> Thorns also and thistles shall it bring forth to thee; and thou shalt eat the herb of the field;[20] In the sweat of thy face shalt thou eat bread, till thou return unto the ground; for out of it wast thou taken: for dust thou *art*, and unto dust shalt thou return."[21]

Indeed, the first writers of the biblical narrative knew a thing or two about storytelling. Our fear of snakes is almost primal. Just imagine if the creature who had seduced Eve to taste the fruit of the Tree of Knowledge had been a Labrador puppy. The first lady of the Old Testament would have been too busy rubbing its belly—and the dog, well, he'd have peed on the tree before running off to chase the world's first squirrel. Western civilization as we know it might have been stillborn. Women might have become the world's dominant decision-makers.

We don't know who told the first lie, but I suspect it came seconds after the ability to communicate. It likely had something to do with convincing a group of humans that the first-ever liar on the planet needed more food, water, or sex than any of the others.

"The world is rife with great liars," said Robert Feldman, a professor of psychology at the University of Massachusetts. He studies lying and deception. "We all lie every day. We live in a culture where lying is quite acceptable."[22]

According to another psychologist, Dr. Alex Lickerman, the fundamental reason for this is that we lie to protect ourselves. In *Psychology Today*, Lickerman wrote that lying is an instinctive defense mechanism intended to protect our interests, our image, our resources, and other people.[23] He also pointed to research demonstrating that our instinct to lie is ingrained so deeply that when you confront a child about a lie, they are more likely to work at becoming a better liar than to learn to tell the truth. We are like professional burglars. When caught, our nature drives us to focus on how not to get caught the next time.

Moreover, the crime of lying, for most of us, is not planned—at least according to Dan Ariely, who studies behavioral economics at Duke University. "One of the frightening conclusions we have," he wrote in his 2012 book, *The (Honest) Truth About Dishonesty*, "is that what separates honest people from not-honest people is not necessarily character, it's opportunity."[24]

The problem that this book examines, however, is not so much why it is in our nature to lie but how and why some very powerful people, along with the organizations they work for, create lies with such purpose and precision. That, and why our first instinct is to believe them. Indeed, despite our loud protestations directed at any politician, athlete, celebrity, business leader, media person, or religious leader who lies to us, our relationship with lies is quite comfortable. The seats in the Theater of Lies are well-padded and inviting.

A deep-thinking philosopher from Israel, Hebrew University professor Yuval Noah Harari, has traced this comfortable relationship (my words) back to what he believes is the driving force in our evolution as a species: our deep-rooted dissatisfaction with human reality.[25] *Translation*: on both a macro and micro level, we are not happy people, so we strive to improve our environment to become so—even if it means lying to ourselves.

In turn, Harari has divided our relationship with falsehoods into two categories: lies and fictions, as if they were on a spectrum. He writes:

> A lie is when you know perfectly well that something is not true, and you say it in order to deceive others. A fiction is very often something that you really believe, which you tell other people *not* in order to deceive them. It can be something small or it can be something big, like a religion or an economic theory or a racial theory.[26]

This is where I call timeout. This is not academic hair-splitting. It is wrong. When you fail to challenge what Harari refers to as *fictions* (what I might also refer to as *myths*), you are padding your seats in the Theater. The lies in your world become more and more comfortable to believe. Worse, each failure to correct these myths and fictions creates further barriers to addressing (in Harari's words) *our deep-rooted dissatisfaction.*[27]

A dissatisfaction that has become deep-rooted in our lives is our propensity to believe these lies and what sometimes we refer to as myths. The late John F. Kennedy shared it, too. In a commencement speech to the graduates of Yale University in 1962, he told them,

> The great enemy of truth is very often not the lie—deliberate, contrived, and dishonest—but the myth—persistent, persuasive, and unrealistic. Too often we hold fast to the clichés of our forebears. We subject all facts to a prefabricated set of interpretations. We enjoy the comfort of opinion without the discomfort of thought.[28]

Fictions and myths are among the first untruths we learn in the Theater. As with a lie, they mislead us—so I place them in the same category. Understanding that the sun does not rise in the morning but that our place on the earth turns toward it, then away, is a fiction based in our bygone ignorance. The sun appears to rise when, in fact, it is stationary (relative to the earth). But that was not what our ancestors saw in the sky, so therefore that was not what they believed to be true.

We know the sun does not really rise or set, yet we repeat this fiction, daily. In Harari's opinion, since we are not trying to deceive someone, this is OK. Yet, we are because such acceptance masks the underlying error that what we see must be the truth.

So, if we see Black people living in urban slums, farming marginal lands, or having a higher percentage of the population in prisons, then we must believe that it to be true that Black people are somehow inferior to whites. If we experience our winters as colder and wetter, we can believe that global warming is a lie and that its promoters came up with a new name for it, climate change, to make the ideas seem more palatable.

If you see an immigrant commit a crime, or someone re-tells a story about such an event, then it must be true that more immigrants will increase the risks of crime. Worse, since the Theater of Lies lets us see all this and because we've been raised to believe what we see, our opinions become more entrenched (and more difficult to change).

Shelby Steele takes on Harari's notion of *fictions* and expands the term to include what he refers to as *poetic truths*.[29] Steele is an American writer and documentary producer who says that when we are confronted by violence and suffering, we tend to retreat to poetic truths that offer deceptively simple explanations for complex problems. A poetic truth, as Steele defines it, is "a distortion of the actual truth that we use to sue for leverage for power in the world. It is a partisan version of reality, a storyline that we put forward to build our case."[30]

The venerable *Scientific American* published a special edition about lies in 2019, under the title, *Truth, Lies, and Uncertainty*.[31] In it, they offer up such terms as "misinformation," "disinformation," and "malinformation."[32] Other terms include "post-truth" (Oxford Dictionary's 2016 word of the year),[33] and, of course, the splatter-gun term— "fake news."

In 2023, the editorial board of Canada's *Globe and Mail* newspaper introduced a deft two-step dance to avoid calling out the Liberal Prime Minister Trudeau as a liar. Trudeau had characterized Canada's failure to adequately rebound from the 2008 financial crisis under the management of the previous Conservative government as "wages did not rise; inequality increased; and the middle class was shrinking."[34] In an editorial harrumph rather than a poke in eye, the *Globe and Mail* wrote, "the numbers do not back up those claims."[35] It then cited Canada's actual economic data from 2009 to 2015—demonstrating that wages did indeed rise, inequality decreased, and the relative number of Canadians who could be categorized as middle class grew larger.

But what caught my attention was not the all-too-Canadian politeness in its pushback on the prime minister's veracity; it was the introduction of a well-established religious term, this time repurposed to describe oft-repeated teachings that evolve into dogma. *Catechism*, as in the teaching pedagogy of the Catholic Church. Theyw wrote:

> "We saw what happened in 2008 and its aftermath," [Trudeau] said, "when GDP started to rise again, wages stayed stagnant. Inequality rose and a lot of hard-working people were being left behind. The middle class was being hollowed out, and people were growing disillusioned." A compelling catechism indeed—if true.[36]

Of course, as the editorial board proved, it wasn't. Trudeau's statements were merely a repeated positioning of the well-trod differences in political philosophy between the Liberal and Conservative parties in Canada. The facts did not matter, only the prime minister's message, delivered to engage the nodding heads of Liberal party's faithful as if they were congregants in a Catholic Church. In the Theater of Lies, familiarity is a load-bearing arch. Even if it is an illusion.

Because whether you use any of these words—Steele's term, *Scientific American*'s, Harari's academic definition, or a borrowed term for religious teachings—none attribute any responsibility of the all-important third party in a lie: the one who repeats it. This is where lies the dangerous power of lies, for repetition breeds consent. As far back as 1977, psychologists proved the more we hear something, the more we believe it to be true.[37] Calling it the illusionary-truth principle, they proved that "subjects rated repeated statements as probably more true than new statements."[38] They also added the editorial comment, "repetition is an illogical basis for truth."[39] Yet, a 1992 study by McMaster University concluded:

> The illusory truth of repeated statements is based on familiarity. Familiarity increases automatically with repetition, and its influence on rated truth is unintentional. Subjects do not spontaneously monitor the source of a statement's familiarity or use that information when rating truth.[40]

The non-academic language translation of the above: repetition is highly effective in convincing people that a lie is truthful, and their acceptance of this is not a conscious act—it is unintentional.

In the Theater of Lies, the producers revel in the audience's unintentional acceptance of these so-called fictions and illusionary truths. Why? In my opinion, we, the audience, are either not curious enough to ask questions or lack the courage to ask them (a problem to which I propose solutions in Act 3). Add to that our inherent need to believe lies, and we have now constructed a theater with a powerful stage from which to perform, persuade, and, in military terms, invade our minds.

Diane Barth is a psychotherapist whose studies have delved deep into this area. She claims,

> We believe lies when we feel too vulnerable to allow the truth and its consequences to manifest in our lives. When truth does emerge, we often feel terribly betrayed, and we can lose faith in our own ability to

make good judgments. To protect against this pain, we sometimes continue lying to ourselves long after reality seems unavoidable.[41]

As I wrote this book, I was reminded of a time when my wife and I had three dogs: a black schnauzer, a gray schnauzer, and a white West Highland terrier. All of them demanded an overly large share of our bed, which, when the cat also wanted a warm spot with us, was quite hard to find. Pepper, the black one, had his own solution. He became the first animal I realized had learned the power of lies.

As the pets began to settle in the bed, if Pepper wasn't comfortable in the spot he'd found, he would stand up, jump off the bed, look at the bedroom door, and bark. In addition to being a particularly smart and beautiful animal, Pepper also had a bark that could peel the paint off the wall. His barking got the immediate attention of the other two dogs, Ty (the gray one) and Buddy (the Westie) would, in turn, leap off the bed to investigate the source of Pepper's trauma. Once these two were off the bed, Pepper would jump back on, select the spot he had wanted, and settle in with a satisfying "huff." Throughout his entire life, he'd repeat this performance whenever he wanted a better place to sleep. The science tells us[42] that there are many animals like my slight-of hand schnauzer who understand the power of lies. It is a survival tool as much as enlightened self-interest.

Lies work. They work because in the beginning of our lives, in the beginning of our history, in the beginning moments of each day, we've used lies—to ourselves—to make sense of the world. They are one of our most powerful tools to make sense of our lives. But they have now become our most dangerous.

"The intelligent, like the unintelligent, are responsive to propaganda."[43]

– H. L. MENCKEN, AMERICAN JOURNALIST AND AUTHOR.

....

2

PROPAGANDA: THE GOOD, THE BAD, AND THE UGLY.

Technically, the word propaganda is a neutral term. The root word "propagate" comes from Latin and means to shoot out or spread. Whether one propagates the roots of a plant, an electrical signal, or an idea, there is nothing inherently bad in the act of so doing. Philip Taylor, a UK professor of communications who has written extensively on the subject, writes that "the study of propaganda itself is not necessarily the study of something evil."[44] But this is a learned academic who also wrote that "the most effective propaganda has evolved through the ages now bases itself on facts and credible arguments . . . upon reason rather than emotion."[45] For me, there has to be more to the investigation of propaganda than academics such as Taylor have pursued. My career as a professional communicator has demonstrated that facts have become, unfortunately, the least important wrench in the propaganda tool kit.

My personal introduction to the term propaganda happened in the back seat of a 400-kilometere limousine ride from Toronto to Sudbury, Ontario. Of course, I was aware of the word, but only in its negative connotation rather than Taylor's notion of neutral. It was 1987, the first time I'd ever heard the word spoken in its native tongue by an Italian, who emphasized the third syllable, making the word sound both powerful and seductive. I immediately understood why Italian is the language of opera (with all due respect to the Germans).

Italians didn't build the first Theater of Lies, but they did institutionalize it. The Vatican brought the word propaganda into to wide use in 1622.[46] But the Catholic Church's headquarters were not the first Italians to practice the art. One of the most propagandic Roman emperor of all time, Julius Caesar, broke custom when he placed an image of himself on the currency of the realm rather than that of a Roman God. He later completed his propagandic vision, declaring himself an actual God. While it settled the convention that only deities had the privilege of having their heads pressed into coinage, it didn't end well for Caesar. He was assassinated shortly thereafter (the Ides of March, 44 BC). Propaganda doesn't always stay true to the plans of its producers (through eager participation of whose minds they wish to influence, propaganda can take on a life of its own) and it isn't always based on lies (more about that in Act One, Chapter Six, The Power of Pathos).

In 1987, I was the director of marketing for the Canadian Track and Field Association (CTFA). A year later, the association and its star athlete, Ben Johnson, were caught up in an Olympic cheating scandal that captured the attention of the world. But a year prior to the world's fastest man being caught with a cocktail of performance-enhancing drugs in his system, the small town of Sudbury was itself just a year away from hosting an Olympic-style event. In the shadow of what was once Canada's largest mining industry, Sudbury had convinced the International Amateur Athletic Federation (IAAF) it could host the World Junior Track and Field Championships. That would be the first time I'd witnessed propaganda in action as the two groups fought each other with different propaganda agendas—different versions of the truth. I also learned that to see how something really works, it helps to see someone break it.

Most any history of the word propaganda begins with the creation of the Sacred Congregation for the Propagation of the Faith (*Sacra Congregatio de Propaganda Fide*) in 1622.[47] The Vatican created this group under the guise of the purpose of missionary work—converting people to Catholicism after dropping the centuries-long convert-or-die strategy of the Inquisition.

The Vatican propaganda machine has been officially in operation for more than 400 years. The irony cannot be lost that by changing its name from the *Sacred Congregation for the Propagation of the Faith* to the *Congregation for the Evangelization of Peoples* (so ordered in 1967 by Pope Paul VI),[48] the Vatican took a term most used by American Protestants—evangelism—and brought it home. This is a classic tactic of most masters of manipulation: they smuggle in the language of their opponents to become more palatable to their detractors.

The Vatican created its propaganda office after a hundred years of fighting Martin Luther's Protestant Reformation. Its previous attempts to deter people from moving over to Luther's less priest-centric version of Christianity included burning heretics at the stake. This failed, as the deaths only created martyrs, providing even more fuel to the antipapist movement. The replacement of Inquisition-style tactics with a propaganda strategy was anything but a neutral move, especially since it was still aimed not at making peace with the reformers but converting them to the Catholic way.

Fast forward to 1987, to the propaganda war between Sudbury and the heavyweight champion professionals of the art at the IAAF. Somehow, they both managed to lose.

I had been assigned the task of escorting the president of the IAAF, Primo Nebiolo, from his arrival in Toronto to the still-in-development site of the following year's World Junior Track and Field Championships. It would only be the second time the event had been held, the first being two years earlier, at the birthplace of the Olympic Games in Athens, Greece.

Nebiolo had created the entire concept a world championship for the next generation of track and field stars. It was part of his plan to make track and field more than just the central pillar of the once-every-four-years Olympic Games. His goal was to raise the sport's support (and fortunes) to the level of the number one sport in the world—football (known in North America as soccer).

He had also been smart enough to stage the first Junior World Championship at the sport's historic starting place, Athens, Greece.

This begs the question: how did a town in northern Ontario, Canada, get selected to become the next host? *That couldn't have been part of Nebiolo's plan,* I thought. It wasn't. It was Sudbury's. I discovered that these earnest Canadians had upset Nebiolo's apple cart.

The mining town and its 50,000 or so residents were out to change Sudbury's image. The source of acid rain for much of southern Ontario and the US northeast,[49] the town needed a tool to pry itself away from its long-standing image as an environmental wasteland destroyed by decades of pollution from nickel mining and smelting.

Other than the nickel industry, Sudbury was famous for its use by NASA as a training ground for its Apollo astronauts. The basin in which the city lies is at the bottom of a huge crater, the result of the impact of a giant comet some 1.8 billion years ago. The rim of that crater and the scattered remains of the impact, NASA believed, were the closest thing on Earth to the moon's surface. So the astronauts were brought up, given vehicles similar in style to the rovers they would use on the moon, and trained to become off-world geologists.

Part of the strategy to change Sudbury's image—its propaganda tactic—was to bring the world's media to the city and showcase the results of decades of remediation that had transformed the region from an environmental disaster to a pristine region of lakes, forests, and a small yet vibrant metropolis. The 1988 World Junior Track and Field Championships, the city's ruling elites decided, could be the draw. The event and its worldwide media coverage were to be a stage for positive messages about a once-polluting mining town made modern and an environmental jewel.

The track and field world had not become excited enough about the junior event to start a bidding war. Other than Sudbury, the only other city to put up their hand as hosts was Cali, Colombia. This was in the late 1980s and, at that time, Cali's major export was cocaine. Cartels, including those of the notorious Pablo Escobar, controlled much of the city and the country. In a two-horse race, the IAAF had little choice in awarding the championships to the Canadian bidders. They wanted the athletes to *run between* the white lines, not snort them.

Nebiolo, however, wasn't pleased—not only by the lack of interest in the rest of the track and field world in hosting this second staging of his brainchild but also that it had fallen to this small Canadian city.

Rumor was that to quell his initial anger at the selection, his staff had told him that Sudbury was a *suburb* of Toronto. True or not, I could see the truth of it in Nebiolo's face as we took the over four-hour limousine drive from the Toronto International Airport to the event site. He seemed to get more frustrated by the kilometer. He regularly pointed to the two IAAF staff people traveling with him, mumbling in Italian. Some of it, I was sure, was cursing.

As our limousine traveled through the beautiful lake country, Nebiolo pulled out the business card I'd given him previously. He stared at it for a moment, noticing my job title: *Director of Marketing*. "Mr. Griffith," he said, "what about the propaganda?" This was the first time I heard the word expressed in terms that positioned it as something desirable—something missing, like a tasty spice.

I was now the rock stuck between four hard places: my employer, the operating committee of the World Juniors, the City of Sudbury, and one of the most powerful men in all of international sports.

Before I could answer the question, he filled my obvious pause with an exasperated sigh. His point: how was putting the next generation of track and field stars to compete in a small mining town in northern Ontario going to advance the sport around the world? The stage was too small, too unremarkable—especially in comparison to its previous host. That was Athens, Greece, remember.

As for any answer that might persuade him that Sudbury could deliver the prestige he was looking for, I had none to give him. When we arrived in the city, he forced a smile for pictures with the mayor, toured the site at Laurentian University, then chartered an airplane to get out of town as quickly as possible. He spent the next year desperately trying to undo the hosting agreement with the city. But with no takers for the event elsewhere, the championships went ahead.

The man in charge of televising the event, Canadian Broadcasting Corporation's (CBC) head of sports, Don MacPherson, later told me that the money paid to the CBC and others to broadcast the event would have been better spent flying anyone who wanted to watch the world junior champions to Sudbury and giving them free tickets—the TV audience was *that* small.

The city was using propaganda to change its reputation. The athletic association was also using propaganda to build the considerable reputation of its sport, even further. But neither Primo Nebiolo nor the Sudbury organizers of the 1988 World Junior Track and Field Championships ever achieved their goals.

What became clear to me over thirty years later was that for propaganda to be effective, it had to have strength in three areas: *a problem to solve, a platform from which to deliver the solution,* and *a personality to express to it.* It also requires the structure of a *compelling story* and a *deep understanding of the tools of persuasion.* These are the tools of the producers in the Theater of Lies, tools honed over thousands of years of manipulating public opinion.

These are the same tools that professional communicators use today to legitimately inform. Using truth as the cornerstone of persuasive communication is not hard, but using lies—as we will discuss further—is so much easier (and, unfortunately, often more effective).

Propaganda is most familiar to us in context of military wars. During the Russian-Ukrainian war, which began in late February 2022, Russian media exposed the Russian government's official yet demonstrably false premise for the conflict.

Soon after the war began, Oliver Darcy of CNN documented the former-Soviet Union's propagandic rationale—aimed mostly at its own citizens. (Note: RT is the acronym Russia's English-language television station and website). Darcy said,

> For several hours I watched the channel and was struck by how brazenly its hosts and personalities worked to mislead its audience and deflect from the issues at hand. The main thrust of RT's coverage presented Russia as a mere victim of western aggression; a country forced to launch a limited "military operation" after its hand was forced by a high-and-mighty NATO that showed no interest in taking Moscow's security concerns seriously. On its news programs throughout the day, RT's on-screen graphics blared breaking news alerts supporting that notion: "RUSSIA: NATIONAL SECURITY THREATS LEFT NO CHOICE BUT TO START MILITARY OPERATION." Another chyron read, "RUSSIA SAYS ITS GOALS IN UKRAINE TO DEMILITARIZE & DENAZIFY THE COUNTRY."[50]

This style of propaganda, Leeds professor Philip M. Taylor describes not as good or evil but in still binary terms as "white"[51] or "black"—the difference being the source of the information (white, known credible source—black, undisclosed source). He also details how the nascent United States of America and one its founding fathers, Benjamin Franklin, was an expert practitioner of the black artform.

Taylor describes an important moment in 1777 when a letter appeared in France that detailed the ruthless behavior of German princes, who like many German soldiers, had joined the British during the War of Independence. For example, these princes were advising the British government that their surgeons had been told to let injured soldiers die rather than be treated. Not only was the letter a fake, but the names of the princes also named fake, their merciless advice to surgeons, fake: Benjamin Franklin was the author of the letter.[52] He later produced a newspaper that featured a story about how the King of England was paying Native Americans for each scalp of a colonial.[53] It, too, was fake, a propagandistic message that achieved two goals— keeping the opinions of freshly independent Americans against their former ruler as well as demonizing another enemy they needed to fight: Indigenous people.

In the end, as Taylor later tells us at the end of his seminal treatise, *Munitions of the Mind*, "Ultimately, propaganda is about sides."[54] In *Theater of Lies*, however, we focus on the use of lies and misinformation as the weapons of propaganda and, in the remainder of this first Act, how we have become so preconditioned as targets that we hardly feel the extensive damage of their impacts.

Propaganda, at least in this book, is not considered a neutral term. It falls into the category of negative, along with its purposefully mind-manipulating cousins: misinformation, disinformation, hyperbole, alternative facts, and fake news.

"We swallow greedily any lie that flatters us, but we sip only little by little at a truth we find bitter."[55]

– DENIS DIDEROT, EIGHTEENTH-CENTURY FRENCH PHILOSOPHER.

....

3

LIES LOOK REAL.

I confess an odd attraction to official government hearings, both in my own country of Canada and in the United States. This stems, I think, from coming home after school to the Watergate Hearings in 1973 as they usurped my mother's afternoon soap operas. For me, it was powerful television, the rows of politicians on the committee, their advisers, passing notes and whispers, sat behind them—and in front of them, the current target of their interrogations (often with a lawyer sitting beside them, passing notes and whispers as well).

Later in life, I had the good fortune, or misfortune, to participate in two official judicial inquiries—Canada's Dubin Inquiry into the role of performance-enhancing substances in sport (post the Ben Johnson steroid scandal in the 1988 Olympics) and the Krever Inquiry into Canada's tainted blood scandal of the 1990s. Until there's a twelve-step program to support my addiction to political theater, I will be as drawn to these spectacles like a fanboy to the next Marvel movie.

The air in these hearings can crackle with electricity with the brightness of television lighting and the combative performances of both the interrogators and the interrogated as they each posture for the cameras and each other.[1]

More contemporary hearings include the series of US Senate and Congressional Hearings into the litany of issues surrounding the presidency of Donald Trump (the Mueller Investigation into election interference, and two separate impeachment processes, among many others). Forbes Magazine called the 2022 House Select Investigating into the January 6, 2021, attack on the US Congress "the best television series of summer."[56] About 20 million people watched the first episode[57] (or should I say, *hearing*) with highlights repeated on most every broadcast and cable news outlet in North America and many more around the world.

Official hearings can be captivating, high-stakes theater. So much so that when you are a producer in the Theater of Lies, distributing a lie through the false *impression* of an official hearing can be a powerful stage. This is what a Republican member of Congress from Florida, Matt Gaetz, tried to do as part of his campaign to foster public distrust in federal institutions. In this case, the Federal Bureau of Investigation (FBI).

The event was advertised as a *field hearing* and part of the constitutional oversight role of the 118th Congress and its investigation into the

....

1   In the Watergate Hearings, so polished a performer was one the congressmen on the government's side, Tennessee's Fred Thompson, he later became an award-winning actor in films such as *The Hunt for Red October* and television's *Law & Order*.

weaponization of the federal government.[58] (Note: field hearings are, defined as hearings held outside of Washington, DC, to "raise public visibility of an issue . . . reinforce a member's relationship with his or her constituents, and attract . . . media attention."[59])

Gaetz's event was held in meeting room CVC-268 at the Capitol Visitor Center in Washington. He sat behind a long table, with the US House of Representatives logo projected on a larger screen behind him and on the sign placed in front of him. Sitting beside him at the table were three other Republican members of Congress, each of them referring to Gaetz as "Chair."[60]

Gaetz's opening words, "I call this field hearing on January 6 to order. From time to time, members of Congress hold field hearings to function as force multipliers for the investigative, analytical, and legislative work of our various committees."[61] Force multiplier is a military term for "a small but highly skilled force may tilt the power balance in domestic wars by acting as a *force multiplier* for existing assets."[62] Strong and very official-sounding words, indeed (though not within any definition of the purpose of a field hearing published by the U.S. Government).

He then played a video beginning with cable news stories that spoke to a conspiracy theory that the government, specifically the FBI, orchestrated the January 6th attack on the US Congress.[63]

Summing up the video play, Gaetz tells the two dozen or so people attending the field meeting (and viewers on the US Congress's own cable channel, C-SPAN), "so much of our work has uncovered some things that initially were deemed as conspiracy theories, but we now have sworn evidence to prove."[64]

Indeed, providing an air of authenticity to the *hearing* were Gaetz's own words, as recorded by *Washington Post* journalist Dana Milbank. She wrote:

He impersonated a chairman — "you are recognized," "thank you for your testimony," "I'll recognize myself [for] questions," "her time has expired"— and the others played along ("thank you for the opportunity to testify," "I yield back")."[65]

The previous day, a press release from Gaetz's office advertised the "field hearing . . . [as part of how] the 118th Congress is investigating the weaponization of the federal government."[66] Without irony, but with purpose, that message is the same one that Donald Trump carried into a federal courthouse in Miami, Florida, as he was indicted on thirty-seven criminal charges. Both Gaetz's event and Trump's appearance before a judge occurred within hours of each other.

The release also identified six witnesses who would appear, without mentioning that two had been criminally sentenced for their role in the January 6, 2021, attack on the US Congress, one was an organizer of the Stop the Steal effort that led up to that day, and another was a former Department of Justice official who had tried to convince several US states to cancel the results of the 2020 US Presidential Election.[67]

It all looked and sounded so real, including moments of faux-judicial gavel-thumpery. Very official. Gaetz said testimony could be used "for the official record [of the] House" or for "work in the Judiciary Committee, upon which I serve, or the Oversight Committee."[68]

And while those statements were true—especially when couched with the word *could*—Gaetz made it appear that his field hearing carried some official weight in law or congressional procedure. It did nothing of the sort. It was theater. It was a representation of an official hearing, produced with the requisite rules of an official hearing, except that Gaetz and fellow presenters were not authorized by either the Judicial Committee or the Oversight Committee to hold such a hearing.[69]

The stage even was merely a meeting of like-minded elected officials and the people who supported their messages. Looking and presented as a credible legislative procedure, what Gaetz actually staged had all the legal power of those same people meeting over lattes and scones at a Starbucks (without the crumbs). In my business, we officially refer to these events as stakeholder relations, or in sometimes pejorative terms, a public relations exercise.

On June 13, 2023, meeting room CVC-268 at the US Capitol was simply a stage for yet another production in the global Theater of Lies. In this case, the goal was the delivery, once again, of the message that government institutions cannot be trusted, especially if they operate under political authorities you do not support.

Propagandists have been borrowing theatrical tactics to deliver their messages for decades. Fritz Hippler was the German filmmaker who ran the film department in the *Reichsministerium für Volksaufklärung und Propaganda* . . . which translates to the Reich Ministry of Public Enlightenment and Propaganda for Nazi Germany. While I am not fond of German opera, I do love the German language for its sense of precision.

When asked in the 1960s how to convince people to go to war, Hippler answered, "simplify a complex issue and repeat that simplification over and over again."[70] This was the man who directed a seminal film of antisemitic propaganda, *The Eternal Jew*. It served as one of the most powerful demonstrations of the Nazi message: that all Jews were parasites and that systematic violence against them was justified. It was propaganda packaged into the most consumer-friendly format of its time: film. And while the format has moved beyond celluloid, the techniques to make lies appear real, as used by Gaetz and so many others, have not.

In terms of the production of lies that are the driving force behind so many of the myths of the twenty-first century, I am going to stick the blame on former prop-boy-turned-Hollywood-director John Ford, who accomplished this in the previous one. From 1913 to 1971, he directed more than 140 films and documentaries. His films were literally theaters of lies, creating myths so powerful they became entrenched in the minds of Americans and how they perceived themselves—at least at the time. He was so good at his job that in the 1940s, the US government hired him to make propaganda films to foster public support for entering World War II.[71]

Congressman Gaetz and others all, knowingly or not, went to his school. Though I think Ford would have fired any writer who put the words *force multiplier* into any of his scripts.

Orson Welles, himself regarded as one of Hollywood's greatest directors, is often quoted as saying, "I prefer the old masters, by which I mean John Ford, John Ford, and John Ford."[72] Summarizing Ford, actor Henry Fonda, who starred in eight of Ford's movies, said, without irony, "Pappy [Ford] was full of bullshit, but it was a delightful sort of bullshit."[73] In the minds of most Americans and people the world over, Ford's bullshit would form the foundation of American exceptionalism, gun culture, and the image of the great but everyday man as hero.

To accomplish this, he needed a star to build his stories around. And perhaps the greatest speciality of Hollywood's moviemaking industry was not storytelling or writing. It was not the special blend of chemistry and light that put images on film. It was *star-making*.

Ford had seen the success of Rudolph Valentino, Hollywood's first superstar. Valentino died at thirty-one, cementing the Hollywood-created myth of him as the world's greatest lover, supplanting the previous title-holder, the historical figure Casanova. Even now, a century later, Valentino's grave at the Hollywood Forever Cemetery draws the most visitors a year. Ford's eventual creation was a University of Southern California dropout who had lost his athletic scholarship due to a surfing injury. His name was Marion Robert Morrison, better known as John Wayne.

While John Ford built Wayne's image into the everyman hero he needed him to be, Wayne—who would later be awarded a Congressional Gold Medal and the US Presidential Medal of Freedom for becoming that hero—was never the horseman, cowboy, or war hero that his movie reputation portrayed. He was too old to fight in World War II and preferred water—being on his yacht or a surfboard—to land.

"The guy you see on the screen isn't really me," Wayne once explained. "I'm Duke Morrison, and I never was and never will be a film personality like John Wayne. I know him well. I'm one of his closest students. I have to be. I made a living out of him."[74] Yet to the world, and especially Americans, his on-screen persona epitomized the quiet, resilient, and rugged individualist that, in reality, he was not. Wayne not only reflected the American psyche (or at least Ford's vision of it) but, through the movie screen, through the shared experience of packed theaters and popcorn, he amplified it.

Ford and Wayne would make twenty-three movies together. In their creative partnership, "the two men succeeded in defining an ideal of American masculinity that dominated for nearly half a century," wrote Nancy Schoenberger.[75] But this ideal was a lie, conjured up like magic.

Ford made US history both patriotic and poetic, and while he made John Wayne its standard-bearer, the actor himself had few, if any, political opinions when he started his career. During the process of playing America's great heroes (real and imagined), however, he slid over to the anti-communist politics of the right—the very political force that saw many writers, actors, directors, and other theater professionals driven out of their professions. Wayne is famously quoted in a 1971 *Playboy* magazine interview as saying,

> With a lot of blacks [*sic*], there's quite a bit of resentment along with their dissent, and rightfully so. But we can't all of a sudden get down on our knees and turn everything over to the leadership of the blacks [*sic*] . . . I believe in white supremacy until the blacks [*sic*] are educated to a point of responsibility. I don't believe in giving authority and positions of leadership and judgement to irresponsible people.

He shared similar judgments about another racial group, Native Americans, the stories of which so many of his films were built around. He said,

> "I don't feel we did wrong in taking this great country away from them . . . Our so-called stealing of this country from them was just a matter of survival. There were great numbers of people who needed new land and the Indians were selfishly trying to keep it for themselves."[76]

One cannot wholly express the irony that the cinematic backdrops for so many Ford westerns—including those starring Wayne—were selfishly shot in Monument Valley, a Navajo reservation on the Arizona–Utah border.

So hardened in his vitriol toward American Indians, six security guards had to hold Wayne back from attacking Sacheen Littlefeather at the 1973 Academy Awards.[77] She had taken the stage on behalf of Marlon Brando, to decline his award for best actor (in *The Godfather*) because, in Littlefeather's words— "[Brando] very regretfully cannot accept this very generous award. And the reasons for this being are the [negative] treatment of American Indians today by the film industry."[78]

John Wayne not only became the icon for propaganda, he swallowed it whole, letting it change his own opinions of America and the world. Orange County, which had named its airport after him in 1971, considered removing his name from the terminal. This came in response to the internet's *never-forget* power, which resurfaced Wayne's racist opinions. However, at the time of this book's publication, years later, the burghers of Orange County seem to have let the outrage fade back into the airport's luggage racks and postponed any decision. It's easier to accept a lie than stand for the truth.

In works of fiction and movies, the process we use to defend ourselves from lies presented to entertain us is called the *willing suspension of disbelief*. With purpose, we park our critical brains and accept the murder mystery, love story, science fiction spectacular, or western adventure as entertainment. As for the truth of the story, as it is not at issue, we never question it. With enough repetition, the process evolves from the suspension of disbelief to the *agreement to be fooled*. Against the Hollywood star-making machine, we can become powerless.

The impact of television allowed the producers in our Theater of Lies a broader, more regular, and less expensive medium to tell their stories. Professional wrestling took the lessons of John Ford and put them on steroids (quite literally). Whether cheering for Haystack Calhoun or Whipper Billy Watson, the wrestling heroes of my generation always took on the bad guys, Killer Kowalski or The Sheik. The bad guys were usually foreign—or at least felt exotic—and had menacing backstories.

These wrestlers are foundational to the misinformation in the process of how we have come to see truth in the Theater of Lies. The sport of professional wrestling is *drama*. It is as though the original Greek writers and actors were sweaty, 250-pound leviathans. From the actor-athletes and their characters and relationships to the pulled-back punches and villains waiting center-ring to be finished off in close to ritual execution, each match is scripted and choreographed. In exchange for not only entertainment but devotion, television wrestling promoters created villains and heroes. And their performers (gifted athletes, for sure) never stopped playing their roles. While we tend to see actors play many different roles, some—like John Wayne, Hulk Hogan, and his comrades—only ever played one.

As the audience for professional wrestlers, we allow ourselves to go beyond suspending disbelief to actually being fooled. We know that the punches, if they land at all, are not hard, and the reaction to them oversold. We know the no-holds-barred tactics are fake, yet we cheer on our heroes and despise their adversaries. Some, like Dwayne "The Rock" Johnson, generate sufficient star power to carry their personas outside the wrestling ring into other forms of entertainment, first television then films.

The very real stages of entertainment theaters—from wrestling rings to films and television—provide the virtual foundations for what is our contemporary Theater of Lies. As we begin to cheer on the reputation that a celebrity has forged on one stage, if that reputation is strong enough, it can lay the pathway to other stages.

Wrestler Jesse "The Body" Ventura, like Dwayne Johnson, went from the wrestling stage to the film stage, then went onto the political stage as the governor of Minnesota. Winning on the stage of body-building's world championship four times, Arnold Schwarzenegger built a path to Hollywood, and there established a new persona as an action hero. He then took that hero persona (one that was entirely fictional) and used it to launch an electoral run at the governorship of California. He won, twice. Each step along the way, we, the audience, transposed our agreement to be fooled from the character's original persona onto the next stage of their careers. To wit, one of the names gaining public support for a future presidential candidacy is none other than Dwayne Johnson.[79]

This process is what I call *reputation creep*. This is when the Theater of Lies becomes truly dangerous: we allow ourselves to be fooled into supporting, say, a racist actor who we'd rather believe was the cowboy hero of our movies, or a billionaire real-estate developer turned reality-television star for the presidency of the United States (and winning). The responsibility, of course, is our own. We give permission to the persona to fool us.

Reputation creep, like propaganda, is not inherently bad. It's just risky as it plays to our most simple decision-making process, bias. In May 2019, Volodymyr Zelenskyy was elected as the president of Ukraine. His prior job was as a comedian with his own television series on which he played a schoolteacher who was persuaded to run for president of Ukraine and won. Few leaders in the world took him seriously until Russian invaded Ukraine in 2022. It was then that the comedian turned politician rose to become an established international statesman—himself becoming the icon of resistance for Ukrainians.

A primary tactic within the Theater of Lies is the strategic packaging of misinformation followed by its weaponization. Its masters use our natural tendency to suspend our disbelief in exchange for entertainment. The next step of our being fooled comes with repetition of these lies over time. Truth fades. We do not see the Theater being constructed around us. Lies overpower reality.

Sometimes, masked as entertainment, they even come with popcorn. Other times, the popcorn is set aside for ceremony, rules of order, and a Congressional Seal—whatever it takes to make the audience believe that the fictions they are being sold are actually real. Unfortunately, while some of our emperors may indeed have no clothes, it is very hard to be the young boy calling out this fact from the sidelines. In the nineteenth-century story, the townspeople realize they have been fooled. Today, that boy would be brought down in a Twitter fight, canceled, and his parents forced to move out of town.

"Totalitarian regimes unanimously brand as nonsensical the idea that there exists a single objective truth, valid for everybody . . . Such being the case, myth is better than science and rhetoric that works on the passions preferable to proof that appeals to the intellect."[80]

– ALEXANDRE KOYRÉ,
TWENTIETH-CENTURY FRENCH HISTORIAN AND AUTHOR.

4

IN THIS THEATER, THEY WEAR MASKS.

If you believe that lies are the most effective way to manipulate opinion and human behavior, then the invention of the notion of race is the second most powerful lie ever told. It's a biggie. In the Theater of Lies, it is second only to the whopper that women are subservient to men. The concept of race is an invention. Its producers were entirely human, and, like all liars, they created their lie for a specific purpose—and it worked.

The word race didn't even come into dictionaries until 1606, when French diplomat Jean Nicot (better known for his introduction of tobacco plants to France and whose name inspired that given to the addictive part of tobacco, nicotine) defined the word in one of the earliest known French dictionaries. "Race means descent," Nicot wrote in *Trésor de la Langue Française*. "Therefore, it is said that a man, a horse, a dog or another animal is from a good or bad breed."[81]

Today, the evolution of our language has separated animals into categories of breeds and human beings into categories of race. But just because race has become such a common part of our language, it does not make it real, especially in terms of biology or genetics.

In an official statement from the American Association of Biological Anthropologists (AABA), the AABA said:

> [Race] does not have its roots in biological reality, but in policies of discrimination. Because of that, over the last five centuries, race has become a social reality that structures societies and how we experience the world. In this regard, race is real, as is racism, and both have real biological consequences.[82]

Race is about culture, not genetics. As Vivian Chou, a Harvard University geneticist, reminds us, "Ultimately, there is so much ambiguity between the races, and so much variation within them, that two people of European descent may be more genetically similar to an Asian person than they are to each other."[83]

The concept of race has been so persuasive, and repeated so often for so long, that it is difficult to pinpoint the precise moment it took root. But historian Ibram X. Kendi, a professor of humanities at Boston University, has done a pretty good job of doing just that. The year was 1453.

In modern terms, I imagine it as a moment when a client with a particularly challenging need met a particularly skilled public relations expert. The client with that need was Prince Henry of Portugal. In addition to his royal duties, he was the Grand Master of the Military Order of Christ, the successor organization to the Knights Templar (of the Crusades' fame). He was also one of the first Europeans to grasp the fact that the emerging industry of the African slave trade was going to be highly profitable.

His nephew, himself a devoted member of the prince's Military Order, was Gomes Eanes de Zurara. In his New York Times bestseller, *Stamped from the Beginning: The Definitive History of Racist Ideas in America*, Kendi writes that de Zurara, the nephew to Portugal's leading African slave trader, positioned Black Africans as less than human and in need of both spiritual and civil rehabilitation.[84]

In marketing terms, we would call this Prince Henry's unique selling proposition. "They lived like beasts,"[85] wrote de Zurara of Africans in his book *The Chronicle of the Discovery and Conquest of Guinea,*

> They are without any custom of reasonable beings. They have no knowledge of bread or wine, and they are without covering of clothes or the lodgement of houses, and worse than all, they have no understanding of good, but only know how to live in bestial sloth.[86]

At the time, the notion that one race of people was better or worse than another was uncommon, if not outright unknown.

If the fifteenth century de Zurara was not the first to think it, he appears to have been the first to write down that life as a slave in Portugal was better than being free in Africa.[87] His words would travel well past his death. After being published in 1453, the book was passed along to most every captain, port master, financier, and person participating in the emerging and rapidly growing trade of enslaved Africans.[88]

De Zurara's positioning of Africans as less than human, according to Kendi, marked the birth of a lie that was supported by at least two fundamental biases of Europeans of the time: first, the Christian drive for conversion, and second, and most powerful, the enlightened self-interest of meeting supply and demand needs. The availability of white slaves was dropping, and the demand could be met by Black slaves from Africa. Kendi writes,

> Zurara distinguished the Portuguese by framing their African slave-trading ventures as missionary expeditions . . . But the market was changing . . . most of the captives sold in Western Europe were Eastern Europeans. So many of the seized captives were "Slavs" that the ethnic term became the root of the term "slave" in most Western European languages. By the mid-1400s, Slavic communities had built forts against slave raiders, causing the supply of Slavs in Western Europe's slave markets to plunge at around the same time that the supply of Africans was increasing. As a result, Western Europeans began to see the natural Slav(e) not as white, but Black.[89]

It was this combination of a supply and demand process masked by the need for Christian conversion that established the belief system not only served to justify Black slavery but drove the colonization of Africa and the founding of the United States (the hypocritical claim in America's Declaration of Independence's claim that "all men are created equal" notwithstanding).

The lie that Black people were less than human gave rise to the idea that white people were better than them. And since that was "true," in a *we're-at-the-top-of-the-food-chain* simile, they raised themselves not just above Black people but any other race.

The through line of that lie continued into 1899, decades after Lincoln's Emancipation Proclamation freed 3.5 million slaves in the Confederate states, when it found expression through the pen of another writer, more familiar to most than de Zurara: Nobel-Prize-winning author Rudyard Kipling (of *The Jungle Book* fame). Here is the first stanza of his poem, *The White Man's Burden*, in which he focused on the "need" for the United States to colonize the Asian people of the Philippines:

> Take up the White Man's burden—
> Send forth the best ye breed—
> Go bind your sons to exile
> To serve your captives' need;
> To wait in heavy harness
> On fluttered folk and wild—
> Your new-caught, sullen peoples,
> Half devil and half child.[90]

Kipling was using the same misinformation technique that de Zurara used. Cause masking capitalism. In de Zurara's case, the slavery of Black Africans was done to save their souls, not to profit from their free labor. In Kipling's case, conversion to Christianity was part of the cause, the other being colonization, so that the economy and international power of the British Empire could sustain itself. As a true believer, Kipling became a legendary producer in the Theater of Lies. His poem and many of his other writings were used both as entertainment and a powerful tool of persuasion to transpose the lie that Blacks were less than human onto other non-white peoples (in his case, onto people of the Philippines).

Kipling's righteous lie—the burden of the white man was to save such peoples from themselves—was told and re-told in Canada, too. The lie is directly connected to the removal of 150,000 Indigenous children from their parents to attend state- and church-sponsored schools, a process that began a few decades before Kipling's words were published.

Officially, the purpose of these schools was to educate and assimilate Indigenous youth into Canadian society. Christian educators from both Catholic and Protestant churches staffed the schools. Officially, 3,213 children died from the abuse of these educators,[91] although the actual number is estimated to be at least twice that high. The last such school closed in 1996,[92] more than a century after the first one opened.

In 1879, Canadian Prime Minister John A. Macdonald, who had previously served as the nation's minister of Indian Affairs, said,

> When the school is on the reserve, the child lives with its parents, who are savages, and though he may learn to read and write, his habits and training mode of thought are Indian. He is simply a savage who can read and write. It has been strongly impressed upon myself, as head of the Department, that Indian children should be withdrawn as much as possible from the parental influence, and the only way to do that would be to

put them in central training industrial schools where they will acquire the habits and modes of thought of white men.[93]

Once again, the notion of saving non-white people from themselves raises its racist head. All this because Prince Henry of Portugal, the navigator who never navigated, had his nephew tell a grand story in the Theater of Lies to justify his new venture: the capture, submission, transfer, and sale of Black African people to white Europeans.

But these questions remain: why was the lie that Black people are less than human so widely embraced at the time and why is it still embraced by many today? The answers must be more than what Nazi propagandist, Hippler, said about simplifying complex issues and repeating them. For others to truly believe the lie and repeat it as truth to others, there had to have been something else at play.

A part of the answer to that question is singular tactic used in each case of the successful telling and re-telling of the less-than-human lie. I call that tactic masking. It occurs when in order to convince people to act in a way that is beneficial to you, you mask your true reason with a rationale your audience is not only more likely to accept, but which is also false. It's a double-blind process that makes your true goal more palatable—like Congressman Gaetz presenting his staged hearing as having legislative authority.

This tactic of masking is used all too often today, like when an industry wraps itself around a flag of environmental sustainability while taking little or no action on climate change. In business and media, in terms of the environment, it is called "greenwashing."

Environmentalist Jay Westerveld created the term in 1986[94] as a pushback on the hotel industry's save-the-towel campaign (hang up your used towel to dry and we'll leave it for you; put your used towel in the bathroom and we'll take it away, wash it, and provide you with a clean one).

> Westerveld noticed the vast amount of waste he had come across throughout the rest of the hotel, where there were no visible signs of efforts being made to become more sustainable. He said that instead, the hotel was simply trying to reduce costs by not having to wash towels as much but while trying to market it as being eco-friendly.[95]

The producers in the Theater of Lies are experts in use of masks to engage you in their stories. It is yet another technique taken from the producers of real theater, in fact, from the original open-air theaters of ancient Greece. You're likely familiar with those today as the two-mask symbol (one sad mask for tragedy, one happy mask for comedy) is an icon for entertainment worldwide. In the case of the Greeks, the actors wore masks to express emotions and characters to the audience. In the case of today's producers of lies and misinformation, multiple masks are used for deception and play upon our biases, a process I will explore further in the next chapter.

"When it comes to controlling human beings there is no better instrument than lies. Because, you see, humans live by beliefs. And beliefs can be manipulated. The power to manipulate beliefs is the only thing that counts."[96]

— MICHAEL ENDE, GERMAN NOVELIST.

....

5

PLAYING TO
THE AUDIENCE.

An expert tailor or seamstress will tell you that the toughest place to cut and sew a piece of fabric is along the bias. In case of cloth, the bias goes against the cloth's natural weave, and it can't be stitched in the same manner as any other piece. Manipulating along the bias takes expertise, in sewing and in propaganda. The producers in our Theater of Lies, however, have found a much more willing audience than a challenging cloth to work with.

One of my favorite conspiracy arguments is that a chain of convenience stores in the United States is called 7-11 because they are run mostly by Arabs, with the name reflecting the year of the first Muslim invasion of Europe. This would be a surprise to the white Texans who started the Southland Corporation and first branded their stores after their hours of operation, from 7 a.m. to 11 p.m.[97]

When Prince Henry commissioned his nephew de Zurara to write the biographical tales of adventures he'd never had, Portugal and Spain were nearing the end of centuries of rule by dark-skinned Africans known as the Moors. In 711 AD, about 10,000 Muslims from North Africa invaded Europe and managed to subdue its population of over 5 million.[98]

It is not ignorance that most everyone has heard of the Crusades but not the seven-century domination of the Moors over most of southern Europe (Spain, Portugal, Sicily, and Malta) that preceded them. It is an example of how the Theater of Lies can close one show and open another, as if the previous production (as in history) had never even happened and rewrite that history in the process.

Eventually, 500 years later, the Spanish monarchy fought back, taking over the Moor capital of Cordoba in 1236. It took another two and a half centuries for Spain to finally evict the Moors from power and the nation when, in 1492, the armies of King Ferdinand and Queen Isabella captured Granada, their last city. It was a good year for Queen Isabella, as she had also financed the first voyages of Christopher Columbus to the New World.

Over the course of their 700-year rule, the Moors brought along with them modern mathematics, sidewalks, streetlamps, science, higher education, and the advancement of literacy—along with a magical component of healthcare called *cleanliness*.

They established the capital at the city of Cordoba and grew it to house a million residents. That scale was enormous, as no other city in Europe had more than 30,000 people at the time. They also built over 900 public baths.[99] To combat the latter, the monarchs of northern Europe and the Catholic Church fostered their own propaganda to convince their subjects that cleanliness, especially the use of public baths, was a sin (though the latter may be linked to sex as much as soap).[100]

There was so much pent-up European bias against the Moors that anyone with dark skin was referred to as a Moor.[101] Today, if you have the name Moore, somewhere in your *Ancestry.com* profile lurks a link to a family of dark-skinned Africans who roamed and resettled in what would become the United Kingdom.

In 1442, at just about the same time that Prince Henry of Portugal was learning about the profitability of the African slave trade, Pope Eugene IV helped the mission along. He declared that not only pagans but also Jews, "heretics," and "schismatics" (dissenters from the Christian faith) would "go into the eternal fire."[102] Later that year, Eugene would decree that "capturing the Moors as slaves was a part of the Crusade and whoever sailed south in this pursuit would receive ablution of his sins."[103]

The year 1492 turned out to be a very good one for white Europeans, as the king of Portugal banished all Moors from the country, forcing 3.5 million to flee as nationless people to cities and towns across Europe. As with the adult children of illegal immigrants whom some US conservatives wish to forcefully expel to the places of their parents' birth, few of the Moors could go "home" to Africa, as it was to them a foreign land. Britain became a popular destination with the name Moore now fully ensconced as a traditional English surname.

The impact of foreign rule over illiterate white Europeans by sophisticated, educated, and highly literate Black Africans had a dramatic effect on the future—a future we now live in. If you thought that

Trump's 2016 election as president of the United States was, in part, a rebound effect from the two-term elections of America's first Black president, Barack Hussein Obama, think for a moment about what nearly eight centuries of Black African Muslim rule might have done to Christian Europeans newly freed from the shackles of bondage found in the availability of libraries, street lighting, and healthcare.

There is one incontrovertible piece of evidence that time has completely pasted over, like wallpaper on a cracked wall. Prior to the arrival of the Moors, Roman numerals were the numerical script (for those who could read). After their arrival, Arabic numerals swept away their Roman forebears, leaving them only on formal documents and statues—in their place was the number zero and the birth of modern mathematics.[104] (I dare you to try to add, multiply, or divide using only Roman numerals).

The vanquishing of 700 years of Moorish rule over Southern Europeans and their cultural dominance is, in my opinion, a production of the Theater of Lies. Just as some conservative governments today are trying to summarize large parts of American history into the category of "we'll have none of that talk, here," we have a tendency to change the meanings of our past to ideas that better reflect—we believe—how we feel about ourselves today. Even if that feel is a based on false premises (such as myths, fictions, and outright misrepresentations of fact). For example, let's dig a little deeper into our collective notion of Thanksgiving.

The first Christian documentation of Thanksgiving comes not from the familiar traditional American story of English Pilgrims feasting with Native American Indians in Massachusetts on July 30, 1620, nor President Abraham Lincoln's long-forgotten declaration of Thanksgiving as a national holiday in 1863 to celebrate the

Union victory at Gettysburg. No, the first widely promoted Christian Thanksgiving was November 25, 1491.[105]

On that day, two things happened. First, the king and queen of Spain accepted the official surrender of the Moors at Granada, then Pope Innocent VII announced that the day would be known as a "day of thanks" or "day of thanksgiving" for the freedoms gained by European Christians.[106] The eating of turkey at the feast comes, again, not from Pilgrims in America but from the strange, large bird imported from the New World (Mexico, actually) and named after the Moors, known often as "Turks." That bird's first English name was "Turkish cock," which was then shortened to the name *turkey*. The English also branded corn as "Turkish wheat" and pumpkins as "Turkish cucumbers," referring to anything foreign as *Turkish*.[107]

But try to find an American who doesn't equate Thanksgiving with the Pilgrims of Plymouth Rock or a European who knows the true source of the term. History has been buried in centuries of propaganda, so often repeated as to excuse the truth as fiction.

The lies used to sell slavery as salvation were communicated at a speed and volume the world had never seen before. It was a deliberate propaganda campaign that concealed its purpose so well that its history is long forgotten. Today, the notion of slavery (to most people) is appalling. But the truth behind why white people imagined Africans as less than human, enslaved them en masse, including their children, from birth, and abused their bodies and minds in multitudes of ways . . . is never questioned. And though the event did occur, the origin story of American Thanksgiving as a celebration between immigrating Pilgrims from England and the local Native population masks the impactful truth of America's history of violence against and relocation of North America's Native populations.

While America annually enjoys the third Thursday of every November as a national holiday, it has buried the truth of its original celebration. Abraham Lincoln declared it a national holiday in 1863 in recognition of the:

> Sacrifices of life, limb, health, and liberty by brave, loyal, and patriotic citizens [to celebrate] victories on land and on the sea, so signal and so effective as to furnish reasonable grounds for augmented confidence that the union of these States will be maintained, their constitutions preserved, and their peace and prosperity permanently restored.[108]

With the Union States' victory over the Confederate States in America's Civil War just two years later, the Lincoln declaration of Thanksgiving goes full circle from the pope's 1491 pontification of the holy day of thanks for God freeing Europe from the Moors. In the pope's case, the Blacks were banished. In America's case, the Blacks were freed.

The why of all this is bias. It is the secret infrastructure of the world's most powerful lies. It is part of the second part of the story of lies—the participation of the receiver, as tapping into the biases of an audience fosters emotional resonance with the speaker. It is the founding ingredient in the recipe for successful propaganda. Let's call it "playing to the audience." Here's how it works:

1. Have an agenda.

2. Create a lie within that agenda's framework reflecting the bias of your audience.

3. Simplify it.

4. Repeat. Repeat. *Repeat.*

5. Do this until your audience starts to repeat the lies for you and foster their spread.

6. Add more lies that reflect your audience's biases until those biases become so entrenched in their psyches that nothing will change their minds.

Throughout the process, remember that you don't need to change or maintain the opinions of everyone—just enough people that will let you achieve your agenda. Once you've got people to believe what you want them to, even if it's wholly based on lies, they will rather fight the people who oppose you than accept that you—and they—are wrong. In psychological teams, this is called cognitive dissonance[109]—the mental discomfort experienced when you try to hold two conflicting beliefs. As a result, you push aside the conflict and focus on the most comfortable of those beliefs and the stress you were feeling is alleviated. You avoid what John F. Kennedy referred to as "the discomfort of thought".

My hope is that one day, American Blacks—and all Americans—will celebrate Thanksgiving as the remembrance of a major milestone in America becoming a unified nation of free people, rather than of people fleeing religious persecution and enjoying a meal with the Native inhabitants of their new home (who they would later kill, conquer, enslave, and redistribute).

Given the dominance of Black players on the field (yet few in the head coaching ranks and none in the owner's box), that day's annual nationally televised football games would be a good place for that true remembrance to be launched into a new American zeitgeist.

"A stupid man's report of what a clever man says can never be accurate, because he unconsciously translates what he hears into something he can understand."[110]

– BERTRAND RUSSELL,
TWENTIETH-CENTURY BRITISH PHILOSOPHER AND NOBEL LAUREATE.

··

6

THE PERSUASIVE POWER OF PATHOS.

Long before mass shootings became part of the ugly fabric of life in America, on September 14, 1989, Joseph Wesbecker walked into the printing plant where he worked in Louisville, Kentucky, and killed eight of his co-workers and wounded another twelve. Commenting on the disaster at the time was the first-term senator for the state, Mitch McConnell. He said, "he was deeply disturbed" and that "We must take action to stop such vicious crimes." He also said, "We need to be careful about legislating in the middle of a crisis."[111]

McConnell fully understood the power of pathos to persuade people—in this case—to persuade people to vote for more control of guns. McConnell knew *pathos*—the Greek word capturing emotions like empathy, care, concern, and even anger—had to be corralled to prevent an assault on the US Constitution's Second Amendment, the right to bear arms. His rationale remains firmly in place in the early twenty-first century, and it comes from a source pre-dating it by twenty-four centuries.

Before the actors can take the stage in a play, someone has to have written a story. In technical terms, you know it as a "script." This script also might inform a speech delivered at a convention, a magazine article, a newspaper clipping, or a webpage. These media are all platforms for stories. Whether the story is a good one or a bad one is often considered a matter of opinion—a "beauty is in the eye of the beholder" situation. But just as trained artists know that a certain structure is required to engage an audience with one of their paintings, effective writers and propagandists know that engaging and persuasive storytelling has structure they must follow as well.

The creators working in the Theater of Lies—the writers, directors, and producers—all use these structures. The best of them can have you completely fooled and eagerly awaiting the sequel. But unlike the storytellers of Hollywood, Bollywood, and almost every entertainment producer worldwide, those who create the Theater of Lies have much more nefarious designs.

Twenty-four centuries ago, about the same time the first mud huts were being constructed along the River Thames in Britain, the Greek philosopher Aristotle identified three pillars of persuasion: *ethos, pathos,* and *logos*. Collectively, he referred to them as "the art of rhetoric."[112] Translated, *ethos* is the reputation of the speaker, *pathos*, the emotional connection between the speaker and the audience, and *logos*, the facts, proofs, and logic of the argument. Aristotle claimed that facts were the least important pillar—especially on their own. [113]

Whether former US President Donald Trump was ever schooled in classical Greek philosophy is up for debate. But however he learned it (in school, by trial and error, or perhaps by a mentor), it's hard to deny his mastery of persuasive techniques. During his first presidential campaign, he stood firmly on his reputation as a successful businessman, billionaire, and dealmaker, establishing his *ethos*. He empathized—with the entrenched attitudes of voters who wanted change and felt that, over the course of their lives, they had become second-class citizens. His emotionally charged rhetoric, such as his "make America great again" mantra, not only reflected their attitudes but also gave them a national platform. In this, he made an emotional connection—*pathos*. His proof points (his *logos*)—cherry-picked data, lies, and "alternative facts"—merely confirmed their decision. While losing the popular vote to former First Lady and Senator Hillary Clinton, his persuasive expertise was sufficient to ensure that Trump won more than enough votes in the US's state-by-state based Electoral College to repeatedly trumpet that he'd won a landslide victory. [114]

In contrast, throughout Trump's presidency, the opposing Democrats demonstrated just how little understanding they had of Aristotelian persuasion. For years, they pounded on facts—*logos* over *pathos* and *ethos*—to persuade the American public that Mr. Trump, both during and after the 2016 election campaign, engaged in behavior worthy of impeachment or even jail.

The Democrats thought US special counsel Robert Mueller was about to deliver their ultimate fantasy live on national television before two congressional committees in what they hoped would be their *coup de grâce*. Mueller was their political version of a nuclear weapon, the ultimate expression of their fact-focused approach. Here was their square-jawed hero, a "just the facts, ma'am" kind of prosecutor with a résumé that included two stints as head of the FBI. The Democrats were certain he would persuade Americans that Mr. Trump had committed enormous misdeeds. They were certain *logos* would win the day. But that only works in a court of law (most of the time). Not the court of public persuasion.

Aristotle had already predestined the impact of the testimony millennia ago: facts, the least effective tool, stand no chance against *ethos* and *pathos*.

So, Mueller, of course, failed to deliver. Called before a Senate hearing in 2019, his most repeated response to almost any question was "I stand by my report" and "to what annotation are you referring?"[115] No passion. No *pathos*. No sense of urgency in his voice.

The Democrats did him and themselves no favors. They carried on like a boxer whose only punch was a right hook, whose response to being pummeled was to throw more right hooks, harder and faster. If Mueller wouldn't deliver the evidence, then they would. So, they led with the facts. They delivered them coldly. Without emotion (*pathos*). And their clear political bias obliterated any of the influence of their reputation (*ethos*). A bad poetry reading would have changed more minds.

The Republicans, on the other hand, appeared well-schooled in the Aristotelian arts of persuasion. They attacked the character of the special counsel's team, weakening his claim to ethos. They positioned Trump as a man who was not obstructing justice but merely defending himself from false persecution, as any good American would do. Thus, they created powerful sympathy for Trump, *pathos*, among the party's supporters—many of whom were united by a sense of institutional injustice imposed upon their lives. They ignored the facts of the Special Counsel's arguments completely.

By the end of Mueller's two-day testimony, those who supported Trump had stood firm. Those opposed remained so but were disappointed they'd lost their opportunity to change pro-Trump opinions.

Trump pushed Aristotle's third pillar, facts, from being the least important to being basically irrelevant—hence the birth of the term "alternative facts"—code for *facts don't matter*. Special Adviser to the President Kellyanne Conway delivered the term into popular culture when she defended Press Secretary Sean Spicer's exaggeration of the number of people who attended Trump's inauguration.[116]

In this case, Conway does what the Greeks would call *sophism*. In their day, sophists were known for their poetic ability and were paid to teach the youth how to speak with authority and persuasion. They were Trump twenty-four centuries before Trump. Their goal was to stir your emotions, to rile you up to the point that you will make choice that any form of logic would not permit. As a professional communicator, you can admire that ability. As a human being, you should fear it.

For sophists, truth was relative. Their goal was to win a debate without any regard to the truthfulness of their argument. Real-world examples can be found on YouTube. Watch Conway debate CNN's Chris Cuomo. In the videos, Conway uses such egregiously fallacious arguments to address Trump's policy or behavior that her post-political career might as well be as a New Age teacher of sophistry. One of my favorites of her responses was to a number of comments about Donald Trump not being "presidential" in his tone and manner. To this, she replied: "Nonsense. He is the president, so, by definition, everything he does is presidential."[117] It was a masterful piece of redirection.

Such deliberately deceitful speech is both an art and a science. It takes practice, skill, and the confidence to spew bafflegab that not only breaks logic down but causes you to throw it out the window in favor of emotion. Once a sophist such as Conway gets their opponent to react with emotions over logic, they have won — as when she used the tactic to attack the credibility of the World Health Organization (WHO) in the early stages of the pandemic (part of the Trump White House strategy to withdraw its funding for the WHO, just a few months later).[118]

> This is Covid-19^2, not Covid-1, folks. You would think that people charged with the World Health Organization facts and figures would be on top of that.[119]

Aristotle proved it. Others perfected it. Pathos, that intangible ability to create an emotional connection with an audience, is the most powerful tool of persuasion. The producers in our Theater of Lies know this, and you will see in the next chapter just how they use storytelling

....

2   International Committee on Taxonomy of Viruses (ICTV) announced "severe acute respiratory syndrome coronavirus 2 (SARS-CoV-2)" as the name of a new virus on February 11, 2020. This name was chosen because the virus is genetically related to the coronavirus responsible for the SARS outbreak of 2003. The World Health Organization (WHO) announced "COVID-19" as the name of this new disease on the same day, following guidelines previously developed with the World Organisation for Animal Health (OIE) and the Food and Agriculture Organization of the United Nations (FAO) that require inclusion of the year the virus was discovered

Source: https://www.who.int/emergencies/diseases/novel-coronavirus-2019/technical-guidance/naming-the-coronavirus-disease-(covid-2019)-and-the-virus-that-causes-it (Naming the coronavirus disease (COVID-19) and the virus that causes it (who.int))

and its purposeful impact on your brain's chemistry to manipulate you into believing whatever they want you to believe.

Put *pathos* and repetition together, and we can see how, despite psychologists concluding that "repetition is an illogical basis for truth,"[120] it matters not. Facts be damned.

This is especially true in oral communications[121]—how most people now digest information (television, video, podcasts, and radio over newspapers and other written media). Because *pathos* is the human touch in communications, the delivery mechanism for *pathos* and the same message repeated on multiple media outlets—those messages come at the audience with the power of a machine gun over a flintlock.

In the case of gun control in the United States, this is why anti-gun control legislators rebuff any discussion of new laws or regulations during major incidents such as school attacks or mass shootings. For them, *pathos* is a Pandora's box to remain closed and locked unless, of course, it can be opened and let loose to further their own objectives. Persuasion is an art form that can have deadly results, especially when powered by lies, misinformation, and pathos.

"The hallmark of addiction is that it changes your brain chemistry. It actually affects that part of your brain that is responsible for judgement."[122]

– MICHAEL BOTTICELLI,
FORMER WHITE HOUSE DIRECTOR OF NATIONAL DRUG POLICY.

....

7

(MIGHT AS WELL FACE IT) WE'RE ADDICTED TO LIES.

David J. P. Phillips is a Swedish communications trainer who has taken a deep dive into the *pathos* portion of persuasion. For the producers in our Theater of Lies, this is their most powerful tool: appealing to our emotions. Though Phillips's analysis is intended to provide businesspeople with better storytelling skills, it is also a lesson in how the producers in our Theater of Lies manipulate our minds.

The first clue of this is what Phillips defines as the foundation of powerful storytelling. As human beings, it is part of our psychological makeup that, as we become more emotionally invested in a particular situation or person (or even a story that we know to be fictional), we reduce our critical thinking abilities about them. We suspend our disbelief more willingly and quickly.

This is how a movie or novel becomes compelling: the more the audience is emotionally invested in the characters and the situations they are in, the less critical thinking they use to understand that it is all made up. The same process works in the Theater of Lies: the producer builds and shapes the story to manipulate your opinions and motivate your behavior.

It is why it took so long for so many people to believe that six-time Tour de France winner Lance Armstrong was a drug cheat. The rumors of his drug use were rampant, but he of course continued to deny them, stating with confidence that he'd passed every drug test he'd ever taken. Moreover, he was a hero who had overcome testicular cancer *before* becoming the dominant cycling athlete of his generation. Armstrong came back from that experience to win the most grueling cycling race in the world, six times in a row. Armstrong knew and exploited the fact that his fans and his sponsors had an emotional investment in his story and thus would ignore the rumors—and often, the hard facts that supported them. He had the *pathos*—cancer survivor. He had the *ethos*—multiple-time world champion. The *logos* could be, and were, ignored.

David J. P. Phillips has analyzed brain chemistry and found one group of hormones that he calls the *angel's cocktail* and another group he calls the *devil's cocktail*.[123] In the Theater of Lies, however, I'd package them all into one single brand: the producer's poisons. They are managed by your body's endocrine system—the quarterback who calls the plays for your hormone-producing glands. Based on the environment it senses, it increases or decreases the amounts of specific hormones active in your body. Unfortunately, though, this quarterback does not know if the situation you're in is real or not.

In the angel's cocktail, Phillips identified three hormones: dopamine, oxytocin, and endorphins. When your body releases dopamine, you become more focused, become more motivated, and have better short-term memory. With increased oxytocin, you become more empathetic. You are more generous. You trust more and bond more easily with strangers and friends. Endorphins, which athletes know as a hormone the body releases after long periods of exertion, make you feel happy. They provide the "runner's high." They also make you more creative and relaxed and, like dopamine, increase your focus. A good laugh will trigger them.[124]

An effective storyteller knows how to craft a narrative to trick your brain into releasing these hormones. Whether the story is true or not, you are chemically persuaded to believe it. One of the most popular films to use these tactics is the movie *Die Hard*, starring Bruce Willis. I've used it for decades as a training aid for aspiring writers. During the same period, it has become my family's favorite Christmas movie. After the turkey dinner, we gather in front of the TV over pumpkin pie and the hostage crisis at Nakatomi Plaza. The story has captured the minds of audiences worldwide, earning more than $1.4 billion[125] since it premiered in 1988, despite winning no major awards.

The narrative structure of the story is iconic and well studied.

In the 1990s, I took a writing course from science fiction author Dean Wesley Smith, a prolific writer and insightful instructor. To attempt to summarize his teaching in a few words would be like attempting to summarize all of Charles Dickens's novels, but Smith first defined for me the "try/fail" cycle of storytelling that both drives a story forward and establishes an emotional connection between the character and the audience, that is, fostering *pathos*. In one of his workshops, he broke down *Die Hard* scene by scene to demonstrate how that script accomplishes it.

Die Hard is about John McClane, who desperately wants to reunite with his estranged wife, Holly, and their children. She has moved to Los Angeles to take on a senior executive position at the Japanese Nakatomi Corporation. Holly invites John to the company's Christmas party in LA, so John travels in the hope of reconciliation. Shortly after McClane arrives at the party, terrorists take over Nakatomi Plaza, holding the party guests hostage. At the time, John is cleaning himself up in Holly's private bathroom, out of sight. This is the first in a series of barriers that the film writers placed between John and reconciling with his wife.

The writers skillfully used what Phillips called "raising the emotional intensity to reduce your critical thinking abilities."[126] The stakes here have been raised from a hoped-for reconciliation with McClane's wife to saving her life along with those of the hundred or so other party guests who have been taken hostage (*pathos*, then more *pathos*). As an audience member, the try/fail nature of his actions on his journey increases your dopamine. At the same time, your brain releases oxytocin as your emotional connection to John McClane intensifies with every expression of his sense of impending loss and realization of his fault in his failing marriage. You empathize with him. Finally, moments like McClane's famous "Yippee-ki-yay, motherfucker" bring comic relief. Endorphins release into your system. You feel more relaxed and focused.

In the movie, it all adds up to a few hours of fine entertainment. In the Theater of Lies, it adds up to danger. The producers here have used the tools Phillips described, plus another, more negative mixture of hormones he referred to as the devil's cocktail—cortisol and adrenaline.

During periods of intense stress (real or imagined), your body releases cortisol. It is the basis of our fight-or-flight response—a healthy, natural response to perceived threats. At the same time, our bodies release adrenaline—especially as our anxieties rise. Adrenaline increases your heartrate, your blood pressure, the ability of your lungs to retain air, and the glucose level in your blood. While these natural stress managers are based on our evolutionary needs, according to Phillips, they also make us "intolerant, irritable, uncreative, critical, and memory-impaired." All of this adds up to bad decision-making.

This is the message structure so often used by the producers in our Theater of Lies—raise the audience's emotional investment in the propagandist's message. This reduces our ability to think critically, manipulating our emotional connection to the propagandist, and the stressors that foster our intolerance, criticism of others, and memory impairment.

David J. P. Phillips tells us that all of this is addictive. And in the world of social media, the internet, and twenty-four-hour news channels, the opportunity for the propagandists to keep feeding us these drugs never stops. Worse, our bodies adjust to the stress levels we're dealing with, and we like it. They produce emotional highs we want to maintain. The Theater of Lies is a provider of addictive substance. We, the audience, keep demanding more.

Addicts will do almost anything to feed their addictions. For street drugs, it may mean shoplifting, breaking and entering, and sometimes selling their bodies. In the Theater of Lies, it means searching out messages that feed those lies and basing our decisions on them, as well as ignoring any messages to the contrary (as they don't feed our addiction).

But there is more to delivering the drug, that is the story, than steadily increasing the stakes. Just as Bruce Willis's John McLean had his antagonist, the master thief Hans Gruber (played by the late Alan Rickman), every successful story needs a villain. In the Theater of Lies, this is no different—like Eve's devil played by the snake rather than a Labrador puppy.

....

8

VILLAINS ARE VERY SEDUCTIVE.

You remember the images. The black-and-white flittering screens of the mustachioed villain grabbing the heroine and tying her to the railroad tracks. The villain's eyes, wide and mad, staring back into the camera. The damsel in distress about to perish, crushed by the oncoming train. There's no way to save her until the hero appears. This is the foundation of almost all of the stories in the Theater of Lies. Today, our productions are more sophisticated, but the message of villainy still resonant.

In June 2015, *The New Yorker* featured a drawing of the contenders in the US primaries for the Republican selection of their presidential candidate for the election, still more than a year away. The setting for the cover art was a men's locker room, with caricatures of the candidates preparing for a workout. The featured candidates were Rand Paul, Chris Christie, Ted Cruz, Marco Rubio, and the presumptive favorite at the time, Jeb Bush. The cover also featured a drawing of Hillary Clinton peering through a small porthole-style window into the locker room. Just seventeen months away from the election, the winner of not only the primaries but the election itself, Donald Trump, didn't even rate a caricature in a magazine based in the city he'd called home all his life.

That very month, he changed all that. Coming down an escalator in a ceremonial entrance to greet a carefully gathered group of supporters and media, he walked to a podium, the lobby of the Trump building echoing Neil Young's "Rockin' in the Free World."

To formally announce his candidacy for president and entry into the Republican primaries, he said, "Sadly, the American Dream is dead— but if I get elected, I will bring it back, bigger and better and stronger than ever before. Together, we will make America great again!"[128]

He went on to attack most of the rest of the world, blaming Barack Obama for letting the country collapse to the level of "a third world country."[129] Most of his wrath was directed at Mexico, which he accused of "bringing their worst people" to America, "criminals" and "rapists." He told the audience,

> They're sending us not the right people. The US has become a dumping ground for everyone else's problems. They're sending people that have lots of problems and they're bringing their problems . . . they're bringing drugs, they're bringing crime, they're rapists, and some, I assume, are good people, but I speak to border guards, and they tell us what we are getting.[130]

He promised that as president, one of his first actions would be to build a "great, great wall on our southern border" and that he would "make Mexico pay for that wall."[131]

Trump said that Obama and previous administrations had allowed Mexico, China, and other countries to take American jobs and prosperity. He continued,

> China has our jobs, Mexico has our jobs . . . our enemies are getting stronger and stronger by the day, and the US as a country is getting weaker and weaker. How stupid are our leaders, how stupid are our politicians to let this happen? Our president doesn't have a clue. . . Politicians are all talk and no action. They will not bring us, believe me, to the promised land.[132]

In less than 250 words, Trump had schooled his opponents on how to launch a campaign. He gave his audience the *ethos*, *pathos*, and just enough *logos* (if false or hyperbolic) to reflect his argument that he should be president of the United States.

The image of him coming down from on high, like a Greek God, following his statuesque wife, would be repeated in newscasts and online for weeks. His most memorable election promise, to build a wall between Mexico and the United States, would be the centerpiece of this campaign. But this, like his entrance, was only an image. They were both props in the Theater of Lies. But he had identified a compelling problem for his likely voters and positioned himself as the only one who could solve it.

Moreover, he had delivered it all in a fashion in which members of the news media had been trained to tell their stories since they first entered journalism school. Reporters along with their editors or producers, listen for these clues. In terms of communications, I refer to this as the structure of a persuasive argument.

1. What is the problem that needs to be solved? How compelling is it? Who are the villains?

2. What will happen if the problem is not resolved? What are the consequences?

3. How have people tried to solve this problem before? Why did they fail?

4. What is your solution to the problem? Why is it a better solution than the ones that have been tried?

5. What makes you the person to deliver this solution?

Trump delivered this structure perfectly. He didn't just leave breadcrumbs in a forest of information for the media to follow. He left them an eight-story carrot cake of lies so large, so colorful, and so clear that the media had to tell his story exactly the way he wanted them to.

The compelling problem:	The American Dream is dead.
Who are the villains?	China and Mexico have been stealing our jobs Previous presidents, who allowed it to happen.
If not solved:	America becomes a third world country. All that America has ever gained will be lost.
The prior solution:	Previous presidents have been weak and poor negotiators.

The solution:	We're going to build as a massive wall and Mexico will agree to pay for it (and provide no details).
Why you:	I am a successful businessman and a tough negotiator.

One of Trump's opponents in the primaries was South Carolina senator Lindsey Graham. Where Trump had based his campaign on the problem of the American Dream being dead, Graham had based his on the idea that the world was falling apart, and he was (according to his campaign slogan[133]) "Ready to become Commander-in-Chief on Day One." While arguably truer and more significant a problem than Trump's theme, to the audience, Trump's message had more resonance. The American voter, Trump realized, cared more for themselves than the world at large. Graham's campaign had all the traction of a set of bald tires in a snowstorm, despite the fact he had substantial international diplomatic and military credentials. And more critically, he hadn't defined a villain and a clear problem that only he could solve.

This is not only the bedrock of media coverage but also the exemplar of some of the biggest stages in our Theater of Lies: election campaigns. Trump's success was based on positioning America's own government, previous presidents, and immigrants—especially Muslims and Mexicans—as the villains. His message was "I alone can fix it."[134] He positioned himself as the hero.

Over my four decades of work in communications and keenly watching others who succeed, or fail, at the persuasion process; then seeing the powerful results that unethical communicators achieve using lies and misinformation – we can officially declare facts the least important component of the modern mass persuasion process. Facts aren't dead, but they don't drive the bus. Pathos is power.

But I have also learned that quoting a Fourth Century BCE philosopher to modern communicators has the same impact of teaching the rules of Latin conjugations to high school students. So, for me, the unexpected consequence of me asking the question, why do people believe lies and misinformation, has made me better understand why people are persuaded to believe anything, whether that be lies or truth.

So, I have modernized the Aristotelian model for twenty-first century. To it, I've added the structure of the persuasive argument and replaced the notion of pathos with a more relevant term in our modern language - emotional resonance (the "you-had-me-at-hello" factor).

$$\int \text{THE ARGUMENT}^n \left(\text{REPUTATION}^x + \frac{\text{EMOTIONAL}}{\text{RESONANCE}}^y \right) + \frac{\text{PROOF}}{\text{POINTS}}$$

In this mathematical-like formula, persuasion is a function of the structure of the argument, repeated first by the personal delivering it, and then exponentially by others (n). The power of that argument is directly related to the number of times it is repeated, over time. The effectiveness of persuasive argument grows exponentially (this is the 'n' factor) – especially if it is simple, memorable, and compelling enough for others to repeat.

The science of this persuasive argument is that it follows the engagement structure of effective storytelling. There are heroes – as we see in cinema - taking on quests (the problem), overcoming barriers (the villains), and bearing the wounds of failure (consequences), all told to an audience now engaged and indeed cheering for the solution and hero to deliver it.

But for persuasion engine to work, the octane-adding impacts of reputation and emotional resonance are needed. So, you add power through the strength (x) of your reputation added to how well the deliverer of the argument emotionally connects to the needs of the audience (y). As we'll see in Act Three – much of this emotional resonance is created by playing off the preexisting biases of the audience.

The final element of this persuasion equation is addition of proof points. But here's the 21st century kicker — whether these proof points are facts, facts stretched to fit the argument, or outright lies or misinformation — makes little difference. Because audiences use proof points to confirm decisions that they've already made (even if they tell you otherwise).

Defining the problem to solve is the ignition that fires the engine of mass persuasion. That's the key that the effective producers of lies and misinformation turn. No villain, no problems, no media coverage, no emotional resonance with the audience. No matter how many jumper cables you attach to that engine, they won't help that engine turnover unless there is clearly defined problem that the speaker needs to solve.

In America, even carrying on the bloodline of one of the country's most beloved and storied presidents couldn't get past his party's nomination process without it.

If there ever was a candidate with the "royal jelly"[135] to become president of the United States, it was Edward Kennedy. Brother to the assassinated President John F. Kennedy and the assassinated presidential candidate Robert Kennedy, the American public and media had been pressing the Massachusetts senator to carry on his family's legacy. In August 1979, Kennedy prepared to take on the incumbent Jimmy

Carter for the Democratic nomination. Carter's presidency had been marred by a massive spike in gas prices and, worse, Iranian revolutionaries had taken over the US embassy and were holding fifty-two Americans hostage. For a presidential candidate, Edward Kennedy had a buffet of problems from which to launch his campaign.

But when ABC News reporter Roger Mudd asked, "Why do you want to be president?" Kennedy had no answer. He mumbled. He hesitated. He talked on live television for just over a minute, but it seemed like hours. He provided no real response. As journalist Chris Whipple (who had been at the interview as a print reporter) wrote decades later, "On the simple question that would define him and his political destiny, Kennedy had no clue."[136] Kennedy had not identified a villain and a compelling problem that only he could solve. He thought his reputation and the hangover of his brothers' reputations were enough to persuade Americans to vote for him.

The most powerful propaganda campaigns have been founded on this clear definition—a problem that has to be solved lest all be lost, then lean heavily into the biases of the audience to entrench emotional resonance.

That's why lies are such easy bullets to fire. If you don't have a compelling problem to solve, you can just make one up.

> *"Democratic governments must tolerate a free press, regardless of criticism. It is a measure of their democracy. Despotic governments must not: press freedom is a sign of weakness."[137]*

– PHILIP M. TAYLOR, PROFESSOR OF INTERNATIONAL COMMUNICATIONS, UNIVERSITY OF LEEDS, UK.

....

9

STAGE-MANAGING THE CRITICS.

Throughout this book, we examine the dynamics of the four principal characters in the Theater of Lies—the producers and the audience (in the generic, them and we), the audience members who step up and join the producers (the "Edgars"), and the curious who question it all. But as in the real world of theater—live stage, films, and television— there is a professional class of critics whose role is to hold the producers to account as well as guide the audience as to what they might expect. That is, the media.

In our Theater of Lies, these theater critics are the free press. And the producers have been trying to manage these critics for centuries— sometimes to great success. Sometimes, not so well. If you ever want to witness at least one manifestation of the critic management process, I recommend watching a US White House Press Briefing. This is where live theater meets the Theater of Lies, and it can play out several times a week.

Governments of all stripes—monarchies, democracies, dictatorships, whether socialist, capitalist, fascist, or communist—have attempted to control the media since the first newspapers hit the streets. Oliver Cromwell, who would later find his head on a spike outside Westminster Palace for trying to change England from a monarchy into a republic, had his government take complete control of all news, mandating state censorship. The acceptance of such heavy-handedness didn't last, so later, leaders went after the pocketbooks of printing barons, creating the *Stamp Act* in 1712.[138] That placed a punitive tax on any publication containing public news or opinions (thus limiting publication to only those with financial means—and government connections).

The size of the tax increased in direct proportion to the number of printing presses each publication operated. To keep up with the numerous shenanigans that publishers used to avoid the tax, the government introduced a new version of the *Act* in 1725 and then again in 1757.[139] This still didn't work. The British press continued to thrive, its publications drawing the attention of most every citizen and in the process, irritate its government.[140]

Napoleon had a simpler idea. If a publication presented information that held him in a negative light, he shut them down. By force. He believed "three hostile newspapers are more to be feared than a thousand bayonets."[141] By the turn of the nineteenth century, he had forced the closure of sixty-four of seventy-three newspapers. By 1810, only four remained. "If I had a free press," he wrote, "I wouldn't last more than three months."[142]

Flash forward to US President Richard Nixon, whose war on the press was so fierce that he played a card typical of propagandists: he changed their name. Nixon is responsible for the traditional moniker for journalism changing from the "the press" to "the media."[143] He believed the term was broader—as it captured television and radio news alongside newspapers—as well as more ominous.

Nixon's vitriol against the media was legendary, especially as he fought the day-by-day coverage in The Washington Post as its Deep Throat anonymous source providing damning details during the 1972 Watergate scandal.

He told Henry Kissinger, "Never forget, the press is the enemy, the press is the enemy. . . Write that on the blackboard a hundred times."[144] The fact that eighty newspapers endorsed him for president in 1968 and 93 percent of those endorsed him again in 1972 did not change his opinion.[145] Nixon's distrust of the media became the status quo for his entire administration. His vice president, Spiro Agnew, gave several speeches that attacked the media, referring to reporters, editors, and publishers as a "small and unelected elite" who possess "broad . . . powers of choice" and "decide what forty to fifty million Americans will learn of the day's events in the nation and the world."[146]

So, while Professor Taylor's academic perspective that democratic governments must "tolerate a free press"[147] may be accurate, the word *tolerate* implies a willingness (if reluctant) to allow the operation of the free press to continue without interference. In practice, this is hardly the case.

Effective free press shrinks the space between the government and the governed. If a government wants to control what the public knows about its decision-making process—rather than just the decision itself—government leaders can see this as a problem and want to keep their distance.

In a White House Press Briefing, the policy makers of government rarely appear. The White House Press Secretary speaks for the leaders and takes questions from the assembled media (known, collectively, as the White House Press Corps). The media then reports on the decisions of the decision-makers, often including commentary from the Press Secretary. The audience—the readers, viewers, and listeners to the media reports—feel closer to the policy makers and their process, as the media attempts to place them "in the room" through quotes and images. This process further reduces the space between the government and the governed when a media reporter gets to ask a question of the decision maker themselves, or even better, a one-to-one interviewer.

At this point, the space has shrunk to what looks like zero, as in the government leader answers questions directly. The communications environment seems intimate, and on television, the closeup shot of the leader becomes personal. Yet, the space only looks like it has shrunk to zero, as in reality the media edits the interview (for clarity, brevity, and points salient to the story they want to tell) and the government leader has been prepared for this interview at times with the same intensity as an actor rehearses for a role.

The rules have changed. Today, with each social media post sent directly from the hands of a propagandist like Donald Trump to their millions of followers, that space has become effectively nonexistent. In the Theater of Lies, the governed can hear directly from the government (or those that wish to become the government). But that still is not enough control for contemporary propagandists. The influence of any source of contrary information, such as the mainstream media, must be mitigated.

During his first campaign and throughout his presidency, Trump used three simple tactics to control the media: endorsing those who praised him, calling any story that he did not like "fake news," and amplifying these tactics by creating his own media outlet: his Twitter page. As he said in a speech to veterans in July 2018,

> "Just remember, what you are seeing and what you are reading is not what's happening. Just stick with us, don't believe the crap you see from these people, the fake news."[148]

No Stamp Act nor Napoleonic stamping-out of media publications: it's as easy as creating your own media outlet and making it more powerful than the ones you wish would go away. You don't have to close them—just push them to the margins of public opinion. Even better, erode the public's trust in what the mainstream media is reporting. Vilification is a common tactic for escalation because at the same, it positions the propagandist as the hero.

While Napolean admitted that if France had a free press, he wouldn't last three months, Donald Trump admitted that without social media, "he might not be president."[149] During an interview with Lesley Stahl of CBS News, he responded to her question about why he is always attacking the media with, "You know why I do it? I do it to discredit you all and demean you all so that when you write negative stories about me no one will believe you."[150] The audacious undercurrent of that statement was, *and you can't do a thing to stop me* (because if you try, then you too become a villain).

Social media has allowed the producers of lies and misinformation to create their own so-called "news" and immediately publish it. Their messages travel far and wide to millions of people who will like, share, and comment on them without a care for their credibility. The filter of the editorial process between the government and the governed has been eliminated, and without it, lies become weaponized. Their power is based on not on credibility, but popularity. Indeed, the editors have become positioned as villains and the only speakers of truth—those people we already agree with.

Yet despite this, some producers in the Theater of Lies still fear the public's trust of mainstream media so much, that they need to threaten not only the livelihoods of journalists, but also their freedoms. To support Russia's invasion of Ukraine in 2022, President Vladimir Putin signed a law that if a journalist or media outlet strayed from the country's approved narrative on what is happening in Ukraine,[151] the offender could be jailed for up to fifteen years and levied a fine of $1.5 million rubles. The law specifically forbade the "public dissemination of deliberately false information about the use of the armed forces of the Russian Federation."[152] Orwellian, indeed.

Russia's internet censor board, *Roskomnadzor*, forced everyone—from teachers, school children, parents, and media—to refer to the country's invasion of Ukraine as a "special operation." Use of words such as "invasion," "attack," or "declaration of war" led to the offending website being blocked and the offending publishers handed off to the authorities for criminal prosecution.[153]

The producers of lies and misinformation no longer treat the media as critics, but as villains. Nowhere is it worse than in the Philippines. Since 1992, 156 journalists have been killed.[154] Rodrigo Duterte, then president of the nation, made his motivations clear, telling reporters,

"Just because you're a journalist you are not exempted from assassination, if you're a son of a bitch."[155]

There is an old joke about politicians . . . *How can you tell if a politician is lying? Their lips move.* I'll provide you with a more accurate tell. A political leader is lying if they continually threaten or malign the free press. It falls under the Shakespearean category of *the lady thou dost protest too much, methinks.*

The Theater of Lies has been successful in reducing the public's trust of traditional media. As a trusted source of information on COVID-19, for example, only half of Americans trust traditional media.[156] A Gallup Poll in 2020 found that 60 percent of people had little or no trust in mainstream media news on all topics.[157]

The mainstream media, however, is not without fault. Three factors are driving lies and misinformation as prime points of amplification for the producers in our Theater of Lies—the competitive need for news outlets to be the first publisher of a story, the slashing of operating budgets and news staff to remain profitable (since 2008, US media outlets have shed over 90,000 jobs in their newsrooms),[158] and the rise of opinion media disguised as real news. More on that later.

"Sometimes you need to lie to make the world go round."[159]

– KOUSHUN TAKAMI, JAPANESE NOVELIST.

....

10

I MAY LOSE MY HEAD
FOR THIS.

I grew up in two countries with the same monarch—Canada and Australia—both under the rule of the queen of the United Kingdom, Elizabeth II. My perspective on the monarchy is, therefore colored by the absentee landlord version of governance that is unique to all Commonwealth nations save Mother England. We sang "God Save the Queen" in school, and any news of a pending visit to our country by any member of the royal family was treated as though it were the announcement of a new holiday. But nothing about living in a constitutional monarchy is real.

The concept itself is about 5,000 years old. The earliest known records of monarchies come from Egypt, where the institution of course thought highly enough of itself to build pyramids for most of its kings—graves that communicate their power and splendor to this day.

Monarchies have not survived as well as religion and agriculture, though, for many years, the monarch was promoted as a direct descendant of a god, a god himself, or at least as having some secret handshake with a god that made it clear to the citizens of the land that this monarch had the god's authority over their lives. Ancient Egyptians considered their pharaohs to be gods, the Romans dabbled with the thought during a few imperial reigns (such as Julius Caesar and Commodus), the Chinese had 2,000 years of emperors defined as the "Sons of Heaven" (until the early part of the twentieth century), and of course, in the world's longest-standing monarchy, Japan, it was only in 1945 that its emperor repudiated his own divinity and declared that those who came before him were a "false conception." He had little choice in the matter, as the United States had just dropped two nuclear bombs on his kingdom.

Forty-four monarchies remain in the world. A few, such as in Saudi Arabia, are absolute monarchies in the Genghis Khan tradition of "do what you are told or die." Most are constitutional monarchies, the most common of which is the British parliamentary model, which, as I said, I grew up with in two countries. Not a one of them has any place on a modern planet. Yet people have been willing to die for them. In World War II, over 3 million of them gave their lives for their emperor.

The Japanese government used loyalty to the emperor as its primary tactic to control and engage its citizens in its war against the United States. In fact, it took direct propagandic action to entrench the notion.

After the attack on Pearl Harbor, elementary schools were renamed "national schools" and charged to produce "children of the emperor," who would sacrifice themselves for the nation. The government bound the religious beliefs of its citizens to the emperor through propaganda, a tactic similar to how Roman Emperor Constantine embraced

Christianity to establish a firmer bound on the broad geographic scope of the Roman Empire.

Japan produced a pamphlet, *Kokutai no Hongi*, and had it distributed to every school, home, and workplace. Its purpose was to instill the belief in every child that being Japanese was wholly unique and that the origin of the imperial dynasty was spiritual. In one part, it read:

> Loyalty means to revere the emperor as [our] pivot and to follow him implicitly. By implicit obedience is meant casting ourselves aside and serving the emperor intently. To walk this Way of loyalty is the sole Way in which we subjects may "live" and the fountainhead of all energy. Hence, offering our lives for the sake of the emperor does not mean so-called self-sacrifice but the casting aside of our little selves to live under his august grace and the enhancing of the genuine life of the people of a state.[160]

So strong was the emperor's fear of America's demand that any Japanese surrender include his abdication, he repeatedly refused it until two nuclear bombs were dropped. What the emperor considered unimaginable (that he would no longer be considered a god) was only overcome by a previously unimaginably powerful weapon.

In *Surviving Hiroshima: A Young Woman's Story*, Anthony Drago and Tony Wellman claimed Japan's internally directed propaganda campaign was wholly directed at hiding the truth. They wrote,

> Despite the bombing raids occurring all around them, the beliefs and opinions of the Japanese people were

largely shaped by the Japanese propaganda machine. What the news media could and could not say was dictated by the government, and Mom [repeating the propaganda] said that appeared to be perfectly acceptable to the people. People in Japan, they're not inquisitive at all. What the parliament said, what the government said, they'd obey whatever they say. Even I didn't know that America was winning—certainly didn't—everything was hidden away from the people.[161]

The Theater of Lies thrives in the light of inherited governance. This goes beyond the demand subjects die for the monarch, as the people of Japan did. This goes beyond any monarch's absolute ability to declare what is true, in the fashion the de facto king of Saudi Arabia, Crown Prince Mohammed bin Salman, denying he and his court had had anything to do with the kidnapping, torture, and murder of journalist Jamal Khashoggi. The primary damage from any monarchy's Theater of Lies is a barrier between monarchs and their subjects.

The lie that monarchies make true is that some people are better than others *by birth*. No matter how hard they work or study or even get lucky, unless a person is born into a royal family, that person will never achieve such stature. And even if that person were born into a royal family, unless that person were fortunate to be born first and (in most cases) male, that person would never become the head of state. The impact of that lie has cascaded through our society our for centuries, like a never-ending row of dominoes.

Monarchies are the living personifications of *I am better than you and there is nothing you can do about it.* This lie would not be so bad if it were limited merely to monarchies, but the societal impact under such a hereditary structure has poisoned the growth of individuals in nonroyal families (i.e., the rest of us). It has embedded the status of women as second-class citizens into cultures and religions worldwide. The lie of the monarchy emboldens misogyny. In a final affront, monarchies reinforce the lie that birth order is the most important factor when determining who is in charge. Even in 2011, as the British government passed legislation to change the order of succession from first male child to first child of any sex, it maintained that birth order was the first criterion.[162]

While many a royal subject will argue that maintaining at least a constitutional form of monarchy reflects tradition, the message remains the same. In partnership with the later manmade construct of race, monarchy is a deadweight lie that holds down individuals and maintains the status and separation of the ruling class (which its subjects are never to enter).

In 2018, British actor and writer Stephen Fry defended his perspective on how what he referred to as the "preposterous"[163] concept of a monarchy manages to survive in modern Britain. In an interview with CBC Television, he proposed that requiring the political leader of the United Kingdom to visit the queen once a month and to bow to her each time kept the politicians in line. He wondered aloud how different Donald Trump might have been if he'd had to do the same. Ignoring that point of fantasy for the moment, what one of the world's finest and funniest thinkers was really saying in his refined Etonian accent was that society benefited from what I would refer to as *respecting your betters*.

Such is the insidious power of the Theater of Lies to shape our opinions of those who govern us, but also our opinions of not just ourselves but others. In the same year Fry made his value of the monarchy declaration, Britain also voted him the second most intelligent person on television[164] (David Attenborough topped the list). That proved, at least to me, intelligence is no protection from the long-term infections one gets from our seats in the Theater of Lies. At least not on its own.

"The Bible has noble poetry in it . . . and some good morals and a wealth of obscenity, and upwards of a thousand lies."[165]

– MARK TWAIN, AMERICAN SATIRIST AND AUTHOR.[3]

....

11

I MAY GO TO HELL FOR THIS.

Imperial Rome's Emperor Constantine established the first official relationship between the Christian Church and government in 312 AD when he converted to Christianity.[166] As the first emperor to march his legions into Rome, he had calculated that the vast geographical area of the Roman Empire (form Northern Africa, Jerusalem, Gaul, and Britain) could not be held together under the auspices of the Roman religion of multiple gods. The further the empire stretched from Rome, the more foreign it became, and many of the conquered regions had

....

3   I dare use a quote from Mark Twain on the veracity of the Bible here, in the hope that it does not give cause for some people to call for banning his books from school libraries based on the author's anti-religion statements.

their own local religious beliefs. Constantine used Christianity and its monotheism as the spiritual authority to rule and bind the highly different peoples and cultures he governed.[167] The process, of course, was not immediate. But sixty years later, another emperor, this time Flavius Theodorus, used his power to "shape the Christian faith so that the Christian faith could shape the empire," says historian Susan Wise Bauer.[168] In her 2010 book, *The History of the Medieval World*, she concludes that "the two traditions [the religion of Christianity and the need to govern] continued to change both of them in ways that would be impossible to undo."[169]

Fast forward to the king (or queen) of England being also the Supreme Governor of the Church of England, and it is the archbishop of the church that places the crown on their head—and the codependence of authority is complete. And so, for every government that requires its heads of state and other elected officials to swear their oath of office on a Bible and close with the phrase "so help me, God."

To be clear, I take no issue with one's personal beliefs. This is not about denying their truth or the values they hold. A great many people in this world take comfort and surety from their beliefs, harming no one in the process.

My problem with religion, any religion, is the use of manipulative methods to propagate themselves. The tools and tactics of propagating faiths like Christianity have used are the bedrock of the lies that form our opinions not only about our religious beliefs but most everything we experience (such as the hierarchy of men over woman, gender issues, abortion rights, and the power of not only being right, but righteous).

Religions, like governing philosophies (whether they be democratic, autocratic, or any other form), force people into binary decisions (softly, as in my way is better than the other way, or harshly, as in my way is the only way and the people who follow the other way are wrong and should be vilified). In Act Two, we will examine the polarity of opinion this causes and damage it does.

Historically, the most important building in a city or town was the tallest. In most cities today, these are monuments to corporate achievement, with skylines dominated by tributes to banks and insurance companies. In the suburbs, these achievements tend not to be corporate but residential: condominium towers raised high so that the wealthiest are both able to gaze far and wide while remaining anonymous in the sky.

The tallest building in ancient Rome was not the emperor's palace or the Roman Forum, though, but the Colosseum. Constructed in the first century AD, geographically and culturally, it was at the very center of Rome. Holding up to 80,000 people (about a quarter of the city's entire population), it was the television set of its day, hosting gladiatorial fights, executions, mock sea battles, and other theatrical productions. Its purpose from day one was the ruling government's demonstration that the most important thing in Rome was its people (and everyone else was, of course, disposable—to wit, the theatrical murder of slaves and criminals before citizens' eyes). The Colosseum was renovated and revered for 500 years of near-continuous use until the Roman Empire itself faded away.

It was perhaps the original, literal Theater of Lies.

Though the feeding of Christians to the lions didn't actually happen there (if it happened at all), it did not stop the Catholic Church from using the myth as a spiritual monument to its martyrs. In the mid-1700s, Pope Benedict XIV declared the Colosseum a sacred site where early Christians had been murdered. He forbade the use of the Colosseum as a quarry, consecrated the building to the Passion of

Christ, and installed the Stations of the Cross, declaring the structure as sanctified by the blood of the Christian martyrs who perished there.[170]

The Church learned many lessons from the Romans, one of which was that buildings were important—and the bigger and grander, the better. After about 400 CE, one would find that the tallest building in almost every town, village, city, or hamlet was a church, its cross-topped steeple a come-hither symbol of salvation. When governing a predominantly illiterate society, spectacle is a powerful tool; and constructing the grandest building in town and making that building open to the public was more about spectacle than anything else. Across small towns in Europe and North America, you can still see the remnants of this strategy. Drive into these communities and look around. Find the church, and in many cases, it remains the tallest building in town. A tour of old churches in Europe is as close to an experience of time travel as one could ever have.

It is a marvel how much time it took to build these churches. In medieval times, the construction period for the church's monuments went well beyond the lifetimes of several generations. England's York Minster Cathedral took 252 years to complete (1220–1472),[171] meaning that the architects who designed the structure, the stonemasons who carved its first stones, and the craftsmen who laid them would be the great-great-grandparents of those who would finally witness the completion of their ancestors' work.

From the current York Minster website comes the story:

> Since the seventh century, the Minster has been at the center of Christianity in the north of England and today remains a thriving church rooted in the daily offering of worship and prayer. The Minster was built

for the glory of God. Every aspect of this ancient building—from the exquisite, handcrafted stone through the unrivaled collection of medieval stained glass—tells the story of Jesus Christ. We invite you to discover this sacred place and the love of God at its heart, which has attracted people from across the globe for more than a thousand years.[172]

York Minster was conceived in 1215 by the local archbishop, who wanted a Gothic structure for the north of England. His goal was a structure to rival Canterbury Cathedral in the south. As it was when Archbishop Walter de Gray first envisioned it, it is today the tallest (and grandest) building in York at twenty-one stories high. It survived the English Reformation, converting from Roman Catholic to the Church of England.

The mortar that has held it together for over 250 years is a centuries-long shock-and-awe tactic to make the church more important than the people it purported to serve (and the people who built it). While, to the faithful, the grandeur of its space may be considered a testament to the power of God and the value of worship, it might have symbolized oppression to others or at least the requirement for obedience. The church design was a demonstration that effective communication is not only about words but also about whatever we purport to be important.

Don't get me wrong. The centuries-old churches that dot the European countryside are spectacular feats of engineering and medieval finance, as well as sheer human will, strength, and steadfast focus. They are marvels to see. But while they may be treated as monuments to God, they are really monuments to the achievements of men. It was men like Archbishop de Gray who demanded the sacrifices of time, money, and human lives to build them. It was men, not God, who demanded these public statements such churches delivered. You might even consider them false idols.

These churches were Marshall McLuhan's "the medium is the message"[173] in mortar and the then-new and magical material, glass. As was common to churches of the day, the over-the-top decoration was intended to reflect the stature of York Minster, and the cathedral was constructed to showcase 188 massive stained-glass windows, each one telling a piece of the story of Jesus. They took over 11 million pieces of glass. And why was this done? Not merely for grandeur but for storytelling, done necessarily in glass because most of the 5,000 or so congregants who regularly filled the cathedral were illiterate.[174]

The Catholic Church of the day was never a promoter of literacy for the general population. The Mass was in Latin (as it remains in some places today), but unlike today, when we expect a Bible and perhaps hymnal in our pews, there would be none of that. The Bible was written not as a book for you to read but as a book to have read *to* you by someone in authority—a priest or a bishop. If you understood not a word that was said, no matter; just gaze about at the beautiful windows backlit from daylight, and you'd get the gist of things. The Moors were much more advanced promoters of literacy. Their testament, the Koran, was written to be read.

While Gutenberg's first major publication was a Bible (1455), it was not until 1522 that Martin Luther published what would become known as the much more read and widely distributed Lutheran Bible. It was published to be read, as it was in German. Gutenberg produced an astounding (for the time) up to 270 copies of the traditional Latin Bible.[175] Seventy years later, the Lutheran Bible's publication numbers overwhelmed that at over 200,000.[176] It drove a literacy craze across

Europe. In Sweden, it became law that everyone had to be literate for the simple reason of being able to read the Bible.[177] So, score one for the Protestants. In fact, their particular brand of Bible drove literacy across Europe, and the number of literate Protestant followers dwarfed the paucity of reading ability among their Catholic brethren.

In a 1988 interview with Bill Moyers on America's public broadcaster PBS, literature professor and comparative religion expert Joseph Campbell said, "television is the church we all go to."[178] He was acknowledging both the past role of churches as a place where people connected, shared stories, and developed similar beliefs, and the present role of television in usurping that role. But that was in the late 1980s. Over thirty years later, the spread of propaganda has found new ways, new places, and new spokespeople for its weaponized lies and misinformation.

"There has never been a time in history when factual truths are attacked with such zeal and efficiency whenever they oppose the advantage or ambition of one of the countless interests groups."[179]

– HANNAH ARENDT, AMERICAN POLITICAL THEORIST, IN *THE NEW YORKER*, 1967.

12

CROUCHING DIRECTOR, HIDDEN PRODUCER.

Decades before Joseph Campbell would call television "the church we all go to," speaking at the Radio Television News Director Association's annual meeting in 1958, Edward R. Murrow, the preeminent broadcast journalist of his time, shocked his assembled colleagues and national advertisers when he told them, "I am seized with an abiding fear regarding what these two instruments [radio and TV] are doing to our society, our culture, our heritage. Television in the main is being used to distract, delude, amuse, and insulate us."[180] He concluded his remarks with a request, or more accurately, a plea. He pleaded with the network executives to use television to "teach," "illuminate," and "inspire." Otherwise, he warned, the promise of electronic media would be diminished to "nothing but wires and lights in a box."[181] Today, our so-called smart televisions are just that—as are our smartphones, tablets, and all the screens we live and work with every day. The screens we hold so dearly in our hands, never going anywhere without them, have become the most pervasive stage for the Theater of Lies. Centuries ago, it was different yet much the same.

Where our medieval ancestors walked into awe-inspiring churches with hundreds of stained-glass windows that told their Church's perspective on the world, today, each of us walks into a church of screens with billions of windows: Internet sites, Tweets, Facebook pages, Google searches. Each of them seeks to convince us of the truth of its perspective on the world. Unlike the stained-glass stories of the past, though, some of these windows on the world are indeed telling us the truth. Most, however, merely *do* distract, delude, and sometimes even amuse. And, while our medieval ancestors had few choices of what church they would walk into, by 2021, there were 1.7 billion websites operating on the internet[182] and almost 4.5 billion people using social media.[183] As we each make what we believe are wholly personal choices about the websites we visit and the people on social media we follow, in this hyper-connectedness of our digital world, the internal can also *insulate* us from contrary opinions and facts that don't support our points of view. So, it has been designed, like churches, where only the beliefs of the congregation are discussed, with no mention of opposing opinions.

The church we all go to today is more akin to all the carnival rides you've ever been on—all at once, all at the same time. All the food, games, bright lights, and hawkers of wares, who only amplify their aggression if you stop for a passing look. The car you searched for, the vacation spot you checked out, the pair of sneakers you looked at—ads for each now chase you for weeks any moment you walk back into our new church, the digital carnival. For while the carnival of content is exponentially larger than what we consumed at our former churches, there remain pastors dictating that content and their doctrine—only now they are hidden behind lines of code rather than a pulpit.

At the real carnival, you walk in knowing you are there for entertainment. You go, money in hand, in agreement to be amused, distracted, and insulated—at least for the moment—from any worries. The rides might thrill, but they are safe. The games may be a bit rigged, but for that big stuffed animal prize, you're willing to go along. The food is sugary and greasy, but it's only a once-a-year treat. The theater is all in front of you, clear as the carnival barker's smile. But on the internet, how can you tell the difference between truth and lies?

Truth is, you *can't*. The internet is a veritable factory of lies and their reproduction. And I am not talking about internet security issues such as fraud, phishing, hacks, viruses, and other outright criminal activities designed to separate you from your money. I am talking about the manipulatory power of something called an *algorithm*. It is the insidious, invisible, and all-powerful computer code that brings the clickbait of social media, traditional media, and internet advertising to bear before your eyes, like magic. Algorithms are the V8 engines of digital machines. They are the hidden pastors of our medieval churches, once the hub of community information and guidance, now made modern.

At its simplest, an algorithm is a series of logical steps, the most obvious analog version being a recipe. Baking bread is a process that starts with a list of ingredients and the order in which you mix them, and the steps you follow between there and making the dough, letting it rise, then baking it . . . all this is an algorithm. Algorithms are not a new, strange, and evil creation. They are as old as human time. In modern terms, think of them as a flow chart.

The next level of algorithm is a series of if-then answers and actions (as in, if I burn the bread I am baking, then I will throw it away). The digital age and the power of superfast servers and computer processes have taken the simple if-then and repeated it, in some cases, to multiple ifs paired with multiple thens, and in turn, repeated these if-thens exponentially. The flow chart goes from simple to three-dimensional—and in terms of super-computers—bordering on infinity in the problem-solving power. The V8 power of the digital engine has now become turbocharged.

Like propaganda, algorithms can be tools for good or evil. They are not inherently bad—in fact, in accessing the internet and the social media world with its billions of sites and exponential connections to make, algorithms are a bedrock process of wayfinding (if biased in their directions). The two most famous are the proprietary programs of Google and Facebook. Algorithms find the content that relates to your history of internet searches, the social media connections you have (and the connections of who you follow), the online shopping, entertainment, and the comments you make on media articles—all processed through a complex logic tree.

With algorithms, the producers of lies and information can slip things into your head and make sure they stay there. These lies grow like a cancer with each new piece of information.

The Organization for Economic Cooperation and Development clarified how dangerous algorithm-driven content can be in its 2020 report on disinformation in the wake of COVID-19. They wrote,

Attention-grabbing headlines with sensationalist content can attract even the savviest internet users and studies have shown they tend to generate more user engagement. As a result, content personalization algorithms can repeatedly expose people to the same or similar content and ads even on the basis of disinformation.[184]

And such internet ads generate levels of revenue that are so high that the sale of misinformation is an important profit center for companies like Facebook, Twitter, and YouTube. David Iche is a former British football player who morphed himself into a self-proclaimed journalist but is really an online spokesperson for conspiracy theories. His claims included the world is secretly run by a reptilian society, Satanists, and pedophiles. Facebook and YouTube took down his sites in 2020, but only after public pressure.[185] And only after he had taken advantage of one of digital media's most powerful attributes: the ability to profit from it. In the past, the primary beneficiaries of lies and misinformation were kings and clerics.

The digital age has created a whole new class of misinformation millionaires.

In 2018, Alex Jones's *Infowars* site generated $800,000 in a single day—with annual revenues of about $150 million, according to the public attorneys prosecuting him in a defamation lawsuit from families of the 2012 Sandy Hook school shooting (Jones had repeatedly claimed that no one had died, the incident was all staged by actors). [186] While the *Infowars* site is one of the primary distribution platforms for Jones's misinformation campaigns, it makes its money selling brain pills, diet supplements, and survivalist gear—often at markups of

100 percent or more.[187] While, in 2018, both Facebook and YouTube removed *Infowars*-aligned sites,[188] in 2022, *Infowars* was still attracting close to 1.9 million unique visitors every month.[189]

The church we all go to now is social media. And 4.4 billion people on earth attend regularly,[190] spending hours a day there, each of us creating content, sending messages, scanning, reading, watching, and sharing what we like with each other.

We pray more on phones than in our churches (Americans spend about 9 minutes a day in religious and spiritual activities).[191] Here are the average hours per day spent using social media by country, head down—as we once were in pews—but now on computers and smartphones.

North America	2 hours and 6 minutes
South America	3 hours and 24 minutes
Africa	3 hours and 10 minutes
Europe	1 hour and 15 minutes
Asia/Oceania	2 hours and 16 minutes [192]

In the pulpits of our old church, we had priests and reverends. On our televisions, we had news editors like Edward R. Murrow and Walter Cronkite, each a voice of trust. The in-between era that separates these periods, from church pulpits to television news, was dominated by print media in all forms—from pamphlets distributed by hand to mass-produced newspapers dropped at doorsteps by young men and boys in the early morning hours, to full-color magazines sold at news-stands and by subscription, coming by mail each week or month. The publishing hands behind all of these—the editors, journalists, artists, and photographers who chronicled the affairs of the day—determined what was newsworthy and relevant to their audiences. And while day-to-day journalists have tended to be more liberal than conservative, their publishers were not. According to Batya Unger-Sargon, deputy editor of *Newsweek*, prior to the digital revolution of news media:

> The publishers, who were often the owners of large corporations, or Republicans, or both. They wanted their newspapers and their new stations to appeal to the vast American middle, which meant that journalists were not at liberty to indulge their own political preferences in their reporting.[193]

In Act Two, we will explore the foundation impact of the evolution of traditional media's business model from advertising-based to subscription-based and how this revolutionized news content. But where traditional media learned its lessons from, today, is from the impact of social media.

Single voices—on the pages of Facebook, Twitter (now X), and Instagram—in some cases have larger audiences than mainstream media. The editors, it seems, have vanished as the audience themselves have not only become empowered to decide what they choose was newsworthy but have also started to create it themselves.

Philip N. Howard, director of the Oxford Internet Institute, calls the period we are in a *"pax technica,"* because "the majority of the cultural, political, and economic life of most people is managed over digital media."[194] During this *pax technica*, the editors are hidden. Facebook, YouTube, Reddit, Twitter, et al. proclaim themselves as just platforms, not publishers. Only recently have some of them taken some action as editors to correct the lies they've facilitated, but only when those messages are put out by account owners that have large followings—and only very rarely. So, while Donald Trump's election fraud tweets were sometimes (but not always) identified as false, the millions of tweets of those who believed him, and that the election should therefore be invalidated were not similarly identified.

Today, there are three groups of editors in social media. The first is obvious: the close to 5 billion content creators like you and me. We, however, are merely repeater stations for the other two: people with lies to propagate and the automated computers with their algorithms that engage us, and the 5 billion engaged to repeat, share, like, and add to the lies that pollute our lives.

Much-repeated lies have fueled the anti-vaccine movement, which has grown more influential throughout the COVID-19 pandemic and the two-shot vaccine solution instituted worldwide in 2021.

The Center for Countering Digital Hate (CCDH) estimates that midway through 2020, the social media accounts of prominent anti-vaxxers had attracted 7.8 million more followers (there were 31 million total anti-vax followers on Facebook and 17 million total anti-vax subscribers on YouTube,). The CCDH also estimated the revenue Facebook had generated through advertising associated with these followers to be worth a billion dollars a year.[195]

Patrick Bet-David founded the YouTube channel and website *Valuetainment,* which he branded as a learning site for entrepreneurs and future leaders. The brand is based on his personal rags-to-riches story as an Iranian who immigrated to the US as a ten-year-old and is now living the American Dream, who selflessly wants to teach others how to do the same. CCDH has labeled his site a conspiracy channel, as it follows a similar editorial plan as Alex Jones's *Infowars.* The site's value proposition is as an independent source of information and support for entrepreneurs that is "not looking to take sides."[196] However, the CCDH demonstrated that it was the second fastest growing source of anti-COVID-19 vaccination propaganda in 2020.[197]

> In just one video on the conspiracy channel *Valuetainment* with 1.8 million views, the host Patrick Bet-David allows his guest Rashid Buttar to claim that COVID is "manmade," that the disease is part of "a depopulation agenda," that 5G (the fifth generation of cellular transmission) is making people ill, and that vaccines are 'causing autism' and 'causing cancer'.[198]

Social media and its algorithms are the building materials for the anti-vaxxers' Theater of Lies. The CCDH identified its four planks. It called Facebook the "shopfront for anti-vax products." They wrote,

> First, campaigners work full-time to foment distrust in vaccines, but they only reach 12 percent of the total audience that follows the anti-vaccine movement. Second, entrepreneurs reach around half of the anti-vaccine following, exposing them to advertisements for products purporting to have health benefits . . . Conspiracy theorists constitute the third category. Finally, there are the [online] communities, which have a relatively small following and are mainly to be found on Facebook.[199]

In my opinion, it is that second category—entrepreneurs—who are the most dangerous. They are the ones profiting from lies and misinformation and, therefore, most likely invest more in both promotion and attraction of larger audiences; because these audiences are not only willing to listen but also to pay to support their beliefs. And if that entrepreneur is a celebrity, that misinformation can be especially dangerous. Alex Jones was a former talk show radio host with a strong bent toward conspiracy thinking and a not-everything-you-see-is-true platform. He moved his audience to an internet platform first produced in his basement (after being fired from his radio station[200]). He grew wealthy not from advertisers on his show, but product sales to what are now called *followers*. In our celebrity-obsessed culture, a carnival worker might refer to them as *rubes*.

....

13

LIES ARE PROFITABLE.

If property developers had a marketing hall of fame, there would be a shrine to Erik the Red. A Viking whose family had been banished from Norway to Iceland in the late 900s BCE (for being a little too Viking-like in their aggression), Erik was the first European to land on the island we know today as Greenland. He named it such, believing this would make the land more attractive to settlers. It worked. In 985 BCE, he led a fleet of twenty-five ships with 500 men and women to colonize his discovery. I would have liked to have seen their faces when the glacial towers of ice came over the horizon, but by that time, only fourteen of the ships remained. They were probably just glad to see land.

It was a prospective customer for radio advertising that told me my first lie in business—at least, the first lie *to my knowledge*. There had been many lies before, mostly involving the mission, vision, and value statements of dozens of companies I either worked for or purchased products from, but these were so general as to pass without notice (like "our people are our most important asset," "the customer is always right," and "made from 100 percent natural ingredients").

Just out of university, I was selling advertising for a small radio station—this time, to a carpet retailer who was telling me why he had chosen a competitor's station over mine. "They have a larger audience and much lower rates," he told me. His claim about lower rates was true, as the competition had a much lower audience to sell to. I showed my prospective client the most recent audience figures for both stations—data directly from the Bureau of Broadcast Measurement (BBM). Our audience was clearly larger. The retailer reviewed the data through thick bifocals. "These numbers are wrong," he told me. "Your competitor uses a much more sophisticated method to determine their audience size. It's much more accurate." Every radio station in Canada subscribed to BBM's services. "They have a helicopter that flies over the city," the retailer told me. "They pick up the signals emitting from each radio underneath them—every house, every car." Radios, of course, receive signals; they don't emit them. That's what radio stations and broadcast towers are for. No matter. "It's true," he told me. "They showed me a picture of their helicopter."

That lie cost me the commission I'd hoped to earn for that sale. It also taught me at an impressionable moment of my career that lying was OK. There was no penalty for the other salesperson's lie, and, they had pocketed the sales bonus that had eluded me.

As a young salesman, I took a lot of sales training courses—one of them from one of America's master salesmen, Zig Ziglar. He was a college dropout who had gone from being a salesman to a sales trainer, motivational speaker, and author of dozens of books. I took the course in my early twenties and have forgotten almost everything. However, I remember him as a tiny man bouncing around the stage with arms waving, his voice shouting to the back rows: "the only difference between a con man and a professional salesman is purpose. The con man seeks to sell you something only he needs you to have. The professional salesman seeks to sell you something you truly need. Their methods, however, are exactly the same."

We've long accepted that people lie—especially in business. We even have a phrase for it—*caveat emptor, buyer beware*—placing the burden of truth on the buyer and not the seller. Despite laws to the contrary, the phrase retains its power. It is all the more true today, the purpose behind many of the lies played out before us in the Theater.

When you walk into a real theater with your partner, a friend, or your children, you unconsciously park your critical thinking at the concession stand. While there, you choose the healthiest or most unhealthy snacks with some modicum of decision-making thought. When you take your seat inside the theater, however, you begin to suspend your disbelief. It's the key to enjoying the movie or play or whatever it is you are about to watch. And in business, people expect it, too.

The buyers of Volkswagen vehicles seem to feel this way. Despite the German automaker's *Dieselgate* scandal in 2015, it has remained the top-selling automotive brand in the world, year after year. Martin Winterkorn was the CEO at the time of the scandal. Five years later, the German court "determined that there [was] sufficient suspicion, that is, an overwhelming possibility of conviction, of the accused Professor Doctor Winterkorn for commercial and organized fraud."[202]

The issue—the crime—was that for at least ten years, Volkswagen had deliberately installed software that controlled the emissions of its diesel engines. In testing settings, the vehicles produced a low and acceptable level of emissions. But the software was designed to allow for increased emissions during regular use (thereby increasing gas mileage). When confronted with evidence of this bait-and-switch technology, Winterkorn denied all knowledge of it, despite his reputation as a fastidious perfectionist with the self-chosen nickname "Mr. Quality." In fact, Winterkorn often boasted about knowing "every screw in [Volkswagen's] cars."[203] When presented with a memo discussing the tampered data module sent to him the year before the scandal broke, the courts were unable to prove he had actually read it. While he could boast about screws, he shrugged at any notion that he knew anything about software issues (or his customers being "screwed").

The company had gone to great lengths to disguise the emissions trickery software, even from itself. Inside VW, the defeat device was referred to in language that obscured its purpose. It was referred as an "acoustic function," "switch logic," "cycle beating" software, or "emissions-tight mode."[204]

To date, the total value of the fines and cash settlements that Volkswagen has had to pay out to resolve the scandal is $25 billion.[205] Yet its customers have remained loyal. The scandal appears to have had no impact on sales, with VW's market share in the years 2015 though 2017 remaining just under 11 percent of all automobiles sold worldwide. *Buyer beware*, indeed.

Whereas VW was caught lying about the emissions quality of its diesels, just a few years later, Telsa, its primary competition for electric vehicles, was caught in a fibbing about the range of its batteries. In

2023, many of its vehicle owners brought a class action suit against the company, stating.

> Tesla violated state consumer fraud statutes when it falsely advertised the range of its electric vehicles. Lawyers representing the owners said that Tesla "grossly overvalued" the range—which is the estimated distance a vehicle can travel on a single battery charge—when selling the vehicles to consumers.[206]

Typically, when a company is caught in a big lie, the CEO takes the fall. The companies that fostered, managed, and propagated the lie often carries on unscathed. Lies, it seems, are personal—not corporate.

Stanford University professor David Larcker and PhD candidate Anastasia Zakolyukina reviewed the transcripts of thousands of earnings calls, the legally required shareholder updates that publicly traded companies are obliged to hold. Most often, the spokespeople on these calls are the CEOs. When examining the calls of companies that had to restate their earnings, which often occurs after a fraud, the Stanford researchers found that "lying executives tend to overuse words like 'we' and 'our team' when they talk about their company. They avoid saying 'I.'" Zakolyukina provided us with the reason: "If I'm saying 'I' or 'me' or 'mine,' I'm showing my ownership of the statement, so psychologically, I'm showing I'm responsible for what I'm saying."[207]

Larcker and Zakolyukina found that hyperbole could also be a lie, or an indicator of one. Just before Enron was about to implode from its own fraudulent activities, CEO Kenneth Lay told employees,

I think our core businesses are extremely strong. We have a very strong competitive advantage. Of course, we are transferring this very successful business model and approach to a lot of new, very large markets globally.[208]

In February 2001, the company's chief financial offer, Rick Causey, told investors, "From an accounting standpoint, this will be our easiest year ever. We've got 2001 in the bag." In another investor call, this time in August 2001, Kenneth Lay said, "There are no accounting issues, no trading issues, no reserve issues, no previously unknown problem issues. I think I can honestly say that the company is probably in the strongest and best shape that it has probably ever been in."[209] Less than five months later, Enron filed for the largest bankruptcy the world had ever seen. On that day, Enron told its thousands of employees they had thirty minutes to pack their belongings and vacate the building.

Larcker writes, "If all my speech is 'fantastic,' 'superb,' 'outstanding,' 'excellent' and all my speech sounds like a big hype—it probably is."[210]

Part of the challenge for us in the audience of the Theater of Lies is the way we continue to reward bad behavior. A 2016 *Harvard Business Review* (*HBR*) report examined thirty-eight cases of corporate lying and found that the consequences for the liars were minimal. Forty-five percent of companies in its sample experienced a significant unrelated governance issue following the event, such as an accounting restatement, unrelated lawsuit, shareholder action, or bankruptcy. As for the CEOs themselves, three were reported to have resigned from other boards because of their actions. Two CEOs who were terminated were subsequently rehired by the same company. *HBR* found that many continued in their positions or were hired by other corporations or investment groups; otherwise, there was nothing notable about what happened to them professionally.

In 58 percent of incidents, the CEO was eventually terminated for their actions. The *HBR* report said,

> "Questionable financial practices" was the only category of behavior that almost uniformly resulted in termination; all other behaviors resulted in both outcomes (termination and retention) across HBR's sample. Even behavior as straightforward as falsifying information on a resume was treated inconsistently by different boards. In a third of cases (32 percent), the board took actions other than termination in response to CEO misconduct, such as stripping the CEO of the chair title, removing the CEO from the board, amending the corporate code of conduct, reducing, or eliminating the CEO's bonus, other director resignation, and other changes to board structure or composition.[211]

If we hope to escape from the Theater of Lies, we have to at least start throwing popcorn at the screen. Our acceptance of lies in business, politics, and most every organizational structure mankind has ever created—must stop (we'll discuss how to do this in Act Three). If not, we will continue to repeat the lies of others and entrench their poisonous outcomes for generations to come.

We support the mangle of misinformation most every time we buy a chocolate bar. Look at the packaging. Somewhere there's a logo or a statement along the lines of "sustainably sourced cocoa."

So let's look at the word *sustainable*. The Cambridge Dictionary defines it as first, "able to continue over a period of time," and second, from an environmental perspective, as "causing, or made in way that causes, little or no damage to the environment and therefore able to continue for a long time."[212]

This is a definition that the promoters of corporate social responsibility (CSR) programs need to heed, especially the world's chocolate industry. It skips madly along the path of its failing cocoa farmer sustainability initiatives—as if each company is one of the Seven Dwarves singing, "Hi ho, hi ho. It's off to work I go." And, between bites of our KitKat bars et al., we're humming along with them.

On the first page of Hershey's *2023 Living Wage & Income Statement*, the $54 billion company (annual revenues +/- $10 billion) states:

> We believe that all individuals deserve the opportunity to earn a living wage & income including the remarkable and diverse group of people who work at The Hershey Company and the many individuals who make their living within our broader supply chain.[213]

That "broader supply chain" is drawn from a pool of 40 to 50 million people worldwide[214] who earn their livelihood from growing, processing, and manufacturing products from cocoa.

That includes over 5 million farmers, most of whom grow cocoa on 10-acre plots of land, or less. Ivory Coast farmer Félicien Angui is one of them. In May 2023, *Globe and Mail* writers Geoffrey York and Adrian Morrow told his bottom of that supply chain story in "The True Cost of Chocolate." They wrote,

Angui has heard little about the global battles over cocoa prices and corporate claims in ethical chocolate. All he knows is that his life is getting more difficult.[215]

Hershey, perhaps recognizing this on page 3 of that same *Living Wage Statement*, writes, "*our research demonstrates that wage and income vulnerabilities exist in multiple parts of our supply chain.*"[216]

The company then points to one of its CSR Programs, *Cocoa for Good*.

Our approach to creating more goodness inside cocoa communities . . . investing half a billion dollars by 2030 to improve resiliency and livelihoods.[217]

As the first link in the industry's supply chain, all Angui and his fellow cocoa farmers want is a decent price for their product. A decent price, being one that feeds their families commensurate with their efforts. The industry's term for this: a *living income.*

Earning a living wage is huge problem for cocoa farmers. Anqui—who has never seen a chocolate bar or even knows what one tastes like—used to be able to use his income to feed his family a kilogram of rice a day. Now, he can afford only half that. And, as the *Globe* reported, cocoa not a subsistence crop like bananas or vegetables. He can't eat it.[218] It's only role in his life is as way to earn money, the jobs many of us have. For that purpose, it's failing.

Nor is this unusual. The *Globe* reported that more than half of cocoa farmers in Ivory Coast earn less than the national poverty line of about US$3 per day.[219]

Fairtrade International, which bills itself as "the most recognized and trusted sustainability label in the world"[220] found that 88 percent of certified farmers in Ivory Coast were still earning less than a living wage. In next door Ghana, cocoa farmers have seen their incomes drop by 16 percent since 2020.[221]

Let's remind ourselves here of the definition of the world *sustainable*. This clearly ain't it.

Cargill Industries is an international food conglomerate with 155,000 employees and is a major player in the cocoa sector. One of its wide-reaching goals is "to ensure a thriving and sustainable cocoa sector for generations to come."[222] Cargill states,

> Our ambition is to accelerate progress toward a transparent global cocoa supply chain, to enable cocoa farmers and their communities to strengthen their socioeconomic resilience, and to deliver a sustainable supply of cocoa and chocolate products from bean to end product.

This is where I want to congratulate Cargill for its candor, if not its language choice (strengthening socioeconomic resilience?) The company is clear that its working toward a goal and not that it has achieved it. In 2021, its program to raise farmer incomes[223] had 244,364 participants. By 2030, it hopes to grow that number to one million. Even if it was successful, that would help only one in five farmers like Anqui.

How long would you last if this was happening to you? Yet, the dwarves of the industry keep singing their song, mindless to the fact that while they tell sing the song of sustainability to their consumers (and themselves), their programs are not working.

Dr. Kristy Leissle is the cofounder of the *Cocoapreneurship Institute of Ghana*. She touts herself as the *Doc of Choc*. When asked if the system is broken, she responds, "What I think people mean by this is that the system is unfair or inequitable. I agree with that. But the system is definitely not broken." She cites the 2 million metric tons of cocoa being exported from the ports of Ivory Coast and Ghana annually, calling it a "remarkable achievement."[224]

Remarkable, perhaps, But with the chocolate industry plastering "100-percent sustainably sourced chocolate" on each and every version of its products, that label wallpapers the living income problem to the point of invisibility.

I can only assume that since the industry believes its system is not broken, that's because it works—for the industry. Yet, what hasn't worked are the sustainability program of the major chocolate manufacturers. We may give suppliers like Cargill kudos for trying, but when the success of entire industry is based on below-poverty-level incomes for the people who grow their product, is trying enough?

According to the *Globe's* investigative report, though the global chocolate market was worth about US$140 billion in 2022, less than 7 percent of that is earned by people who grow the cocoa it's based on.[225] By 2026, revenues are projected to rise to $171.6 billion.

By comparison, in 2022, the US Department of Agriculture estimated the average income of a US-based farmer at over $100,000 a year[226]—and that's about ⅓ more than the average income of all Americans. StatsCan finds similar data for Canadian farmers.[227] But we don't see flour companies or bakeries labeling their products with *100-percent sustainably sourced* messages.

The sustainability programs of the chocolate industry have become part of the fabric of lies and misinformation that we accept as true—as so the people who make our chocolate bars. And their motivation, I believe, is not evil—its shared beliefs seem real. But not to the farmers who have to live the cocoa industry's sustainably sourced message every day, while feeding their children meager portions of rice.

The director general of the Ivory Coast's state regulatory body believes the only sustainable results from these programs are the incomes of the consultants. He told the *Globe*, "They make a lot of money from these sustainability programs. Of course, the consumers are deceived."[228]

Dr. Leissle, one of those consultants on whom the industry relies, blames the mass market for cocoa, not the industry.

> The fact is that moving so much cocoa around the world relies upon a great deal of inexpensive labor. That's what it takes to achieve the processed food abundance we see in 'developed' countries today. Bananas, avocados, petroleum, tilapia, cocoa. If there is a mass-market for a product, its supply chain almost certainly exploits many people, and their environment.[229]

That's sixty words to say *that's the way the system works*. I think we heard words to that effect during the slave trade.

The industry and its companies share a lie with their consumers so that we can all feel better—the companies with profits earned and their consumers with chocolates enjoyed. A 2020 study of 7,000 Europeans by Cargill found:

70% of consumers factor sustainability into their food and beverage purchase decisions, with an even higher percentage of frequent chocolate purchasers, nearly three-quarters, reporting they prefer to buy sustainable products.[230]

The respondents' highest concerns about chocolate were child labor, farmer income, and deforestation. The majority also said they'd even pay more if the product was made with sustainable cocoa.[231]

When consumers purchase chocolate, they think they are paying for the above, but the facts tell us the cocoa industry is not delivering the goods, just the sweet taste of success.

But of this I am certain: if these companies were investing hundreds of millions of dollars a year on product that consistently loses money to the point it was a billion-dollar sinkhole in their balance sheets . . . they'd either kill the product or fix it. I don't see any CEO, CFO, shareholders, or board member agreeing to the status quo. Yet this seems the case with this same investment in their sustainability programs. Around the boardroom table there must be either a shared misbelief that these programs are actually working, or a shared belief that, as long as consumer keep buying the sustainability lie, they'll keep selling it.

So, for we, the consumers or chocolates and other products, *caveat emptor* is simply not enough. It places all the responsibility on the audience for the message and not the producer who published it. And we need to remember that sometimes the audience has few, if any, choices to make—like between two choices for high office, the availability of a place to live (any place) for some, and the same for a job.

We need more tools at our disposal to understand, with confidence, that not everything is as it appears to be (and that we have a right for it to be so). Ask the people who used to work for Enron. Nearly 62 percent of the 15,000 employees' entire retirement savings plans relied on Enron stock that was purchased at $83 in early 2001.[232] The Theater of Lies cost them their pensions.

*"I think the problem is worse than it's ever
been, frankly."*[233]

– NINA JANKOWICZ, DISINFORMATION EXPERT,
US DEPARTMENT OF HOMELAND SECURITY.

....

14

A SNAPSHOT OF THE
THEATER IN ACTION.

The Theater of Lies is more akin to Las Vegas than Broadway, as it operates 24/7 and its entire production process is designed to keep you in the (virtual) building. No matter who you are, the productions run quietly in the background, part of the day-to-day fabric of your life, there but unseen.

The goal is of this book is not to uncover lies, but help you recognize and challenge them. I have no desire to be a factchecker or to provide you a list of lies as they emerge (there are others far more skilled and devoted to this). During the course of writing, lies paraded across my desk as if I was stopped at rail crossing and forced to endure the world's longest train.

But what is relevant, I believe, is to give you a snapshot of the Theater in action over a very short period, just a few weeks. We can examine the back-and-forth dynamics of the Theater's production in as close to real time as possible and demonstrate the lies lying behind its every working moment.

There was a particular period during the last weeks of May through the first weeks of June 2021 when, as I was writing this book, an avalanche of real-world truths pushed back at the Theater of Lies. It was then that I witnessed the industrial power of the Theater's producers to re-establish their false narratives—to get the audience back in their seats, believing what they have been told for decades. As our societies begin their slow crawl out of a lie that has dominated our beliefs for centuries, the believers of the lie and its mythic corollaries showed us just how the Theater of Lies thrives.

The last time Bilal Farooq saw her friend, Madiha Salman, Salman was organizing a science, technology, engineering, and math event for young children at her child's school. That was June 6. The next day, Salman, a forty-four-year-old PhD candidate in engineering at the University of Western Ontario in London, Canada, was taking an evening walk in the city's west end with her husband, Afzaal, their two children, and Afzaal's mother. The family had emigrated from Pakistan fourteen years earlier, with their eldest and a baby. That baby, Yumna, had become a ninth-grade honor student and decided to paint large mural at her high school. Despite the COVID-19 pandemic stopping in-school learning, Yumna would go to the schoolyard every day to paint. She also helped her mother care for her Canadian-born brother, Fayez, then nine years old.

Nathaniel Veltman was twenty. He lived alone in small apartment in London, Ontario. He had a part-time job in the shipping department of an egg producer just a few miles outside the city. The morning of June 6, he dressed himself in faux body armor before getting into his pickup truck.

Paige Martin witnessed what happened shortly thereafter. She had stopped at a red light while heading southbound down Hyde Park Road when she saw "a flash of black" and her car shook. She said she saw a vehicle come over the median that looked to her like it had come from the other side of the road. She said:

> About five minutes later, after I got some gas, I headed back and that's when I saw, after I came up over Sarnia Road, just cars backed up and there weren't that many emergency vehicles yet, but I could see in my rearview mirror that they were all coming from behind me. . .
>
> Then it was just chaos and there were people every-where and running, citizens trying to direct the emer-gency vehicles where to go and there was a lot of point-ing and screaming and arms waving.[234]

Veltman had driven up on the curb and turned his pickup truck directly at Bilal Farooq and her family. They were waiting at a cross-walk. The women were wearing niqabs, a veil that covered their heads, leaving their eyes exposed, identifying them as followers of the Prophet Mohammad.[235]

London Police Department Det. Supt. Paul Waight said, "There is evidence that this was a planned, premeditated act motivated by hate. It is believed that these victims were targeted because they were Muslim."[236] The police department later categorized the attack as an act of terrorism and a hate crime.[237]

What the police didn't say, of course, was that the Farooq family were victims of the Theater of Lies. Veltman had become an Edgar (the man searching for Democratic Party pedophiles), moving from the audience to the stage, and had become one of its actors. His weapon was his pickup truck, but it was lies and misinformation that fueled his racism and unrelenting need to act upon it.

In reaction to the crime, the leader of Canada's New Democratic Party said, "The reality is our Canada is a place of racism, of violence, of genocide of Indigenous people, and our county is a place where Muslims aren't safe."[238] A candidate for the Conservative Party in the same riding where the murders had occurred was even more explicit: "This terrorist may have been acting alone in that truck on that day, but he was not acting alone. He was raised in a racist city that pretends it isn't."[239]

Indeed, a national poll of close to 2,000 Canadians published two weeks after the crime found that only a third of respondents thought Canada was a racist county.[240] Three-quarters of people over the age of fifty-five didn't think the country was racist at all.[241] In two western provinces, Alberta and Saskatchewan, close to half of respondents thought that "exaggerating discrimination is a larger problem than seeing it where it does not exist."[242]

The Theater of Lies, it would seem, is skilled at fostering racist attitudes within many minds all the while adding the tranquilizer of denial. Hubris tells me I am not a racist, through I see it in others. A lifelong barrage of misinformation and lies, however, and rip that veneer of some people, like Nathaniel Veltman, and allow racist beliefs to drive their actions—and in the worst way possible.

During the snapshot we are examining, Canadian Prime Minister Justin Trudeau provided a textbook example of doublespeak. He said,

"We need to recognize mistakes made by the past, learn from them, and be resolute on demonstrating that the kind of hatred that, in this case, gave rise to such horrific tragedy is not encouraged, even accidentally." Then he added, "I don't want to start looking to the past." [243]

If you can tell me what he means, please write.

Perhaps, in his Canadian way, he was avoiding criticizing his predecessor, Stephen Harper. In the 2015 federal election, Harper's Conservatives had two strong Islamophobic planks in their platform: a general promise to protect Canadians from "Islamic terrorists" and a "Barbaric Culture Practices Hotline"[244] (concerned citizens could call to inform authorities about any disturbing rituals their neighbors might be indulging). To shore up the platform, Harper and his party called for a ban on the wearing of the niqab during the swearing in at citizenship ceremonies. They also mused about extending the ban to anyone working a job in civil services[245]—as the Conservatives failed to win that election, the platform was not further pursued.

On June 8, 2021, two days after Veltman's attack, the former prime minister avoided any mention of his previous attempt to win the favor of voters by leveraging any fears they may have had of Muslims when he wrote, "Canada is a place of tolerance and pluralism. Cruel acts of racial and faith-based hatred must be unequivocally condemned by us all."[246]

Un-cruel acts, like those in his election platform, apparently, were OK. Denial, obfuscation, and distraction using nice-sounding, but ill-understood words are power tools in the Theater of Lies. Participants spout words like "pluralism" in full knowledge that few people can actually define the word and fewer still would ever use the word in regular conversation. It does, however, make them feel like they have provided a *learned* answer.

The message from the Theater of Lies that certain people are intrinsically different from and alien to "us"—and are responsible for what we do not like about our own lives—has sunk deep roots into our consciousness. As Boston University professor Ibram Kendi introduced to us earlier, the notion of one race being better than the other was fiction produced to rationalize Portuguese slave trading—some 600 years ago. The producers of lies need only to lean into the bias of their audience's racism to leverage it to their advantage.

Yet, the week of the so-called hate crime in London, Ontario, was also the 100th anniversary of a far larger hate crime in the United States—one of the worst massacres of Black people in America.

Between May 31 and June 1, 1921, hundreds of Black men, women, and children were murdered in Tulsa, Oklahoma. At the time, the Greenwood District was home to dozens of highly successful businesses owned by Black Americans, earning itself the nickname *Black Wall Street*.[247] Over a 48-hour period straddling the month of May and June, mobs of white residents attacked Black residents, destroying their homes and businesses. City officials had deputized many of the attackers, giving them weapons. Some flew airplanes, lobbing homemade bombs at the homes of Black residents.[248]

The rage was ignited by lies. A Black shoeshine boy had, without evidence, been accused of assaulting a seventeen-year-old white girl in a department store elevator. White residents wanted to lynch him. Black residents wanted to protect him. In the aftermath of forty hours of continuing violence, 10,000 Black residents were left homeless.

The 35 acres what comprised the bulk of the Greenwood District were destroyed. More than 1,000 houses were burned or demolished. Hundreds of bodies were buried in mass graves.[249]

If you haven't heard about the event, don't be surprised. As Dean Obeidallah, a columnist for *MSNBC News* wrote in 2021, "this horrific incident in Oklahoma was intentionally covered-up for decades by White people in power and their allies."[250] US historian Scott Ellsworth said,

> The mayor and other city officials realized that the massacre was this horrible public relations problem, so they actively sought to erase records of the attack. This cover-up worked, which is why so few people outside of Black communities have heard much, if anything, about it until very recently.[251]

The deeper story behind the white residents' anger was that Black Americans in the area, their section of town with fine homes and successful businesspeople, did not reflect the lie that, as a race, they were less than white people. They were, in fact, the most prosperous community of Black people in America. At that time, in Tulsa, they were more financially secure than most of their white neighbors. In fact, while the state of Oklahoma had only two airports, six Black families owned private planes.[252] At this early age of aviation, that could only be considered astounding. But worse, white attackers used these planes, stolen from their Black owners, to drop Molotov cocktails and lit sticks of dynamite on their defenseless neighbors.

Just a few weeks before events commemorating the 100th anniversary of the crime, the commission formed to manage it fired Oklahoma's governor, Kevin Stitt, from its committee. His crime? He had signed into law a bill that prohibited the teaching of what is known as critical race theory (CRT) in Oklahoma schools. It you are unfamiliar with the theory (as I was), CRT argues that race is not a natural, biologically grounded feature of physically distinct subgroups of human beings, but a socially constructed (that is, culturally invented) category used to oppress and exploit people of color. It is the twenty-first-century pushback on the 600-year-old narrative of Portuguese slave traders that encircled the world.

One could dismiss the governor's prohibition of CRT as tone-deaf, but in my opinion, it was propaganda from the Theater of Lies of the highest order, seeking to bury the historic notion of race precisely when the state of Oklahoma was most ready to discuss it. The teaching of CRT subject matter is now banned in almost all Republican-led states in America.

But let's return to Canada during what I may refer to as *Hell Week* from the theater.

During these same weeks, a hundred years after the Tulsa Race Massacre, what appeared to be the remains of 215 Indigenous children were found in a mass grave. They were buried outside a residential school in Kamloops, British Columbia. The youngest was about three, and the oldest under twelve years of age. All of them had been under the care of their Catholic teachers and caretakers, the pointy end of the spear of the Canadian government's plan to "take the Indian out of the child."[253] In 2008, Canada's highly regarded Truth and Reconciliation Commission had previously determined that only sixty children had died at the school, which had operated from 1890 through 1969.[254]

Mary Ellen Turpel-Lafond, director of the Indian Residential School History and Dialogue Centre at the University of British Columbia, summarized the discovery, stating:

> The discovery confirms what community survivors have said for years—that many children went to the school and never returned. There may be reasons why they wouldn't record the deaths properly and that they weren't treated with dignity and respect because that was the whole purpose of the residential school . . . to take total control of Indian children, to remove their culture, identity, and connection to their family."[255]

As soon as the bodies were discovered, the Theater of Lies went into full performance mode. On his Twitter feed, the head of the Catholic Church, Pope Frances, wrote:

> I join the Canadian Bishops and the whole Catholic Church in Canada in expressing my closeness to the Canadian people, who have been traumatized by shocking discovery of the remains of 215 children, pupils at the Kamloops Indian Residential School.[256]

In language that was both sanguine and noncommittal, he neither apologized nor admitted to any responsibility of the Catholic Church for their deaths. Many leaders of the church in Canada lauded his words and wrote about how the Catholic Church had successfully dealt with the matter years prior.[4]

Father Raymond Souza is a contributor to the Canadian newspaper *The National Post* and a parish priest who also writes for the *Catholic Register*. Rather than confirm and accept any culpability of the Catholic Church for the deaths, he chose to go on full protect-the-church mode. On June 4, he wrote, "There has been much commentary about a Catholic apology for residential schools, even in these pages, that I prefer to think is ill-informed rather than ill-motivated."[257] A few days later, he published another article in *The National Post* under the headline "Justin Trudeau Can Learn Something From the Church About Apologies."[258] This is a standard tool of propagandists—the hubris of telling their audiences that they are better than others (in an evasion of a worse crime, the deaths of 6,000 or more Indigenous children).[259]

Another stage management tool of the Theater of Lies is deflecting attention in order to get people to ignore any truth that challenges the misinformation messages. Like a police office blocking a crime scene telling passersby, "Move along. Nothing to see. Everything is fine."

....

4   It should be noted that it would take another year for the Pope Francis to officially apologise. To an assembled group of Indigenous peoples, including residential school survivors, he said, "I am sorry. I ask forgiveness, in particular, for the ways in which many members of the church and of religious communities co-operated, not least through their indifference, in projects of cultural destruction and forced assimilation promoted by the governments of that time, which culminated in the system of residential schools. . . It is painful to think of how the firm soil of values, language and culture that made up the authentic identity of your peoples was eroded, and that you have continued to pay the price of this. In the face of this deplorable evil, the church kneels before God and implores His forgiveness for the sins of her children. I myself wish to reaffirm this, with shame and unambiguously, I humbly beg forgiveness for the evil committed by so many Christians against the Indigenous Peoples."

The full text is available at https://www.cbc.ca/news/canada/edmonton/pope-francis-maskwacis-apology-full-text-1.6531341

With the discovery of the 215 graves, a retired judge in another western Canadian province took it a step further. He used a barrelful of tactics to minimize the importance of the discovery and the critical need to address the issue—including pronouncing it as conspiracy theory, and white children had it just as bad, and one of my personal favorites, *enough is enough already.*

His name is Brian Giesbrecht. He wrote an opinion article in the *Winnipeg Sun.* Giesbrecht is a senior fellow of a thinktank called the Frontier Centre for Public Policy (FCPP). I include most of his opinion article here because it is so instructive on the tools—like misdirection, gaslighting, and minimizing any actual harm done—the producers in Theater of Lies will use to influence their audiences.

First up—it's a conspiracy theory. He writes,

> It's not clear that there was anything sinister about the discovery. In fact, it is shocking that many people seem quite willing to accept slanderous conspiracy theories about teachers and priests murdering and secretly burying hundreds of children. . . It is far more likely that the deaths simply reflected the sad reality of life back then.[260]

Next, he says "our" people were treated badly, too.

> In our comfortable times, we forget how hard life was a hundred or more years ago—Dickens's world of chimney sweeps and the poor house. Stories are being written about Canada's "home children," for example. These were mostly English orphans and children from

poor homes who were taken from their parents and sent by themselves to Canada . . . some received good treatment, some were treated very badly. Many died alone and forgotten.[261]

Finally, for his enough is enough message, he tells readers,

The residential school story has now been exhaustively told. Canadians have heard it—and we get it. We have sympathized, and billions of dollars have been paid by people, most of whom weren't alive then, to people who mostly weren't either. It is time to move on.[262]

Move on . . . in the same tone and manner used by the people who don't wish to discuss in the impact of racial discrimination in America and Canada or any other past mistakes.

Giesbrecht's editorial was produced from a source that peddles critical, independent thought as its stock in-trade, a think tank. The published mission of the FCPP is "to analyze current affairs and public policies and develop effective and meaningful ideas for good governance and reform."[263] Yet, in my experience, think tanks can suffer from group think as much as any organization, and in cases such as FCCP, exist purely to influence public, academic, and government policy. Thinks tanks, especially those that are ideologically based, can be elite production facilities for the Theater of Lies.

During that three-week period in 2021, a confluence of grievous anniversaries, heinous discoveries, and instances of contemporary violence flooded into our minds—and they were reflooded, repeatedly, by traditional and social media. It was as though the producers of the

Theater of Lies felt that a series of revival shows were needed to slap some sense into us, the audience.

The lies. They keep coming. They will keep coming. Stopping them is impossible. Yet if we do not take action to stop their assault on our lives—or at least to manage them—the liars will achieve their goals. Fooling you is only their first step. They have more nefarious goals; goals they believe cannot be met through truth, and goals so important (to them) that will take whatever steps necessary to achieve them.

In Act Three, we will examine what we can do to protect ourselves and our society from the influences of lies, misinformation, and propaganda. But before we go there, I want to examine the real-world consequences of the Theater of Lies, because it goes beyond manipulation. It threatens our health, our minds, and our ways of life.

········· ACT TWO: ·············

WHY WE MUST GET OUT (AND WHAT COULD HAPPEN IF WE DON'T)

"It's a beautiful thing, the destruction of words."[264]

– GEORGE ORWELL,
BRITISH AUTHOR, ESSAYIST, AND POLITICAL CRITIC.

....

1

WE WERE WARNED.

In February 2022, the world's best athletes were descending in Beijing, China, for the Winter Olympic Games. Just hours prior to the opening ceremony, when the flags of ninety nations would be carried into the Beijing National Stadium, the host nation and its freshly re-minted strategic partner in world affairs published a 5,400-word statement. The following is taken from the Kremlin's English-language version:

> The sides [earlier defined as Russia and China] share the understanding that democracy is a universal human value, rather than a privilege among a limited number of States, and that its promotion and protection is a common responsibility of the entire world community . . . that democracy is a means of citizens' participation in the government of their country with

the view of improving the well-being of population and implementing the principle of popular government . . . There is no one-size-fits-all template . . . It is only up to the people of the country to decide whether their State is a democratic one.[265]

With that statement, the two nations proclaimed their leading roles as producers in the Theater of Lies, so powerful their misinformation and propaganda, that the most dangerous consequence of sustained and all-encompassing lies had been realized. For now, the people of China and Russia no longer only lived in the Theater of Lies, they were *governed* by it. I call this the Rule of Lies, and I see it creeping into mainstream democracies at an alarming pace.

As I read the Russia-China statement, my head twisted like a confused terrier. I'd read these words before. Not word-for-word, but certainly from their intent. It was if the statement had been ripped out of a George Orwell essay from seventy-six years prior and been held up to a mirror. The two documents even had the same word count, 5,400. It was if someone had taken Orwell's 1946 essay *Politics and the English Language* and re-written it as satire.

Under the subheading of MEANINGLESS WORDS, in that essay, Orwell shows how the words democracy, socialism, freedom, patriotic, realistic, and justice have so many different interpretations to so many different people that their use in political language is abusive. Their use allows the speaker to say one thing and the audience to hear another. Orwell wrote,

> In the case of the word democracy not only is there no agreed definition, but the attempt to make one is resisted

from all sides. It is almost universally felt that when we call a country democratic, we are praising it: consequently, the defenders or every kind of regime claim that it is a democracy, and fear that they might have to stop using that word if it were tied down to any one meaning.[266]

In their pre-Olympic statement, the Russian and Chinese governments tell us that the meaning of democracy is *up to the people of the country to decide whether their state is a democratic one.* Their truth however is quite the opposite—it is not up to the people of these two nations to make such a determination. It is up to their leaders. The summation of the section quoted above, more simply, is *our populations live in a democracy because we tell them they do.*

Such is life in the Rule of Lies. Truth be damned.

Two internationally recognized organizations that rank democracy globally (the University of Würzburg's Democracy Matrix,[267] and the publisher of *The Economist*'s Intelligence Unit) both rank Russia and China near the bottom (for China, Democracy Matrix rank—172nd out of 176 countries, *The Economist*—148th out of 167 countries,—and for Russia, Democracy Matrix rank—144th out of 176 countries, *The Economist*—124th out of 167 countries). For both ranking organizations, Russia and China are summarized as the opposite of democratic, falling under the title "Authoritarian."[268]

The "war on the truth is a central pillar of the CCP's [Chinese Communist Party's] strategy for survival," claims Dan Blumenthal, the director of Asian Studies at the Jewish Policy Center.[269] This is so much the case that in an editorial in the state-run newspaper *Beijing Daily*, party leaders admonished local media for truth-telling and balanced journalism, stating, "Chinese media interested in negative news have been seduced into wrongdoing by Western concepts."[270] The People's Republic owns its theater—right from the producers to the actors, the playwrights, and, unfortunately, much of its audience.

In fact, Blumenthal identifies at least nine departments that the Chinese government uses to control every possible message that any individual, group, corporation, or government department publishes: The **General Administration of Press and Publication** (GAPP), which drafts and enforces restraint regulations; **State Administration of Radio, Film, and Television** (SARFT), which controls the content of radio, film, and TV aired in China.; **Ministry for Information Industry** (MII), which regulates the Chinese telecommunication, software industries, and internet-related services; **State Council Information Office** (SCIO), which promotes Chinese media to a global audience and is also responsible for restricting news that is posted on the internet; **Central Propaganda Department** (CPD), the party organ that works with GAPP and SARFT to monitor content; **Ministry of Public Security** (MPS), which monitors and filters the internet and punishes and detains those who speak out; **General Administration for Customs**, which collects books, videos, and other information that China does not want inside its borders; **State Secrecy Bureau** (SSB), which enforces state secrecy laws, which are often used to punish individuals who write undesirable content; and finally (though likely not all) the **Central Party School**, which since 1933 has trained every political and bureaucratic staff member of the government from the municipal level and above (it is always headed by a member the CCP's Politburo, the communist version of what Western democracies would call a cabinet).[271]

As a final touch, or perhaps *touché*, China's **National Security Commission** identifies democracy activists as one of the nation's five poisons to the country's stability (the other four being Taiwan separatists, Tibet separatists, Falun Gong practitioners, and its Muslim Uyghur population).[272] Try to square this with the joint Russian/Chinese proclamation at that *democracy is a universal human value.*[273] As governments and lie producers continue to redefine words to fit their own purpose, dictionary publishers may want to consider adding asterisks to certain words—especially political terms (*such as "the political use of this word may not be exactly as shown"*).

However, if trust in government is the sign of a healthy society, the Chinese people seem to believe what their government tells them. In 2021, a rather robust and independent survey of about 20,000 Chinese citizens (though perhaps the respondents feared answering the poll honestly for fear of retribution) found that their trust in their national government had increased to 98 percent that year from 91 percent in 2018.[274] So if Xi Jinping et al. are telling the people of China they live in a democracy, then okay, they do.

But that trust, according to Chinese American public affairs commentator Kaiser Kuo, may have more to do with the unwritten social contract between the Chinese government and its people— "You stay out of politics; we'll create conditions in which you can prosper and enjoy many personal freedoms."[275]

According to Kaiser, that contract began in 1979 with the reforms of its then-president, Deng Xiaoping.

> Since Deng inaugurated reforms in 1979, China has not experienced significant countrywide political violence. GDP growth has averaged close to 10 percent per annum. Almost any measure of human development has seen remarkable improvement. There are no food

shortages and no significant energy shortages. Nearly 700 million Chinese now use the internet. Over 500 million have smartphones. China has a high-speed rail network that's the envy of even much of the developed world. China has, by some measures, even surpassed the US as the world's largest economy.[276]

That, of course does not explain why Russians might believe they live in a democracy. A 2019 international survey by the global public relations firm, Edelman, placed Russia at the bottom of the list of governments trusted by its citizens. (China was near the top, reflecting the Chinese government's powerful influence on the beliefs of its citizens.) [277] Though, it might at least be part of the explanation why Vladimir Putin wanted to sidle up next to China on its democratic, new world order messaging.

In clear legal wording, the Russian Constitution's first article defines the nation as "a democratic federal law-bound State with a republican form of government."[278] Its third article states that "*the supreme direct expression of the power of the people shall be referenda and free elections.*"[279] Yet, in reality, the Kremlin selects the candidates who run for office. That would be like the King of England hand-picking all the candidates who could run for office in his government. Democratic in form, perhaps, but not in function. Added to the tendency of the Russian government to silence, upon threat of imprisonment, any media commentary (including citizen journalism) that does not follow the government's messaging and the statement *Russia is a democracy* is about as hollow as an empty nesting doll.

Which brings me back to George Orwell, the godfather of dystopian fiction. Russia and China had Canada's ambassador to the United Nations, Bob Rae, reflecting on him as well.

> Working at the United Nations has me thinking of Orwell and his observations more frequently these days. . . The UN at its best can be an institution that serves the greater good, but it has also, especially in recent months, been a place where words are twisted and lies abound. As certain state actors attempt to rewrite history and facts are turned on their heads, I often look to Orwell for guidance and wisdom. Russian President Vladimir Putin's ongoing "special military operation" to "destroy Nazism" by attempting to annex eastern Ukraine is a case in point. At the UN we've also become accustomed to constant attempts by the Chinese government to insert President Xi Jinping's thoughts into official resolutions, compromising and qualifying commitments to human rights, democracy and the rule of law by making them subject to the "spirit" of the "equality of nations" and "mutual respect." (Translation: Stay out of our business).[280]

Most people are familiar with at least two of Orwell's most famous novels: *Animal Farm* and *1984*. They are required reading in most high school curricula. The former was a clever and biting satire of the Soviet Union, disguised as story of farm animals working together to overthrow the farmer. The latter was a similar attack on Nazi Germany, the title coming from the inversion of the last two numbers of the year it was written, 1948.

But two years prior to that, Orwell wrote the essay *Politics and the English Language.* I often use the essay as a teaching aid for writers because of its focus on brevity, clarity, and advice on the use of simple language. Relevant here, however, is the rising bile that Orwell must have been feeling when he wrote the essay, as he damned almost every statement made by governments as "largely the defense of the indefensible."[281] In his closing paragraph, Orwell wrote,

> Political language—and with variations this is true of all political parties, from Conservatives to Anarchists— is designed to make lies sound truthful and murder respectable, and to give an appearance of solidity to pure wind.[282]

Orwell is number one on my list of dead people I would love to have dinner with, along with his eighteenth-century precursor satirist, Ireland's Jonathan Swift (famous for his novel *Gulliver's Travels*), and America's top societal commentator, the late George Carlin (famous for just about everything he said).[5]

In Orwell's 1946 essay, he warns of us of the power tools used to build what I am calling the Theater of Lies. We'll get more into the details of those tools in Act Three (such as the overbearing use of words with Latin roots rather than Saxon, like *plurality*). Act Two, however,

....

5   For the record, my complete list includes former prime minister of Pakistan, Benazir Bhutto, astronomer Carl Sagan, and when she passes away, former managing director of the International Monetary Fund (IMF) Christine Legarde. Julia Child, too, as she could cook, entertain, and debate public affairs with the best of them.

focuses on the consequences of living the Theater of Lies and why, as individuals and a society, we must take concrete steps to defend ourselves. As a world, we are already experiencing the consequences of pervasive lies and misinformation. Like climate change, inaction fosters negative impacts.

Seventy-six years before this book was written, Orwell told us, "If thought corrupts language, language can also corrupt thought." [283] It is even more true today. This is how the purveyors of lies, misinformation, and propaganda manipulate us. And their actions have consequences.

"The more we want it to be true,
the more careful we have to be."[284]

– CARL SAGAN, AMERICAN ASTROPHYSICIST AND AUTHOR.

··

2

NEWS MEDIA AND LIES: A CODEPENDENT COUPLE.

One of the most insidious consequences of the Theater of Lies is the economy we have built around it. This economy is like the ticket sellers or the concession workers pushing popcorn and sugary snacks in a traditional theater. Their work has nothing to do with the production and presentation of lies on the stage, but their livelihoods depend on their continuance (in fact, in the cinema industry, the prime driver of profit is often not the films, but the food).[285]

The candy sellers in the Theater of Lies are mainstream news media. The larger the audience, the higher the revenue—whether from advertising or subscription fees. Misinformation has become a particularly powerful tool for attracting audiences (whether in the need to call them out or debate their veracity). Mainstream media and producers of lies have become the twenty-first century's most influential codependent couple.

A snapshot of the US cable television news sector is indicative of this relationship. In 2016, the year of Donald Trump's first presidential campaign and electoral win, CNN had its highest audiences ever. It leaped up the cable television ratings from twenty-fourth place overall (including sports, news, and entertainment channels) to eighth—driven mostly through its lie-by-lie coverage of Trump's campaign announcements. It created a massive audience for a *Toronto Star* reporter, Daniel Dale, who first started tracking and reporting on each of the Republican candidate's lies for the Canadian daily newspaper. Dale went from being the writer of a unique series of sidebar stories, to a special guest on CNN, to a regular guest on CNN and finally, in 2019, a full job at the work. CNN's audience reached its peak during its coverage of the Capital Hill Riot on January 6, 2021—topping 10.7 million viewers.[286]

Much of that audience went elsewhere after its primary carnival barker lost the bully pulpit of his presidential office. In from 2021 to 2022, CNN's total audience fell off a cliff to land uncomfortably (for its management and shareholders) at 750,000.[287] That's a ninety percent drop in viewership.

But it's not lies that the media are hunting. It's eyeballs. And lies are incredibly good bait.

Anyone who tells you that traditional news media is dying has never seen a story in any newspaper or broadcast outlet launch a tsunami of social media commentary. What is not dying, but *has* died, is a business model that once focused on advertising—classified and display—to fund a relatively independent editorial process. But in 2010, a seismic shift in revenue sources flipped the page on the editorial policies of major newspapers. It was that year that revenues from individual sub-scription payments (mostly digital) first exceeded advertising revenues. Outside of a very few daily newspapers (notably *The Washington Post* and *The New York Times*), the power of digital subscriptions caused the publishers of major media outlets to push out stories that attracted readers to click and buy subscriptions.

In essence, according to Toronto-based media researcher Andrey Mir, traditional mainstream media were now following the well-cut path of early social media adopters and developers—publishing stories with the specific goal of attracting readers—readers who'd have to pay to read them. "The shift from advertising to digital subscriptions invalidated old standards of journalism and led the emergence of post-journalism," [288] writes Mir in *City Journal*, a public policy maga-zine. Post-journalism, Mir defines as the audience's change in how they consumed media. Where once we read newspapers or watched a news broadcast to get the news, today's digital-first consumer uses traditional media as a place to have a story confirmed. [289] That may appear like a good place for traditional media, but the consequences of what may seem an evolutionary change are actually quite radical. Post-journalism media requires what early internet advertisers called *clickbait* to drive readership.

The *Merriam-Webster Dictionary* defines *clickbait* as "something (such as a headline) designed to make readers want to click on a hyperlink especially when the link leads to content of dubious value or interest." [290]

The impact of words as clickbait has been quantitatively defined as massive through the research efforts of three social science research-ers, David Rozado, Musa Al-Gharbi, and Jamin Halberstadt, and a connect-the-dot exercise by the deputy editor of *Newsweek*, Batya Urgar Sargon.

The trio of social scientists (working out of universities in New Zealand and the United States) published their work in 2021. As the abstract of their paper, "Prevalence of Prejudice-Denoting Words in News Media Discourse: A Chronological Analysis" states:

> This work analyzes the prevalence of words denoting prejudice in 27 million news and opinion articles written between 1970 and 2019 and published in 47 of the most popular news media outlets in the United States. Our results show that the frequency of words that denote specific prejudice types related to ethnicity, gender, sexual, and religious orientation has markedly increased within the 2010–2019 decade across most news media outlets.[291]

London's *Guardian* newspaper investigated the trio's work with rigor. While the trio's work was limited to newspapers, the *Guardian* also used a tool known as the Stanford Cable News Analyser to demonstrate that cable news outlets followed the same pattern. What was most interesting, however, is neither the *Guardian* nor the trio of social scientists could define specifically why this pattern had and was continuing to occur.[292] This is not uncommon in journalism, as a reporting of the facts often takes precedence over any analysis (leaving that to opinion writers and others).

Batya Urgar Sargon did the analysis. She connected the dots. Money. In her 2021 book, *Bad News,* she writes about how articles containing words that attracted audiences had become more and more frequent after a seminal event occurred.

> Around 2011, the New York Times erected its online paywall. It was then that articles mentioning "racism", "people of color", "slavery" or "oppression" started to appear with exponential frequency at the Times, BuzzFeed, Vox, The Washington Post, and NPR.[293]

By 2010, traditional news media had gone from attracting readers to hunting them. In digital media, that meant using words and terminologies that reflected specific readers with specific ideologies—like bait. When you combine this new model with creative abilities of the producers in the Theater of Lies, this makes traditional media a prime target for manipulation. Indeed, as clickbait headlines drive media revenue from paywalls and subscriptions, what we once believed was the foundation of good journalism—the truth—is not an incentive for publishers. If people are more attracted to the drama, lies, and misinformation, truth is secondary to the story. The editorial cliché—*if it bleeds, it leads*—has been placed, in my opinion, with *if it lies, it flies, and we follow it.*

I am not saying that mainstream media is not ethical (opinion on this is clearly divided, at least in the United States, by party affiliation)[294]—but I am saying that other than the ethical standards of the journalist and media outlet of concern, there is no incentive for them to be ethical or truthful. That will only come from audience demand (and knowledge).

Another media tool emerged about the same time as its subscriber-hunting tactics were launched. Previously, the likelihood that the story you were reading in your newspaper was either written by reporter employed by that newspaper, or a wire-service—such as United Press International (UPI) or the Associated Press (AP). The drop in advertising revenue forced publishers to make cuts to its largest budget item, the salary cost of their reporters. Cuts to newsroom staffs had an immediate impact on the sources of content. Newspapers became distributors of information that others generated. The accountants working for media outlets could tell you clickbait headlines drive revenue, but the better bottom line requires cost cutting. That means if free content (or cheaper than can be produced in-house) is available, why spend money to produce it? Especially if truth is not driving the bottom line.

A Pew Research study in just one American city (Baltimore, MD) found that, in 2019, over 70 percent of all media stories in that city were generated by governments (federal, state, and municipal). Just 7 percent of stories were original content—that is, created by the media outlets' own reporters.[295] That means, at least in the crab capital of America, the chances that a journalist actually wrote the story from their own efforts and investigation rather than relying on press releases and interview opportunities (like a press release, but the reporters are invited to interview a specific person) is less than one in ten. In reference to the previous chapter, this means the propagandists, whether they are using truth or lies as their tactic, are succeeding in controlling their messages and having these well distributed. And despite any cries to the contrary, a story published in top-tier media (daily newspapers, television network, and cable news), is a credibility platform for lies and misinformation.

Part of the emerging structure of the Theater of Lies is that the worst place to find news is any radio and cable outlet promoting itself as being solely focused on news. Pew Research (an independent source of media research and insight) found that on all-news radio stations, "there was little of what could be considered reporting."[296] Most segments, the study found, were anchors doing monologues or taking call-in comments from listeners (yet often referring to themselves as "journalists").

Cable news today—CNN (including its international outlet), Fox News, and MSNBC—was built on the radio news model. Most of these 24/7 news channels do not produce what one would traditionally call a newscast. They have opinion hosts, opinion guests, and paid opinion consultants. When news does appear, it falls into the category of "breaking news," giving a false importance to the story. The places for true news coverage in America are the television network news, local television news, and newspapers, as well as internet sites such as AP and Reuters. National Public Radio (NPR) and its website often rank as the most neutral.[297] When one considers the hundreds of sources from which Americans get their news, very few play host to edited, fact-checked, editorially controlled content.

National broadcasters such as the CBC and the internationally delivered British Broadcasting Corporation (BBC) have yet to fall into the-all-news-means-no-news trap, perhaps because they are publicly funded and do not have to compete for advertising dollars in the same way that private media outlets do. But all media outlets are still generating less of their own content, relying on others to deliver it to them.

There is a danger in this. Misinformation, hyperbole, and lies can slip through unnoticed or be caught only after publication. More so, since mainstream media are no longer the primary supplier of news, but its distributor, mainstream media becomes the source of validation and amplification for news others are creating—whether that be governments, companies, or people with a large social media presence.[298]

As-seen-on-TV works as well for the producers of lies and misinformation as it does for sellers of real products.

Once a mainstream media outlet distributes a message produced in the Theater of Lies, it becomes more credible—but that does not by definition make it true. And broadcast news becomes as much of an entertainment source founded on the topic of current affairs, that the codependence with lies become more difficult to break, primarily because of its profitability for both partners—the media and the producers of lies.

All of this makes truth harder to find. Yet, once found, it may not be truly relevant. In the next chapter, we'll examine our collective tendency to stretch the truth to make it better fit the hole we are trying to fill.

"The stronger our commitment to an ideology or philosophy of life, the harder it is to accept evidence that we might be wrong."[299]

– CAROL TARVIS, AMERICAN PSYCHOLOGIST.

....

3

SILLY PUTTY LOGIC.

If the mainstream news media and the Theater of Lies are a codependent couple, then their shared audience is struggling to make sense of it all. They do not do this vainly. As human beings, the need to make sense of things is hardwired into our thinking processes. It is particularly prominent in "justifying and explaining uncontrollable bad and confusing events," says Aditya Shukla, the publisher of *Cognition Today*.[300] Canadian psychologists Sally Maitlis and Marlys Christianson defined sense-making as "the process through which people work to understand issues or events that are novel, ambiguous, confusing, or in some other way violate expectations."[301]

As the traditional news media work hard to attract the eyeballs so naturally embedded in their profit and loss statements, the use of the *novel* and stories that *violate expectations* is powerful tool. But we before dig deeper into the relationship between the audience's need to make sense of the news, and the news distributors themselves, I think we should answer the question, what is news, anyway? Outside of dictionaries, there are not a lot of definitions about what *news* really is.

Fakhar Naveed is a Pakistani academic who has provided what I believe is comprehensive view. He has defined news as:

> Anything out of the ordinary, an unusual picture of life, anything that people talk about (the more it excites the greater its value), current activities of general human interest (the best news interests most readers), anything that enough people want to read, the report of an event that is fresh, unusual and which is interesting to a great number of people, and finally, like a hot cake coming straight from oven.[302]

All of which makes news a pretty broad term (and something that is appetizing, if not always fulfilling). Naveed's list, however, gives you some insight into the decision-making process of a news editor. And, with the extreme time pressures of getting a story written, produced, and published, these decisions can take place in minutes. Fact-checking can be cursory.

For example, let's look at a 2014 story about an Australian woman named Belle Gibson (no relation to the Aussie actor with whom her name rhymes, Mel Gibson). A local television news station in Australia first reported on Gibson—as her story checked almost every one of Naveed's "what is news" qualifier.

Gibson had been diagnosed with brain cancer and decided that after two months of traditional chemotherapy and radiation, the treatments were not working. Instead, she chose to cleanse her diet of all meats, went vegan, and undertook an intensive meditation and exercise regime. She was cured. To invite others to participate in her cancer-killing lifestyle (and make a fair bit of cash), she developed an app called The Whole Pantry (it was downloaded 200,000 times) and later, with publisher Random House, wrote a book under the same title. It sold 300,000 copies in its first year.

Gibson's story was news, proliferated across social media, and made the twenty-one-year-old woman an icon for the alternative medicine industry and quite wealthy. At the time her story was being widely story in traditional media, she was moving on to the highroad of celebrity occupations - philanthropy.[303]

Alex Edmans, a professor of finance at London Business School, reviewed Gibson's story. He found two problems: one if the story was false, and two, if the story was true.[304]

Why? Because stories are not data. They are instances. Edmans reminds us that even when these stories are true (that is, factual), they are not evidence. "Stories are powerful," he says, "they're vivid and they bring a topic to life. But a single story is meaningless and misleading unless it is backed up by large scale data."[305] And, damn, do the media love to tell stories. Their power to do so is their bread and butter. In the quick decision-making environment of newsrooms around the world, a great story is very powerful bait. For them, its clickbait.

So let's look at how the media manages data.

At some point in your education, you likely came across the notion of a bell curve. For me, it always seemed to come up around exam time when someone would ask the teacher or professor if they were "grading on the curve." A bell curve is a particular way of visualizing data that shows normal probability distributions.

Here is what a typical bell curve looks like. Relevant to our discussion about media is that the most tempting stories to publish are outside the norm, not within it (the cliché is true: dog bites man is not news, but man bites dog is).

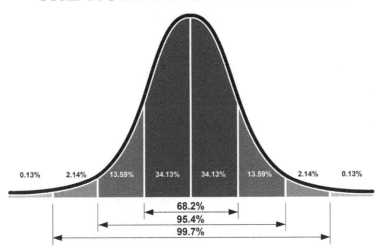

THE NORMAL DISTRIBUTION

The middle of the curve marks the median in the curve. But the interesting part is when one adds lines of standard deviations (from the median, or the norm in the case of news interest). While these lines look evenly spaced, the data within them is not.

Bell curves follows the 68-95-99.7 rule, meaning that about 68% of all the data lies within one standard deviation of the median, 95% of all the data is within two standard deviations, and 99.7% is within three standard deviations. While three standard deviations looks like it is three times as much one deviation—that's not relevant. What is relevant, and overlooked, is that the data reflecting three standard deviations represents only 0.3% of whole. That means, it is an extreme outlier.

Gibson's self-healing cancer story fell into a spot that scream for attention, well past even the three standard deviation points. Her story became news because of its rarity—not because of its normalcy. And, with the aid of media exposure, Gibson was able to earn hundreds of thousands of dollars selling books and advice to people who wanted the same cure.

So, let's now go from statistical analysis to something a little more fun, but just as relevant to codependent relationship between the media and lies. A toy.

Lies are often at the end of the bell curve. The tendency of the audience, or a producer in our Theater of Lies to stretch a fact to fit a pre-determined conclusion they already want to make. I call this *Silly Putty* logic.

Silly Putty is a soft silicone toy, packaged in a plastic egg. Invented[6] (as a toy) in the 1950s and marketed worldwide, the Crayola company sells 6 million of them a year.[306] One of the fun features of the toy is that if you press it onto a newsprint photo, the image of the photo is retained on the putty. As a child in the 1960s, my friends and I had lots of fun pressing the putty onto images in comics, then stretching the transfer images of Archie, Batman, or Popeye into shapes that made their faces unrecognizable. It's what I think of today when I see a person—journalist or not—take one piece of data and stretch so far to make their point that the data is evidence of the story they want to tell.

The fundamentals of this process are, unfortunately, baked into journalism. Credible, fact-checking reporters and editors avoid it, but the notion of news needing to be novel can be overwhelmingly seductive to a journalist seeking to break a story.

....

6   Silly Putty was invented by a Scottish engineer, James Wright, as a by-product of research into substitutes for rubber (in short supply due to World War II).

About eighteen months after the first story about Gibson broke in the press, the Australian version of CBS's *60 Minutes* exposed her as a fraud.[307] She had never had cancer. I want you to think about this: *eighteen months* from the telling of her original story to a mainstream media outlet doing a deep dive into fact-checking it.

Despite this, the editorial decision (pre-knowledge of her fakery) was that Gibson's miracle sure was news. And, by definition, it was.

But Professor Edmans was right: if Gibson's story had been true, it would have been only one data point in time. In no way did Gibson's return to robust health prove that fruits, vegetables, and exercise were better at curing brain cancer than chemotherapy and radiation. Yet the media coverage of her "success" would have indeed driven many a real cancer patient away from their doctor's advice, toward salad bars over cancer clinics. Even if they still chose traditional courses of treatment, well-meaning friends might still insist Ms. Gibson's methods were better. In the meantime, to use the vernacular, Gibson and her publisher made bank.

This is where traditional news media is culpable, if unknowingly, in spreading misinformation—and, in Gibson's case, outright lies. While a news editor might take an outlier of a story such as Gibson's and present it as interesting, audiences might take this information as data, as evidence. Even if the news media presented a warning, such as *please talk to your doctor before following this treatment*, audiences will tend to ignore it, as their use own use of Silly Putty logic will stretch that data point into a tantalizing and highly relevant truth.

Later in this book, we will discuss understanding how we understand. A story such as Ms. Gibson's is an example of *confirmation bias*. We are attracted to information that confirms the opinions we already hold.

The Silly Putty logic sets in. Especially for the growing audience of journalists whose objectivity, as Ungar-Sargon and others have demonstrated, is often based on what an audience wants to hear rather than news that needs to be told. Naveen's "like a hot cake coming out of the oven" seems more relevant all the time. Except that is the quasi-journalists, or opinion hosts, that are baking most of those cakes.

Once the primary profit for large radio networks (Glenn Beck has weekly audience of 8.5 million listeners, Sean Hannity—16 million, and The Mark Levin Show—8.5 million . . . all conservative talk show hosts),[308] cable news networks have developed similar shows, all of which are the highest rated of any programming on their networks (CNN—Anderson Cooper, audience 791,000; Fox News—Tucker Carlson, 3.16 million; and MSNBC—Rachel Maddow, 2.0 million).[309]

This all reminds me of a carnival barker shouting, "Come see the man-eating chicken!" So, people line up and pay their dollar or two. What they see inside the tent is a man, eating a chicken. At least my carnival friends and their audiences were all in on the joke. With traditional news media, sometimes not.

The audience, however, is complicit in its use of Silly Putty logic. The publisher of *Cognition Today*, Aditya Shukla, has identified seven strategies that people tend to use to help them make sense of things. One of them is "plausibility versus accuracy."[310] He says "sense-making, by definition, is about justifying or explaining an action retrospectively, so there is a tendency to think about what a believable and plausible story is."[311] Accuracy of the information presented is not a primary influencer.

Other ways, Shukla has identified include "enacting"—relating stories of what has happened in the past to the issue a person is trying to make sense of today and "social elements"—making sense of things in way that meets the social standards of the day. [312] To this "of the day," I would add—*and of their environment*—as the abortion debate teeters on both sides of the argument, pro-life and pro-abortion. As part of their own sense-making, each person in the debate may be centering at least part of their logic on the Christian or liberal values of their personal environment.

Silly Putty logic enables all these strategies. If I like who is telling me the information, I will find that story more plausible. If I once felt unwell after a vaccination (or know someone who did), I am more likely to believe that a COVID-19 vaccine is dangerous. If I have visited Africa and only been exposed to struggling, low-income, low-education laborers, then you may also believe that all Black people in America were better off having their ancestors enslaved, because *you've seen people in Africa, personally*. All of what you've seen may be true, all lies, or likely a mix of truth, lies, misinformation and hyperbole—but as a member of the audience in this Theater of Lies you take these single data points and stretch them into evidence of what you need to make sense of your world.

Do that at a dinner, you have a conversation. Do that with hundreds and the strings of stretched Silly Putty, start to form a web. Post that on social media with thousands of followers and you have the lie, so believed, and conspiracy theories are born. All of this to snare the attention of everyday people who just want to make some sense of their world and find a place for their anxiety. In Belle Gibson's non-cure cancer cure, her story fed not only the desire of the media to tell an extraordinary tale, but the need for cancer patients for extraordinary hope.

Sick people can become desperate and the Theater of Lies provides an insidious solution. While providing false senses of hope, it also makes more people sick.

"A crisis has to be created. No man is willing to die for the eight-hour day."[313]

– JOSEPH GOEBBELS, GERMAN AND NAZI PROPAGANDA DIRECTOR.

....

4

THE THEATER IS MAKING US SICK.

The con job is a classic: create a crisis, then sell the mark a fix only you can deliver. The more people are afraid, the easier the sell.

This con job is so old that in 1957 it was the source for a Broadway musical, *The Music Man*. More famously, it was made into a movie in 1962, and returned to Broadway in 2022. The original productions starred Robert Preston as traveling musical instrument salesman Harold Hill, who comes to the fictional River City, Indiana. He finds he needs a reason for the town to have a marching band—and, therefore, buy all the instruments and uniforms from him. His strategy included some of the fundamental tools in the Theater of Lies: create villains and victims and play to peoples' biases.

Hill fabricates the evils a new form of entertainment that has come into River City, the pool hall, and amplifies it with the compelling need to protect the children from its nefarious embrace. He then raises the stakes to show that pool halls will be the end of their town as they know it. Only he can save the day, he tells them, by teaching the youth of River City how to play music—on the bright shiny instruments they would first need to buy from him. All summarized in rhapsodic harmony that first declares to all who'll listen River City has "trouble".[314]

If this tactic sounds familiar, here is a sample of Donald Trump's speech to the cheering members of the Republican Party who had just named him as their candidate for 2016 presidential election. While it lacks the poetry and rhythm of Harold Hill's song and dance, the message of impending peril and him as the sole person to address it is eerily the same—*I am the hero to fix all your problems.*

> Our Convention occurs at a moment of crisis for our nation. The attacks on our police, and the terrorism in our cities, threaten our very way of life. Any politician who does not grasp this danger is not fit to lead our country. Americans watching this address tonight have seen the recent images of violence in our streets and the chaos in our communities. Many have witnessed this violence personally; some have even been its victims. I have a message for all of you: the crime and violence that today afflicts our nation will soon come to an end. Beginning on January 20th, 2017, safety will be restored.[315] . . . I have joined the political area so that the powerful can no longer beat up on people who

can not defend themselves. Nobody knows the system better than me. Which is why I alone can fix it.[316]

Harold Hill was a con man. He identified the game of pool as the threat and music as the solution. This was not the con, however. He might have even been right that if the youth of River City were engaged in music, they'd have no time for or interest in the devilry of that had set up shop in the local pool halls. The problem was, while he could deliver the bright shiny instruments, colorful uniforms, and batons that could be twirled and thrown skyward, Hill had no abilities in music. As a musician and teacher, he was a fraud. His goal was to get all the cash he could from the citizens of River City—for instruments and uniforms—then depart in the night without teaching anyone how to actually play a note.

> HAROLD: I have a revolutionary new method called the Think System where you don't bother with notes.
>
> MARCELLUS: But in four weeks the people will want to hear the music! You'll have to lead a band.
>
> HAROLD: But when the uniforms arrive, they forget everything else—at least long enough for me to collect and leave. Oh, this is a refined operation, son, and I've got it timed right down to the last wave of the brakeman's hand on the last train out'a town.[317]

Hill's fraudulent Think System promised that the children could learn to play their instruments by merely thinking the melodies ("as simple as whistling").[318]

Of course, the story being fiction, his Think System worked—to the surprise of no one greater than Hill himself, the woman he was trying to woo (a word in keeping with the Depression-era dialogue of the play), and the townsfolk who were about to run him out of town for fraud. A happy ending for all.

In real life, the Theater of Lies provides no such joy.

Whether one considers Donald Trump a conman or not is of no concern to me. Nor is it relevant to this book. What is relevant is that, like the fictional Harold Hill, Trump not only identified a crisis and amplified its impact on his audience, but he also identified himself as the only person who could solve this crisis. But for the Hollywood miracle of his mythical Think System (or a late train), Hill would have failed. In our Theater of Lies, however, the only crisis solutions that its producers can truly offer is more crises.

Con artists need a crisis to solve. To attain and maintain their positions as saviors, they have two options. One, they must be clearly seen to have solved the crisis (in which case they are no longer con artists at all, like Hill). Or two, they must continue to create more crises—all through repeated lies and misinformation. If the crises are never-ending and the blame can be put onto others for not only the crises themselves, but as barriers to the savior's ability to solve them, then the con artist can continue. And this is where consequences of lies, misinformation, and propaganda are realized.

This is where, how, and why Donald Trump has continued to re-position every legal claim against him as not so much as a problem for him, but as a barrier to the beliefs and ambitions to all who support him ("every time the radical left Democrats, Marxists, communists, and fascists indict me, I consider it a great badge of honor and badge of courage").[319]

Through its constant need to maintain a state of crisis, the Theater of Lies has measurably raised the stress levels of we, its audience. The American Psychological Association (APA) conducts an annual stress survey in the US. Its 2020 report states that for eight in ten Americans "the future if our nation is a significant source of stress."[320] This is the highest the organization has ever recorded (the previous high had been seven in ten in 2018).

Dr. Arthur C. Evans Jr. is the APA's chief executive officer. In the 2020 report, he said:

> We are experiencing the collision of three national crises, the COVID-19 pandemic, economic turmoil, and recent, traumatic events related to systemic racism. As a result, the collective mental health of the American public has endured one devastating blow after another, the long-term effects of which many people will struggle for years to come. We don't have to be passive players in mitigating the rapidly increasing stress Americans are facing and its consequences on our health.[321]

But it's only getting worse. The APA has been conducting this survey since 2007, and its 2022 results showed that the daisy-chain of stressors Americans have been experiencing (such the COVID-19 pandemic, Russia's invasion of Ukraine, political uncertainty, and racial issues) were taking their toll on people's lives. Respondents to the APA survey reported unintended weight gain (as well as unintended weight loss), increased consumption of alcohol and drugs, and strained or ended relationships.[322]

The APA's chief executive officer states, "The data suggest that we're now reaching unprecedented levels of stress that will challenge our ability to cope."[323]

Similar data has been found in Canada. The annual Mental Health Index report by human resources consulting firm Morneau Shepell in March 2021 found many of the same stressors effecting Canadians.

> March 2021 marks twelve consecutive months of diminished mental health among Canadians. The current state of mental health is eleven points below the pre-pandemic benchmark and indicates that the working population is as distressed as the most distressed one percent of working Canadians prior to 2020 . . . Beyond the economic and health crises of the pandemic that have led to profound change for Canadians, social justice issues dominated headlines in 2020, calling attention to systemic racial inequalities, including the significant rise in anti-Asian racism and increased focus on the Black Lives Matter movement . . . The length of time that we have been under undue stress is itself the greatest risk at this point, threatening to further deteriorate our mental health.[324]

The issues that are stressing Canadians and Americans are, in my opinion, transferrable to much of the world. The similarity is that each of these stress-driving issues has been and continues to be amplified in the Theater of Lies. As I have presented, producers lean heavily on established and well-accepted lies that support racism, political uncertainty, and gender issues. The amplification of lies, often with purpose to raise our fears, is directly to increased levels of stress. Stress, in my opinion, is often the fruit of the poisoned trees of lies, misinformation and their rocket-launching partner, hyperbole.

When we think of how lies can kill, we often turn to military, police, and terrorist actions that were result of lies—such as the death of police officers and the January 6, 2021, riots on Capital Hill in Washington, DC, or race-based shootings in the United States and Canada, and Russia's invasion of Ukraine (based on the lie of de-nazifying the country). But stress is a silent killer. Our body's main stress hormone is cortisol. When stressed, our bodies release more of it—interfering with our memory, ability to learn, lowering our immune function, decreasing our bone density, and increasing our blood pressure, cholesterol, and heart disease.[325] Long-term stress also leads to depression.

"If we stay under chronic stress, our physiological stress response is taxed beyond what it's designed to do, and it starts to impair us," says David Prescott, PhD, associate professor of Health Administration and Public Health at Husson University in Bangor, ME.

Stress is making us sick. Stress is killing us, and these outcomes are direct consequences of lies, misinformation, and propaganda. In Professor Hill's real theater performance, we sing along, applaud—then go home. In the Theater of Lies, we argue, raise our stress levels, remain trapped in our seats, and get sicker.

This can't end well, unless we do something. Quickly.

"Without facts, you can't have truth. Without truth, you can't have trust."[326]

– MARIA RESSA, 2021 NOBEL PEACE PRIZE WINNER.

....

5

LIES ERODE TRUST.

Trust is fundamental to our lives, beginning at birth. According to Erik Erikson—a twentieth-century developmental psychologist who defined eight stages of human psychological development—the first year of our lives is the crucible in which we learn to fundamentally trust (or mistrust).[327] He identified that as infants, we depend on our caregivers for our basic needs and develop trust when these needs are met. If these needs are not met, we are more likely to grow into adults who are suspicious and mistrustful.[328] Attachment theory is a complicated psychological debate with, like much in science, the adaptation and addition of new interpretations. But this much is without debate, trust is fundamental to our feelings of personal well-being. As such, it is a primary target for the Theater of Lies.

Its relevance to our mental health is so hardwired into our psyches during these earliest years that it is the most attractive target for weaponized lies. Like a sniper firing a head shot. Only in the Theater of Lies, that shot is more like the *drip-drip-drip* of Chinese Water Torture.

The producers of lies have two complementary goals. One, for you to trust their message rather than any messages you may have previously trusted (or believed). And two, for you to distrust any person, organization, brand, or ideology, that is delivering any messages to the contrary—whether those messages are true or not.

Upset the foundation of anyone's belief system, the rest of their mind will follow—and the behaviors the mind generates (how you vote, what you buy, who you trust).

We trust the elevator we go into (if not, we take the stairs). We trust the building we are going into is not going to collapse. And, if a fire alarm goes off in the building, we don't go screaming out the door and dash down the stairs in a panic. We wait and see if the alarm is a real fire, trust that someone one will tell us, and even if it is a fire—we trust that the firefighters will come and take care of it. Only when we actually smell smoke or hear a voice we trust do we drop everything and get out of the building.

Same thing for our brand of ketchup—trusting it will taste the same every time we dip our fries into it. We trust that the twenty-dollar bill in our pocket can be exchanged for the cost of those fries or anything else we want to use it for. We trust that when we use a plastic card with an embedded computer chip inside it, instead of that cash, the money comes out of our bank account swiftly and accurately. So does the person who accepted the card in lieu of the cash. They trust that the money will magically vanish from your bank account and appear in theirs, all in a heartbeat.

Trust is interpersonal—I trust you and you trust me, or we don't work well together. It is also societal—we trust that certain institutions function properly, notably our governments, police departments, and yes, our aforementioned fire departments. One of the most damaging consequences for the productions coming out of the Theater of Lies is this erosion of trust in these and many of our established institutions. Worse, extending from the previous chapter, our crumbly faith in our society to function is even affecting our health (and not because we have trouble getting to see a doctor). The Theater's practice of other-ing—sets us up to distrust other groups in society (by religion, race, sex, or otherwise grouped) and creates barriers to education and career growth as well as a host of societal deficits in healthcare, the economy, and freedom of choice.

You may be familiar with Maslow's Hierarchy of Needs. In the later half of the twentieth century, it became part of the bedrock teachings in two disciplines—psychology and marketing. The latter being the most important use of Abraham Maslow's purported analysis of the process of needs fulfillment that human beings follow, by nature. Meeting human needs, that is—consumer needs—is a foundation of business education and strategy. A version of the famous diagram is below.

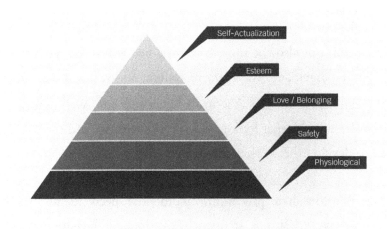

Maslow's Hierarchy of Needs

Psychologists and academics have debated the Maslow's conclusions (which he published in 1943), but the business world ate it up as if it was the secret sauce for understanding consumer behavior.

The irony in doing research for this book is finding that while Maslow did intensive research to define and publish his hierarchy of needs, he never created the diagram that made it famous.[329] Yet, it was this diagram that simplified its complication and eased its adoption by marketers, advertisers, and business strategists.

What I would add to the bottom of the pyramid is trust, for without out it, the other needs cannot be fulfilled. Trust is bedrock. Crack that and the rest crumbles.

What the producers in the Theater of Lies discovered, long before the business community adopted the hierarchy's principles, is that if you create lies and distribute lies that threaten the most basic needs in the hierarchy (physiological, safety, and social), you can motivate changes in human beliefs and behavior to your own goals. The legitimate business version would be, for example, a home alarm company running advertisements that show escalating crime rates[330] and images of burglars breaking into homes. These ads would hit not just at the safety need, but also the most basic one below it—that your life may also be in danger. So, buy an alarm system, and you will feel better.

Researchers and the Victoria University of Wellington, New Zealand, took a deeper look into Maslow's theories and the process he used to develop them. They discovered:

> Maslow had preconditions for his need hierarchy to work. This is frequently overlooked. Freedom to speak, to express oneself, to live in societies with fairness and justice, these are some of his preconditions.

Censorship, dishonesty, inability to pursue truth and wisdom work against us.[331]

To this, I add the notion of trust. Because even if you have achieved some or all of your own hierarchy of needs, if you don't trust that these needs can be maintained—especially by forces outside or your own control—then your fear of loss is fundamental to your decision-making process. In Maslow's hierarchy, trust is the foundation of *each* level—as even though you may have reached a supposed place of fulfillment by reaching any level—a lack of trust that you can maintain it will strip that feeling of satisfaction away as quickly as an earthquake makes you fear for the stability of your entire house.

Phillip Bump, an opinion writer for *The Washington Post* characterizes the trust-destroying messages from commentators such as Tucker Carlson, when he was on Fox News, as:

> Every night, he tells his audience that *they* (Democrats, the government, doctors, women, you name it) want to attack and undermine *us*. These claims are often existential: *They* are going to riot; *they* are going to harm you; *they* are going to ruin your life and the country.[332]

In 2016, three researchers (two in Canada, one in South Korea) teamed up to take a deeper dive into three internationally recognized measurements of trust—the Gallup World Poll, the World Values Survey, and the European Social Survey.

John Helliwell (University of British Columbia), Shun Wang (KDI School of Public Policy and Management), and Haifang Huang (University of Alberta) demonstrated that while people are more trustworthy than most of us perceive, social trust—trust in our institutions to operate well—is quite low. [333] Moreover, they found:

> Living in a high-trust environment makes people more resilient to adversity. Being subject to discrimination, ill-health, or unemployment, although always damaging to subjective well-being, is much less damaging to those living in trustworthy environments.[334]

In 2000, the global public relations firm, Edelman, began publishing an annual research report titled *The Edelman Trust Barometer* (full disclosure—I was a vice president at the Canadian division in the early 1990s). In its 2023 report, its online survey of over 32,000 people across 127 countries found that what was worrying respondents, globally, was: on a personal level—economic fears of job loss and inflation were felt by an overwhelming number of people (89% for job loss, 74% for inflation). And, on a societal level—fear of energy shortages, food shortages, nuclear war, and climate changed was causing anxiety for 66, 67, 72, and 76 percent of respondents, respectfully.[335]

These worries are at two foundational levels of Maslow's hierarchy—physiological and safety. Compare that against what Helliwell, Wang, and Huang reported seven years earlier. At that time, they had already concluded:

> There are significant additional benefits from trust in three aspects of the institutional environment: the legal system, parliament, and politicians.[336]

Trust makes us more resilient. Distrust, less so. And if you are fight-ing a war—a hot one or a cold one, a political or business one—a tactic you'd like to have at hand is any way to make your adversaries less resilient. This is where the Theater of Lies is a weapon, producing lies and misinformation that generate distrust in our institutions (such as the verbal attacks by Donald Trump and his supporters like Matt Gaetz on the FBI and the Department of Justice, as well as the Center for Disease Control and the WHO).

When you add political polarization to the mix, you have a danger-ous combination, says Adam Enders, an associate professor of political science at the University of Louisville in Kentucky. In an interview with NPR, Enders said:

> Because the more that people lack confidence and trust in institutions, the more they're willing to buck norms and ignore institutions when it's good for their side . . . That's when we see institutions start to fall apart, and norms crumble—and that's an environment that we can't really predict. . . While false conspiracy theories have always been around, . . . they've been embraced and promoted by growing number of influ-ential leaders in recent years—from former President Trump to pastors to prominent business owners. And they have political reasons for doing this, whether it's their consumer base or their congregation, winning this culture war or something along those lines.[337]

A second step comes, in part, from what public relations practi-tioners like me preach to our clients. Just as parents need to earn the trust of their children, for companies, politicians, and every individual, trust must be earned. It takes a lot of time and energy to accomplish it; mostly based on a series of promises made and kept. Yet, a single event of breaking any of these promises can leave an individual's—or an organization's—trust in tatters.

In the Theater of Lies, however, there is little or no need to keep promises. The producers of lies lean heavily on another time-tested method to create trust—the opinions of people whom their audience already trust. That may be a talk show host, a social media site, a celebrity, or (as will be discussed in Act Three) people who share the same biases.

Those messengers often become surrogates who don't even know they are now part of the production process. Like Edgar Welch, who went to a pizza parlor in Washington, DC, to personally investigate the ruse that leaders from the American Democratic Party were part of a secret ring of pedophiles (bringing along a cache of weapons), are pawns in a larger game. Lies produced to erode trust and its more engaging cousin—the embrace and entrenchment of distrust.

How the producers achieve this is through the expert use of a fundamental tool of what PR professionals call advocacy communications—though for nefarious purposes.

It's called the *bowtie model*—first developed in the Australian mining industry a century ago. Then it was created to promote workplace safety and later adapted by many cause-related businesses and organizations that wanted to foster this persuasion model to convince people to change their habits. Fundamental to that process is hearing the message from a person they trust.

The bowtie process looks like two funnels—one with communications directed to a wide group of prospective messengers who are likely to be persuaded to advocate for the cause, and another funnel pointing away from the now-persuaded messenger and providing them with the communications—and motivation—to carry the cause message to as wide a possible audience as possible. The second funnel, the advocacy funnel, is better thought of as the horn end of a trumpet—ringing out advocacy for change at the head of parade.

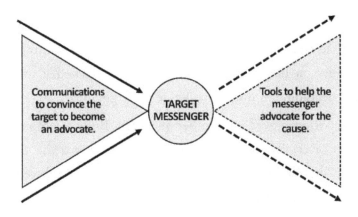

We should remember here that the definition of propaganda, for the purposes of this book, concerns the intent of the communications, not the communications itself. In a non-propaganda world, the source of the communications on the right side of the bowtie is clear and their messages neither lies nor misinformation. In the propaganda model, the one used in the Theater of Lies, that source and their motivations are often not clear (as that would often limit the effectiveness of the campaign) and the messages they use to convince their targets to become advocates are most often lies or facts stretched to create absurd conclusions (i.e., Silly Putty logic).

For a real-life example, we need look no further than an athlete turned unwitting advocate for the anti-vaccine movement (all the while screaming he was not).

Aaron Rodgers is a world class quarterback in the National Football League. If he was running a skills workshop for aspiring football players, I'd highly recommend attending. As an expert on vaccinations and the COVID-19 virus, his advice should be ignored. Yet, many have embraced his messages, or at least used his beliefs to justify their own.

In August 2021, during training camp with his then team, the Green Bay Packers, sports reporters asked him if he was vaccinated against COVID-19 (it was an NFL requirement that all players and coaches had received it). His answer was, "Yeah, I've been immunized. There's guys on the team that haven't been vaccinated. I think it's a personal decision, I'm not gonna judge those guys."[338]

The reporters moved on to other questions. But a few months later, the thirty-seven-year-old quarterback test positive for the virus. His response—he'd been taking a holistic treatment for over three months, prior to his immunization comments—involving, among other things, micro doses of the virus and extensive use of vitamins. The NFL suspended Rodgers for ten days for violating its COVID-19 protocols.

In a media blitz after the suspension, Rodgers told various radio and internet interviews that he'd "done his own research"[339] after "hearing of multiple people who had adverse events around the getting the Johnson & Johnson [version of the vaccine]."[340] He also said he had "concerns about potential fertility issues had he taken one of the vaccinations."[341]

As for consequences of lies and misinformation, this is informative—not that Mr. Rodgers did his own research based on either misinformation or misunderstanding facts, but that it underscores the larger issue, the erosion of trust.

By his actions, Rodgers demonstrated that he did not trust his employer (Green Bay Packers Football Club), his governing body of his sport (the National Football League), medical experts hired by the NFL, the US government, the US Center for Disease Control and Prevention (CDC), and the WHO. That's a long list not to trust. Instead, Rodgers leaned on his own trusted sources (mostly himself), which he identified in a 500-page document he submitted in his defense to the NFL (which the league rejected). [342]

The post-suspension media blitz was the trumpet end of the bowtie model. One of those was the *Joe Rogan Show*, hosted on the Spotify podcast network. Rogan's audience is about 8 million people. He, too, is an advocate for vaccine hesitancy, insisting that young people didn't need them. Taking a lesson from the radio talk shows of the past—controversy builds audiences—he defended his choices, telling his viewers, "I'm not an anti-vaxx person. In fact, I said I believe they're safe and I encourage many people to take them. My parents were vaccinated. I just said I don't think if you're a young healthy person you need it."[343]

Rogan, focusing his anti-vaccine sentiments on young people was, in fact, further eroding public trust in the US government, the CDC, and the WHO (which Donald Trump threw under the trust bus by officially withdrawing the USA from the organization in July, 2020[7]).

Canada is not without its own athletic ambassador against vaccines and government in general, Jamie Salé. She is a former world and Olympic champion figure skater who sums up her approach to the Government of Canada as "we been led by a bunch of criminals, basically, our whole life."[344] In 2023, she announced the creation of her own media company (her own trumpet horn, so to speak) because "media and our government has sold out."[345]

....

7   Note, the United States officially rejoined the WHO in January 2022.

How powerful is the bowtie model? Data gathered by Pew Research in 2021 confirmed that people who relied on family, friends, and community connections as their most important source of COVID-19 news were the *least likely* to be vaccinated[346] (practically in a dead heat with those who relied on Donald Trump as their information source[347]).

The purpose of the bowtie model it to create and enable messengers who will advocate for causes. In the Theater of Lies, that takes people out of the audience and brings them onto the stage as part of the production.

In the case of vaccines and their effectiveness (or harm), the anti-vaccine movement shifted its trust from governments and the pharmaceutical industry to purveyors of anti-vaccine information, who turned out to be, primarily, companies that produce and distribute natural supplements and holistic medical treatments.

Indeed, 40 percent of the funding for one of the world's most established anti-vaccine organizations (with the authoritatively neutral-sounding name, the National Vaccine Information Centre), comes from a physician-turned-businessperson, Dr Joseph Mercola. [348] According to *The Washington Post*, Mercola has "amassed a fortune selling natural health products, court records show, including vitamin supplements, some of which he claims are alternatives to vaccines."[349]

The CCDH adds Bernard Selz, a Wall Street fund manager, to the top-heavy list of anti-vaccine propaganda funders. Through the Selz Foundation, he funds 75% of the annual budget of the Informed Consent Action Network (ICAN).[350] The charity touts its mission as "promoting drug and vaccine safety and parental choice in vaccine decision."[351] Up until 2012, the foundation had previously focused its philanthropy on education and culture. Then, for unknown reasons, it switched its focus to anti-vaxx causes, beginning with a $200,000 donation to Andrew Wakefield[352] (whose 1998 study connecting the measles vaccine to autism has been widely published, promoted, and then found fraudulent. His medical license was revoked in 2010[353]).

In the case of COVID-19, the messengers attack the truth about the success of the worldwide vaccination process, despite peer-reviewed research to the contrary. In December 2022, the Commonwealth Fund and Yale School of Public Health published a study that identified:

> From December 2020 through November 2022, we estimate that the COVID-19 vaccination program in the US prevented more than 18.5 million additional hospitalizations and 3.2 million additional deaths. Without vaccination, there would have been nearly 120 million more COVID-19 infections. The vaccination program also saved the US $1.15 trillion (Credible Interval: $1.10 trillion–$1.19 trillion) (data not shown) in medical costs that would otherwise have been incurred.[354]

In Canada, the negative impact of vaccination misinformation was clearly demonstrated. In their 2023 report title *Fault Lines*, the Council of Canadian Academies states that during just a 6-month period between March and November 2021, "misinformation contributed to vaccine hesitancy for an estimated 2.35 million Canadians."[355]

During this period, the *Fault Lines* report estimated that without such misinformation, there could have been "198,000 fewer cases, 13,000 fewer hospitalizations, 3,500 few ICU patients and 2,800 fewer deaths."[356] CCA estimates that misinformation cost hospitals $299 million dollars—and as a reminder—all the CCA's findings were focused on a single six-month period (not the twenty-four months of the official pandemic period). [357]

In summary, the CCA concludes that misinformation resulted in lower institutional trust.[358]

The 2023 Edelman Trust Barometer also reflects the CCA's Canadian research, but internationally. Forty-six percent of respondents do not trust governments as sources of information (versus 36 percent that that do) and for businesses, their opinions flip. While 30 percent of respondents do not trust businesses as sources of information, 48 percent do.[359] What's important about this? Less than half of people trust information from the government or business. We live in a world where most people do not trust organizations that, arguably, have the most impact on their lives.

The Edelman research demonstrates that trust follows a similar path to the Law of Conservation of Energy. That is, it can neither be created nor destroyed; it can only be transformed or transferred from one form to another. In this case of trust, since people need to trust something . . . or someone . . . when they lose their trust in one source of information, they look to another to fill that void. This was another conclusion of the Helliwell, Wang, and Huang's 2016 study.[360] For the producers of lies, this is combination punch: the first lie to foster distrust of its target, and then a quick follow-up lie to transfer that trust to the liar. Repeat until victorious.

As Canada's former figure skating hero, Jamie Salé, has demonstrated, the road to distrust of government institutions, governments, and democracy is merely an extension of the distrust for vaccination that was given oxygen during the COVID-19 pandemic. Since Salé publicly transferred her distrust in the latter, the former—the number of her Twitter account followers—has grown tenfold (there, she identifies herself as part of the group "Freedom Fighter Canadians for Truth").[361] The former Olympic gold medalist is wandering down the path to destroy democracy and with a megawatt smile and decades of experience as performer, her stated goal is foster an environment "full of energy, hope, healing and awakening."[362] To me, this sounds like the foundation of a career future based on misinformation rather than medals (while maintaining a Harold Hill-like ability to dance to new music.

Such is the real danger when lies erode trust. Yes, democracy is at stake. But that is not the only consequence of living in the Theater of Lies. It may not even be the worst.

....

6

FROM POST-TRUTH
TO POST-TRUST.

I have often wondered if there is a secret school for dictators and their twenty-first-century brethren, elected autocrats. By and large, the leaders of most nations are highly educated, many from private schools and elite universities.[364] Dictator or democrat, socialist or capitalist, it is rare for the leader of a nation to have less than a basic university education or even an advanced degree: the exception to the rule, perhaps, being Poland's Lek Wałęsa. He was a shipyard electrician with a vocational school certificate before coming a union leader and eventually president. Even the founder of modern communist China, Mao Zedong, was broadly educated (if not degreed) in law, economics, manufacturing, and police studies, all while working as a librarian at Peking University. [365]

Whereas much research has gone into this book, I must confess that I have not looked through the course calendars and syllabuses of the world's universities to come to this conclusion: no formal educational institution in the world offers a degree program or even a night course on how to become a dictator.

If there were one, it would need, of course, a textbook. I'd highly recommend Levitsky and Ziblatt's *How Democracies Die* (Broadway Books, 2018). While it is a forensic accounting of the crumbling democratic processes around the world, it could be used—unfortunately—as a playbook for autocrats-in-training. In it, they write, "one of the great ironies of how democracies die is that the very defense of democracy is often used as a pretext for its subversion"[366] (reflecting Orwell's disregard for the term). That is, in terms of this book, the use of lies, rather than truth, to achieve one's goals.

Steven Levitsky and Daniel Ziblatt are Harvard University professors focused on political science and government. In *How Democracies Die*, they remind readers that most democratic governments do not die at a crucial moment with military generals leading coups, but mostly from elected leaders "who subvert the very process that brought them to power." "Democracies erode slowly," they write, "in barely visible steps."[367]

The professors identified four behaviors of elected officials that portend a threat to the democratic processes that elected them. One, the rejection or weak commitment to the democratic rules of the game. Two, the denial of the legitimacy of political opponents. Three, the toleration or encouragement of violence. And four, the readiness to curtail the civil liberties of opponents, including the media.[368]

Each of these behaviors share a common goal, according to the Harvard professors: creating "a climate of panic, hostility, and mutual distrust."[369] Combined, of course, so that the hero can come in and save the day (that is, society from a corrupt government).

Earthquakes destroy buildings and entire communities. Distrust—developed, nurtured, and entrenched—is more slow and subtle, like waves breaching on a rocky shoreline. It can even look as lovely, but over time that shoreline crumbles to sand. The geography in the case of democracy is political. Levitsky and Ziblatt's work proves the power of repetitive lies can forever alter political geography.

But that is not all that is lost from the erosion of trust. When lies are used to attack governments, their institutions, and the corporations they do business with, they foster significant collateral damage. Lies stall progress. Not only scientific, but also economic and social.

In 2022, the World Economic Forum (WEF) commented on that year's Edelman report, drawing the conclusion that "distrust has become society's default emotion, with 60% of people inclined to distrust until they see evidence something is trustworthy."[370] The WEF sees what they call this "cycle of distrust" as a barrier to action on global challenges in climate change and public health. They also quote Richard Edelman, Chair of Edelman Public Relations, who shows that people's notion of from whom they deem trustworthy has swung away from experts to people closer at hand.

> Classic societal leaders in government, the media and business have been discredited. Trust, once hierarchical, has become local and dispersed as people rely on my employer, my colleagues, my family.[371]

In the case of COVID-19, writers in *Foreign Affairs* (Larry Brilliant, Mark Smolinski, Lisa Danzig, and W. Ian Lipkin) demonstrated the erosion of trust was not only a barrier to defending public health during the 2019–2022 pandemic but will also be a barrier to future ones.

> Trust is the difference between calling a hotline and choosing not to, between sharing information internationally and hiding it, between following quarantine rules and flouting them, and between sharing vaccines and hoarding them. Without trust, even the best public health policies will fail. It is this human element that will, above all, determine whether the world can use modernity's gift of science to stave off catastrophe.[372]

An October 2020 study of 7,537 Americans found that "intentions to be vaccinated against COVID-19 have declined rapidly during the pandemic, and close to half of all Americans are undecided or unwilling to be vaccinated."[373] That same study also found that unwillingness to be vaccinated rose from 18.5% in April 2020 to 32%[374] - almost doubling the number of people refusing to get the jab. That's a huge gap in trust. The result, according to *The Atlantic* writer, Derek Thompson, is that we have become "culturally unready"[375] for progress.

While the world wanted the pharmaceutical industry's international cadre of scientists to work 24/7 to create a vaccine for COVID-19 as soon as possible—the mere months it took to accomplish this (due to the successful application previously developed mRNA technology) was vilified, by some, as proof of a conspiracy between government and industry toward imaginary ends (inserting microchips into our bodies, controlling our minds, manufacturing massive profits, and even the initial virus being created to fulfill these imaginary objectives).

The foundation of these conspiracy theories is a lack of trust. Anti-vaccination promoters point to the massive whole-of-government approach of the US government's *Operation Warp Speed* and collaboration with the pharma industry as a conspiracy rather than proof that when governments and industry are focused, collaborative, and under intense public pressure and media scrutiny—great things can happen (the last example in memory would be President John F. Kennedy's promise to send a man to moon and bring him home safely before the end of the decade in the 1960s—though there remain a small number of conspiracy theorists who tell us the moon landings were faked).

Of course, billions of people weren't sitting beside the NASA astronauts on that high-risk journey. Vaccine willingness required much more personal participation. But if our trust in government is in decline (which it is) and our trust in the pharmaceutical industry is under attack (which it also is) the results of the partnership between them were viewed, by many, with great skepticism.

As Derek Thompson wrote in *The Atlantic*:

> In a country where people don't trust the government to be honest, or businesses to be ethical, or members of the opposite party to respect the rule of law, it is hard to build anything quickly and effectively—or, for that matter, anything that lasts.[376]

Canada's Institute on Governance examined the relationship between trust and the public's social acceptance of science in its 2022 discussion paper, *Trust, Integrity, and Science Ethics*. The think tank wanted to examine the decline of the public's relationship with science and innovation. One of the institute's goals is laudable—taking responsibility for what scientists and governments can do to increase the public's trust of science. But through the process, they exposed a contradiction, an anomaly that the COVID-19 pandemic exposed. That is, how "the pandemic also brought about new challenges for public trust in science as people look to scientists to develop and deliver adequate responses in a highly uncertain environment." [377]

The lie producers in our Theater of Lies target a principle of science that, for most of its audience, is either unknown or misunderstood—that uncertainty is part of the scientific process. Consensus among scientists can take decades to achieve and two key audiences in the Theater of Lies have no patience for that: the public and mainstream media. The discussion paper's author, Dr. Ravtosh Bal, reflects this book's position that media reports tend to be at the opposite ends of the Bell Curve, writing that "media reporting on science veers between the two extremes of hyperbole and failures . . . the exaggeration or misrepresentation of scientific findings by the media contributes to public mistrust as expectations are belied in the long term." [378]

Act Three of this book will discuss some suggestions on how to overcome this (such how to increase science literacy, as identified by Dr. Ravtosh and others). The Institute on Governance also published another study—this one on the other side of the science trust coin—Canadians' trust of government. In that study, the Institute concluded that:

> Declining trust means that citizens are less likely to support government direction, making widespread consensus difficult. Trust is required for citizens to accept government information over misinformation. Lack of institutional and social trust can lead to

populism, which in turn leads to further criticism of government and its institutions. [And] declining trust has led to the far right questioning the very legitimacy of elections and public institutions.[379]

In 2016, Oxford Dictionaries declared "post-truth" as its word of the year.[380] That came on the heels of the 2016 US presidential election campaign and Britain's vote to leave the European Union (a process known as Brexit). At the time, Casper Grathwohl, product director for Oxford University Press, said, "post-truth could become one of the defining words of our time."[381]

Just three years later, Shiv Singh, an author and writer for *Fast Company*, coined a new term to describe this new period in our lives: post-trust.[382] It was a *wish-I-had-thought-of-this-first* moment for me, for it truly defines our new reality. Perhaps this book can help push it into more into mainstream use.

If I were leading a course for wannabe dictators and elected autocrats, I'd ask them to write an essay on how to achieve their goals by using lies or truths to reduce public trust. I think we know which one they'd choose.

The short version would be this—with apologies to Odgen Nash.[8]

Truth, like candy, may be dandy.

But if it's trust you need to bust,

Lies, like liquor, are much much quicker.

....

8   The original "Candy is dandy, but liquor is quicker" is a quote from the American poet Ogden Nash, from his poem "Reflections on Ice Breaking," in 1931.

This may be funny, except when you see a sitting US Member of Congress uses lies to call for a "national divorce"[383] (splitting of America into two separate countries, one liberal, the other conservative). This, said Marjorie Taylor Greene was needed, because of "the sick and disgusting woke culture issues shoved down our throats to the Democrat's traitorous America Last [meaning, liberal] policies."[384] She finished her tweet with, "we are done."[385] The message had 24 million views.

Sometimes, you just gotta laugh. One of our defenses is to find the humor in such lies, so much so that we look to the professionals to do it for us. We also look to them for the truth.

"I'm not a comedian. And I'm not sick. The world is sick, and I'm the doctor. I'm a surgeon with a scalpel for false values."[386]

– LENNY BRUCE, AMERICAN COMEDIAN.

7

SEND IN THE CLOWNS.

We don't go to war; we send soldiers. We don't make our clothes; we have others manufacture them. We might build hundred-thousand-dollar kitchens, but we still like our meals delivered. We love passing on responsibility to others. Delegating is natural, and it provides us with even more opportunity to complain if we don't believe the job has been done as well as we'd like (or would have done ourselves). It should come as no surprise, then, that our first choice in dealing with living in the Theater of Lies has been to outsource it, too.

What is surprising is to whom we most often delegate the burden of truth-telling. You might first think it is to journalists or news media in general. That fits the way we delegate things only to complain about those we delegate *to*. But in the United States, less than 50 percent of people trust traditional news media, and that number continues to decline year to year.[387] A 2020 study by Gallup found that only 9 percent of Americans wholly trust the media while 31 percent don't believe a word they say.[388] Reuters *2022 Digital News Report* (DNR) had the American number dropping to 26 percent.[389] In Canada, a 2021 poll by Ipso Research showed a continuing decline, with over a third of Canadians surveyed (34%) having little or no trust in traditional news media—following a consistent path of decline since 2017.[390]

Worse, the *DNR* survey of 46,000 people worldwide found that 36 percent said media was having a negative impact on their mood.[391] Maybe that's the reason people are looking elsewhere for their information, and particularly from sources that can make them laugh.

In the 1989 reboot of *Batman*, the villain who first grabs the attention and trust of the people is none other than the Joker. Just before he poisons the citizens of Gotham, he asks people who do they trust? As satire, it was perfect, though the audience, I suspect, might not have gotten it. Yet, since the Middle Ages, we've looked to jokers to be our messengers of truth.

In the 1500s, King James VI of Scotland had a jester named George Buchanan. If there were a patron saint of jokers—or professional fools—Buchanan would be it. His boss had a bad habit: regularly signing documents without reading them. So, George the Jester, as only a professional fool could do, provided his liege with a royal comeuppance. He wrote up a document for King James to sign, which, of course, the Scottish king promptly did. Unfortunately for the king, the document was his abdication, and, in his place, the court comedian had assigned himself to the throne.

> No sooner had he received it, but he goes to the king, and told him it was not time for him now to be sitting there; with that, the king, greatly amazed, started up,

and George, in great haste, set himself down in the king's chair, forthwith declaring himself king, saying, you, who was king, must be my fool, for I am now the wisest man. The king, at this, was greatly offended, until George shewed him his seal and signature. From that day the king always knew what he signed.[392]

American media is perhaps at the height of its joker-turned-truthteller ways. From Lenny Bruce in the 1960s to George Carlin in the 1970s through to the early part of this century, many comedians have used their stages for political commentary. In the mid-1970s the NBC show *Saturday Night Live* established a new form of satire: the comic news show, a send-up of the traditional six o'clock news. The show-within-a-show had the newsy title "Weekend Update" and was hosted by comedian Chevy Chase, who, in it, put a humorous spin on the week's news. Its first episode was broadcast live on October 11, 1975. It has since gone on to become the centerpiece of *SNL*'s forty-plus seasons. Two dozen comedic news anchors have followed in Chase's footsteps. It would also inspire later productions like Comedy Central's *Daily Show* and *The Colbert Report*. I am certain the court jesters of the past would have been proud, as would the writers who followed in their footsteps, from Jonathan Swift to the communism- and imperialism-bashing Englishman, George Orwell. They each used absurdity, humor, and fantasy to skewer the political machinations of their day.

As the audiences of these supposed truthtellers rise, the political and upper-class targets of their satire fight dual urges to flee from the barbs or run toward them. In Canada, the CBC's *This Hour Has 22 Minutes* has had cabinet members and even a sitting prime minister appear on the show (some of which saw as a form of populism that demonstrated their ability to laugh at themselves). One of the show's stars, Rick Mercer, went on to host his own show, the *Rick Mercer Report*, which included a two-minute rant about whatever political, social, or economic struggle he deemed worthy of his 750 words of contempt (which was written to be pointed, not funny). Mercer now appears on television election coverage, side by side with journalists and professional political commentators, to provide his play-by-play political insights. Though he remains an actor and comedian, he is still looked to for truth (if only it remains his opinion).

The internet has only expanded opportunities to move from stand-up to one's own political and cultural commentary platforms, often in the form of talk shows, as with figures like Bill Maher on the left and Joe Rogan on the right. Sarah Silverman, who gained her fame in stand-up, took advantage of COVID-19, putting a stop to in-person events to create an Instagram Live series where she acted as an advice counselor on issues ranging from dating to the Jewish occupation of Palestinian lands to dealing with evangelical Christian upbringing.

This clown-as-truth-teller phenomenon is not limited to North America. In Britain, the BBC has established a reputation for adroit satire under many different show titles—most famously *Monty Python*, with John Cleese and his "Ministry of Silly Walks," among other political arrows. The people of the Ukraine went all in with their choice of truthteller in 2019, electing a comedian as their president. Prior to his election, Volodymyr Zelenskyy's only experience in politics had been pretending to be the president of Ukraine in his popular television show *Servant of the People*.

The fight between the jokers and the journalists came to a head on October 15, 2004, when, on America's CNN, the host of *The Daily*

Show, Jon Stewart, was a guest on CNN's debate show *Crossfire*. On his show, Stewart had regularly berated the two hosts (Paul Begala, representing the left, and Tucker Carlson, standing in for the right) for their hard-fought attacks on each other, politicians who reflected the other's views, and most anyone who disagreed with either of them themselves. Stewart's message, delivered moments after he was introduced, could be summed as "please stop." Interrupting the usual format of the show, where Begala and Carlson set the stage for their guest to defend themselves, Stewart went immediately on the offensive: "Thank you very much. Can I say something very quickly . . . ah . . . why do we have to fight? The two of you. Can't we just . . . say something nice about John Kerry. Right now."[393] John Kerry was the Democratic Party's candidate for president at the time.

At this, Carlson later asked, "But of the nine guys running, do you think [Kerry was] the best? Do you think he was the best, the most impressive?"

In his response, Stewart used his skills as a comedian and actor, his ability to rehearse and prepare not possessed by the hosts of *Crossfire* (nor prepared for).

> The most impressive? I thought Al Sharpton was very impressive. I enjoyed his way of speaking. I think that oftentimes the person that knows they can't win is allowed to speak the most freely . . . because otherwise, shows with titles such as *Crossfire* or *Hardball* or *I'm Going to Kick Your Ass* will jump on it. I made a special effort to come on the show today because privately, among my friends, and in occasional newspapers and television shows, I have mentioned this show as

being . . . b . . . b . . . bad." (He said this last sentence with a pleading voice). "And I felt that that wasn't fair, and I should come here and say that it's not so much that as bad as it is hurting America. Here's what I wanted to tell you guys . . . s . . . stop. Stop hurting America. And come work with us, as the people.

Tucker Carlson then made the mistake of trying to take on a professional comedian—one who had learned his stock-in-trade doing improvisation. He attempted to berate Stewart for asking so-called "softball" questions when John Kerry appeared on *his* show. Carlson's position was that because Stewart had a politician on his show, he had a responsibility to be tougher. Carlson said: "When politicians come on, it's nice to get them to try and answer the question. In order to do that, we get them to answer pointed questions. I want to contrast our questions to some of the questions you asked John Kerry."

To this, Stewart responded,

> You know, it's interesting to hear you talk about my responsibility . . . I didn't realize . . . and maybe this explains quite a bit . . . is that the news organizations look to Comedy Central for their cues on integrity. If you want to compare your show to a comedy show, you are more than welcome. If that's your goal. I wouldn't aim for us. I would aim for *Seinfeld*. My point is this. If your idea of confronting me is that I don't ask hard-hitting news questions . . . we are in bad shape, fellas.

Carlson then stepped into the deep end, attempting to lighten mood through humor, like an amateur going into a light saber match with Darth Vader and expecting to win. "We're here to love you, not confront you," he told Stewart.

In response, Stewart said, "What I am saying is this . . . I'm not . . . I am here to confront you because we need help from the media and they're h . . . hurting us," (repeating his pleading style).

Carlson began to grow exasperated. He was used to controlling the narrative on his show. "I thought you were going to be funny. Come on. Be funny."

Stewart then gave Carlson a verbal slap across the face. "No. No. I am not going to be your monkey." He later said: "You are on CNN. The show that leads into me is *Puppets Making Crank Phone Calls*. What is wrong with you?"

Prescient for my purposes was what Stewart then said, in 2004, to the two astute political commentators: "This is theater."

Even without the power social media has today, this line found its way around the world.

The audience in the Theater of Lies cheered. Somebody with the same skills—or better —than those the producers of the theater possessed had stood up and fought for truth. Moreover, the attack worked. Within days, CNN canceled *Crossfire* and terminated both hosts.

While all this was happening, Jonathan Klein had just taken on the role of president of CNN. In a statement to the *New York Times*, he said that he agreed with much of Stewart's indictments against the media and the program specifically. "I agree wholeheartedly with Jon Stewart's overall premise." He said he believed that especially after 9/11, viewers were interested in information, not opinion.[394]

So, on that day in 2004, Jon Stewart joined himself in history to the jester George Buchanan. Five hundred years earlier, he had delivered the message to the King of Scotland that he had better start reading what he was signing—and it worked. By taking charge of the conversation on *Crossfire*, Stewart killed off at least one stage in the Theater of Lies. In both cases, the audiences cheered.

Yet, in our lifelong—centuries-long—battle to free ourselves from the powerful influence of the Theater of Lies, these are two instances I can find where the truthtellers took on the liars and won. Change *happened*. But that change did not last, and these single changes didn't damage the power of the Theater in any lasting way. Until his firing in 2023, Tucker Carlson had the number-one-rated show on *Fox News*. (Noteworthy of mention is that Fox News fired Carlson because of a discrimination lawsuit brought by a former producer, not for the content of his show being based on lies, misinformation, and/ or hyperbole).[395]

The reality is that to live and thrive in the Theater of Lies, we cannot expect others to fight our battle(s) for us. We must learn to defend ourselves.

> *"Truth is a revenge because we live in a world of lies, about poor people, about gay people, about what we are, what we experience. Every time, truth is a fight."*[396]
>
> – ÉDOUARD LOUIS, FRENCH WRITER.

....

8

THE THEATER IS BECOMING MORE DANGEROUS.

The world's Theater of Lies has always been a dangerous place, but it's growing ever more so.

Hate crimes are rising in most parts of the world. The data has been challenging for many countries to put together, as the categorizing a crime as based on hate (that is, a bias motivation for the crime being race/ethnicity/ancestry, sexual orientation, religion, gender, gender identity, or disability)[397] is relatively new. In the United States, the FBI released a report showing that hate crimes had risen 11.6 percent in 2021 from 2020,[398] with the largest number caused by hate "against Black people, followed by crimes targeting victims for ethnicity, gender, and religion."[399]

Canada has seen similar increases in hate crimes. In the first year of the pandemic (2019), police-reported hate crimes increased 37 percent over 2018.[400] In 2020, the increase grew to 80 percent with—like the United States—the crimes targeting Black people, East or Southeast Asian people, Indigenous Canadians and those of South Asian descent. Crimes against Black people and Jews were the most common hate crimes. Particularly troubling was that the youngest victims of hate crimes, tracked over a nine-year period (2011-2022), tended to be Indigenous Canadians or those based on sexual orientation. These young victims of hate also sustained the highest proportion of injury.[401]

World over, crimes against religious groups continue to rise. Jonathan Greenblatt is chief executive of the Anti-Defamation League (ADL). In response to the publication of the FBI's 2021 statistics, he confirmed that the ADL had identified 2,717 antisemitic incidents in 2021 (the highest total since the organization started tracking the data in 1979).[402]

In March 2023, the Turkish ambassador to the United Nations told UN General Assembly that hatred against Muslims has become a major threat to democracy and that desecration of copies of the holy Quran and mosques was on the rise.[403] He made a point that Muslims were facing:

> Increasingly systemic practices of denial of freedom of religion, hate crimes and various manifestations of Islamophobia. [This] goes hand-in-hand with the rising tide of populism and polarization that tend to dominate political discourse in many countries.[404]

In the United Kingdom, the *Guardian* summarized the nation's 2021 hate crimes statistics with this double-barrel headline:

> Racist hate crimes pass 100,000 in England and Wales for the first time—disability, sexual orientation, and religious hate crimes increased last year while anti-transgender crimes rose by 56%.[405]

Echoing the sentiments of the Turkish ambassador and the US-based ADL, the *Guardian* reported that Muslims were the most targeted group, followed by antisemitic hate crimes.

Some of these increases may not represent a complete increase in the overall number of hate crimes. Those associated with creating and analyzing the data believe that more crimes are being reported as victims are becoming more comfortable with coming forward. Nonetheless, the trend is alarming—and in my opinion—the producers in the Theater of Lies bear much of the responsibility. The perpetrators of the hate crime are merely members of the audience who took the lies as a call to action, enabling them and their brethren to violence. More and more of us are becoming Edgars.

To address these rises in hate crimes, ADL's Greenblatt said, "a whole-of-government, whole-of-society approach will be needed to address these extremely disturbing trends."[406]

Lies are killing us and enabling us to kill others.

The automated machine gun fire of lies in the Theater has chipped away at the people's bedrock faith in America's democratic process in a way that has never been seen before. While there is no proof of election fraud, the allegations persist, such that Ted Cruz, a Canadian-born US senator from Texas and former presidential candidate, called for the election process to be reviewed based on allegations. To do so, he used the language of his law-abiding opponents, citing the US Constitution. Cruz said, "We went into this election with the country deeply divided, deeply polarized, and we've seen in the last two months unprecedented allegations of voter fraud, and that's produced a deep, deep distrust of our democratic process across the country. I think we in Congress have an obligation to do something about that. We have an obligation to protect the integrity of the democratic system."[407]

Out of context, his arguments sound reasonable, something election deniers can point to (it's a good trick for the Theater). But Cruz went so far as to call for the opposition to calm down, as though it were the people calling for the rule of law who were causing the problem. He said:

> I think everyone needs to calm down. I think we need to tone down the rhetoric. This is already a volatile situation. It's like a tinderbox and throwing lit matches into it.[408]

In short, the one-time presidential candidate positioned himself as the sane voice in the Theater of Lies when he was, in fact, one of its producers.

People opposed to vaccinations of any kind (referred to as *antivaxxers*) are reviewing the list of ingredients in the COVID-19 vaccines and publishing the toxicity of each one (in reality, most every component is toxic, though only at doses thousands of times higher than are contained in the vaccines, as with most pharmaceuticals). Through a destabilization of governments and businesses by way of false-flag social media campaigns, the Russian government has spread its negative influence across the world, well past its military or economic might. And careers in Hollywood, politics, business, and academia are being destroyed by the practice of *doxxing* (the search for and publishing, with malicious intent, of private or identifying information about a particular individual).

The world is long past the fraud of a Nigerian prince asking you to help extract his money from a corrupt government. The next iteration of this has been highly personal; the practice on the internet today is called *spear phishing*. Through it, a fraudster finds out just enough real information to convince their targets to hand over their most private information. They tell you where you shopped, what you bought, and when, and then they tell you that they are the bank, just wanting to verify the information . . . *Please enter your password.*

Online bullying, unfortunately now a staple in our school system, is only going to grow as the world's online bully-in-chief, Donald Trump, has demonstrated its effectiveness and has given permission to engage in it.

The consequences are real. It has trickled down in the minds of students. In 2016, the Southern Poverty Law Center (SPLC) surveyed over 2,000 teachers on the impact of the vitriol and lies emanating from the US presidential election. In their report, they found:

> The gains made by years of anti-bullying work in schools have been rolled back in a few short months. Teachers report that students have been "emboldened" to use slurs, engage in name-calling and make inflammatory statements toward each other. When confronted, students point to the candidates and claim they are "just saying what everyone is thinking." Kids use the names of candidates as pejoratives to taunt each other.[409]

And,

> Students have become very hostile to opposing points of view, regardless of the topic," a Jefferson, Georgia, high school teacher wrote, adding, "Any division now elicits anger and personal attacks."[410]

Our schools and universities have become minefields, where teachers, professors, and even students have to mind every word they say for fear of triggering other to act against them.

This behavior, on a student-level, should concern all of us—as these children will become adults, voters and citizens who may not be able to unlearn messages within the Theater of Lies and the behaviors they foster. But within that concern is a glimmer of hope. If our students are modeling the slurs, slang, and lies of what they see adults doing, then changing adult habits will create better ones in the coming generations.

For if we do not do something to protect ourselves from the lies, the liars will control the world. The doors to the Theater will be locked. We will never be able to leave. Good people will exclude themselves from leadership positions. Scientific results will be appraised based on political and economic motives, as with Galileo being convicted of heresy for claiming the earth revolved around the sun. One of history's most ground-breaking scientists, authors, and artists was confined to house arrest for the last nine years of his life.

Yet such draconian measures remain commonplace today. In 2015, Chinese courts sentenced a human rights lawyer, Yang Maodong, to six years in prison for "picking quarrels and provoking trouble."[411] In 2018, Zhang Zhan, one of the first Chinese journalists to write about the struggles of the doctors and healthcare workers to control the initial outbreak of COVID-19, was charged and sentenced under the same law.[412] She spent four years in prison.

In India, there is a conspiracy theory that Muslim men are marrying Hindu women to convert them to Islam. The Modi government, which had already passed many laws that were clearly anti-Muslim (for example, the *Citizenship Amendment Act*, a bill that offers amnesty to non-Muslim illegal immigrants from three neighboring majority Muslim countries: In 2020, Bangladesh, Afghanistan, and Pakistan), has allowed one of its states, Uttar Pradesh, to pass "love jihad" legislation. Uttar Pradesh's chief minister, Yogi Adityanath, said,

> I warn those who conceal their identity and play with
> the honor of our sisters and daughters, if you don't
> mend your ways, your final journey will begin.[413]

Yet this same government has acknowledged that it has no official evidence of Muslim men marrying Hindu women for the purposes of conversion. Just as Senator Cruz and others have used the language of defending democracy when their actions actually threaten it, the Indian state of Uttar Pradesh has characterized the new law as justice for women when the truth is exactly opposite. This is an example of how propagandists take advantage of current news topics to press their own agenda (in the communications business, we call this hanging your story on a *newspeg*).

Robert Kennedy, Jr., nephew of former President John F. Kennedy, demonstrated his affection for Winston Churchill's propaganda-empowering belief in "never [letting] a good crisis go to waste."[414] Kennedy, Jr., an ardent anti-vaccination campaigner, published an op-ed on the Washington, D.C., website *POLITICO*, in which he wrote, "Coincidence is turning out to be quite lethal to COVID vaccine recipients."[415] Kennedy described any deaths after receiving the vaccine not yet attributed *to* the vaccine as suspicious, accusing medical officials of following an "all-too-familiar vaccine propaganda playbook" and "strategic chicanery."[416] The truth, in fact, is that in most all developed nations, Canada and the US included, healthcare departments are required to report *any and all negative outcomes*, so that further investigations can be made to determine if the medication, vaccine, or procedure was directly linked to that outcome or if it was merely coincidental (like getting hit by a car after walking out of the clinic where you received a vaccine).

But Kennedy's leaping on incident reporting as reflecting true vaccine dangers is just part of the Silly Putty logic that producers in the Theater of Lies rely on.

In early 2023, when a National Football League player dropped to the field, unconscious, after tackling an opponent, the in-stadium of thousands and television audience of millions gasped as they learned—in real time—that Damar Hamlin needed immediate on-field CPR and an ambulance to rush him to a local hospital. His heart had stopped twice and he was unable to breathe on his own. The game between the Buffalo Bills and the Cincinnati Bengals was first paused, then delayed, as the live television audience and the 85,000 people at the game waited for over an hour to hear news of Hamlin's condition and the any decision to restart play.

But we no longer sit and wait anymore. We have computers in our hands. Access to search engines and social media at our fingertips—and in the case of sporting events such the NFL—we are sitting beside people—friends, family, and strangers—having a shared experience. The Theater of Lies knows this—and reacted as quickly as the emergency physicians and on-field medical staff of the two foot-ball teams.

As the audience searched for answers online, the Theater of Lies went into full production mode. As reported in *The Washington Post*,

> "Everybody knows what happened to Damar Hamlin because it's happened to too many athletes around the world since COVID vaccination was required in sports," said former Newsmax correspondent Emerald Robinson, in a tweet that was viewed more than 2 million times and visible under the #DamarHamlin hashtag trending in the United States.[417]

Congressman Marjorie Taylor Greene tweeted the following, as the ambulances were coming on field for Hamlin while paramedics and doctors were fanatically providing him with CPR to restart his heart.

> Before the covid vaccines we didn't see athletes drop-ping dead on the playing field like we do now. And we never saw the CDC [Centers for Disease Control & Prevention] say things like this. How many people are dying suddenly? Time to investigate the covid vaccines.[418]

Quick social media responses are a tool for the producers of lies. They can react to and communicate with their audiences faster than any scientist, journalist, or knowledgeable at-the-scene person can react.

Even 24 hours later, while doctors in Cincinnati were still working to determine the cause of Hamlin's heart stoppage, mainstream producers joined the chorus, like players piling on each other in the chase of a fumbled football.

Fox News' Tucker Carlson brought a cardiologist onto his show, in the hope, I assume, of providing credibility and perhaps a note of journalistic integrity. There, Dr. Peter McCullough stated that "vaccine-induced myocarditis may have caused Hamlin's episode."[419] Carlson introduced McCullough by stating the doctor discovered "more than 1500 total cardiac arrests had occurred among European athletes since the vax campaign began."[420]

All the while, Carlson and others ignored a 2021 study of 789 professional athletes in the United States conducted by Columbia University. The study examined the possibility of COVID-19-associated cardio injury and found "few cases of inflammatory heart disease [had] been detected."[421]

The success of the Theater of Lies most public proponents—such as Donald Trump, Vladimir Putin, Narendra Modi, Xi Jinping, and others—has empowered a new generation: thousands who have learned just how successful these tactics are. As we've learned about persuasive communications, to believe fact-checking is the way to prevent these abuses from recurring is self-deception. Emotion resonance, *pathos*, always wins over facts.

Repeating here the quote of American actor, Groucho Marx, from this book's opening chapter, "I don't mind lying if it gets me somewhere": our world has evolved into *I don't mind repeating someone else's lie if it gets me somewhere.*

To wit, Fox News host Sean Hannity admitted, under oath, that be never believed that voting machines manipulations caused Donald Trump to lose the 2020 US Presidential election. "I did not believe it for one second," Hannity testified in his deposition by a lawyer for

Dominion Voting Systems. [422] In a separate deposition, Fox News' executive vice president, Meade Cooper confirmed, also under oath, that "she never believed the lies about Dominion."[423] It was under her leadership that all Fox News commentators pushed out the voting machine issue lie on most all its shows. And the network's Trump-friendly status pushed Hannity's own audience over the 5-million-view mark—the highest in its history.[424]

The truth may set you free but lies will make you rich.

Worse, the Theater of Lies has evolved to the point that the truth no longer matters because it too is open to interpretation—interpretation that has risen quickly from anti-vaccine messages to hate crimes around the world.

Alternate facts aren't required if you can convince your audience to ignore the facts completely.

"Speaking your truth is the most powerful tool we all have."[425]

– OPRAH WINFREY, AMERICAN TALK SHOW HOST,
ACTOR, AND ENTREPRENEUR, ACCEPTING THE CECIL B. DEMILLE AWARD FOR
OUTSTANDING CONTRIBUTIONS TO THE WORLD OF ENTERTAINMENT IN 2018.

"You want the truth? You can't handle the truth!"[426]

– JACK NICHOLSON, AMERICAN ACTOR,
AS COLONEL NATHAN JESSOP, IN *A FEW GOOD MEN* (1992).

....

9

DANCING WITH TRUTHS.

Each of the preceding chapters has started with a relevant quote on the chapter topic from a person with knowledge of the subject matter, and perhaps a little pithy about it. In this penultimate chapter of Act Two, *Dancing with Truths*, I needed two quotes to set it up. Beyond the Silly Putty stretching of truth discussed in Chapter 5 as a now-common consequence of the Theater of Lies, the producers of lies and misinformation have established two more powerful barriers to truth that will be discussed here: cognitive dissonance and truth being used to argue both sides of an issue. The latter is like the family patriarch (or matriarch) sitting at the head of the dinner table and saying with perhaps only a mere raise of an eyebrow, "We'll have none of that talk, here, or anywhere."

So, with all due respect to Oprah Winfrey, US-based talk show host and known as the "Queen of all Media,"[427] speaking your truth is not the most powerful tool we have. If it was, truth would stop lies in their track. If truth alone is what we are going to rely on while living in the Theater of Lies, most of the time, it only has the power of stale popcorn for satisfaction, whereas the lies are delivered hot, fresh, and well-buttered. Truth is a weapon, but it has become, unfortunately, not the most effective weapon in our arsenal. We need more.

I hope the examples and details set forth in this book have proven at least that much to you. Lies are more powerful than truth, traveling faster and farther than any fact. Truth may have righteousness on its side—as one can hear in Winfrey's voice (she was speaking to an audience of Hollywood industry elites at the 2018 Golden Globe Awards)—but it is usually late to the party.

What has instead occurred is that the Theater of Lies has shown us that, if truth be told, there are some dance steps we can use to get around them. The first being to agree, but use it to your own advantage, no matter which side of an issue you support.

In 2023, the US Centers for Disease Control and Prevention (CDC) published its *Youth Risk Behavior Survey Data Summary & Trends Report: 2011–2021*. The report covers "10-year trends, on health behaviors and experiences among high school students in the United States (US) related to adolescent health and well-being."[428] The report identified particularly concerning data about students who identify as lesbian, gay, or transgender (LGBQ+).[9]

> LGBQ+ students and those who have any same sex partners were more likely than their peers to have used or misused all substances included in this report (i.e., ever used select illicit drugs, ever or current prescription opioid misuse, and current alcohol, marijuana, and electronic vapor product use). They were also significantly more likely to experience all forms of violence. The differences in terms of mental health, compared to their peers, are substantial. Close to 70% of LGBQ+ students experienced persistent feelings of sadness or hopelessness during the past year and more than 50% had poor mental health during the past 30 days. Almost 25% attempted suicide during the past year.[429]

Through looking at the initial media coverage of this report, I learned that there are well-organized, well-funded, widespread, and well-opposed sides to the diverse range of issues concerning gender identity. (Full disclosure: I have a transgender niece.)

In one corner, I present a committee of the United Nations, *UN Free and Equal* (unfe.org). Its mission is to "stand up for equal rights and fair treatment for lesbian, gay, bi, trans and intersex people everywhere."[430]

....

9   The term LGBQ+ is taken from the CDC report. Other terms such as LGBTQ, 2SLGBTQ, and 2SLGBTQ+ should, for the purposes of this book, be taken as interchangeable while recognising the unique need for each expression and its interpretation.

In the other corner, I present, as one representative of the opposing view (there are many), the International Organization for the Family. Its mission is "to unite and equip leaders, organizations, and families to affirm, celebrate, and defend the natural family as the only fundamental and sustainable unit of society."[431]

Critical to that statement is the word *only*.

At the time of the CDC's publication of its report, PBS News interviewed Dr. Sharon A. Hoover from the University of Maryland School of Medicine. Hoover is a licensed clinical psychologist and professor. She is also a "director of the National Center for School Mental Health (NCTSN) Center for Safe Supportive Schools (CS3), focused on building trauma-responsive, comprehensive school mental health systems that attend to social determinants and injustices and engage and support marginalized populations."[432] She does not identify herself as having any association with the United Nations and its Free and Equal committee, but I think it is safe to assume she would fall into its side of the gender debate.

On *PBS News*, she commented on the CDC's report:

> It's one of our greatest worries, that some of the controversy right now and some of the legislation and just discussion even at the school board level about making our environments and our schools less inclusive for LGBTQ+ youth could really negatively impact this group of students, who are already vulnerable. We know that LGBTQ youth are much more at risk of suicidality, of depression and anxiety. And we also know there are solutions that can be put in place to help them not only with getting mental health supports,

but also, at a more public health level, to really make schools a more inclusive, accepting place, where they can feel that they belong. [433]

On the same day, the International Organization for the Family posted this commentary on the same CDC report.

> These rates clearly show that students who have succumbed to the LGBT agenda are not doing well and that their life outcomes are significantly worse than those of students who are heterosexual. For educators and other woke elites to constantly indoctrinate our youth in the LGBT lifestyle is child abuse; indeed, these leaders need to be alerting our children to the dangers of the LGBT agenda. [434]

This reminds me of two things that my forty years of communications experience have taught me about research. One: for experts, the data speaks for itself. And two: for people who don't like what the data is telling them—if you torture the data long enough, it will tell you exactly what you want to hear.

Shortly after journalist Maria Ressa had been co-awarded the 2021 Nobel Peace Prize,[10] she spoke at Penn University. There, she said, "Facts, truth, trust. Without these three, we have no shared reality, we cannot solve any problem together, and we cannot have democracy."[435]

But as I wrote about in previous chapters, there is more than democracy at stake. The international debate on gender, as just one example,

....

10   Ressa was co-awarded the 2021 Nobel Peace Prize with Russian Dmitry Muratov, who co-founded the newspaper *Novaya Gazeta*.

is affecting children and young adults (who, if they are confused about their own genders, have enough emotional strain on their lives).

And it is here that the Theater of Lies has re-baked truth to the point that the producers tell their audience: if you even talk about it, life as you know it will end. Dancing with truth, in turns out, is two-step. It runs to the beat of binary thinking. Next, let's look at the example of the word *woke* and its binary opposite, *anti-woke*.

....

10

WOKE GETS BROKE.

Let's take a step back in time to the year 1772. It was in that year that a slave-trading sea captain turned pastor, John Newton, wrote the now-classic hymn "Amazing Grace." In the modern era, it has become much more than a hymn. It is a civil rights anthem, a civil religion anthem, a folk song, and a pop culture icon, says Daniel Johnson, a PhD researcher at the University of Leicester.[437] He notes that the song has entered popular culture through its use on television, including *The Simpsons, Cheers,* and *Star Trek,* and has been covered by such artists as Johnny Cash, Willy Nelson, Aretha Franklin, and Cold Play. After the terrorist attacks on September 11, 2001, the song was sung as an allegory of redemption for the deaths and destruction.[438]

Below is the first verse, lyrics written to convey the revelation of truth against previously long-held convictions:

Amazing grace, how sweet the sound
That saved a wretch like me
I once was lost, but now am found
Was blind, but now I see.[439]

The song was written as part of Newton's atonement for his time as slave trader and his need to find forgiveness. After coming to his epiphany that the slave trade, and particularly his own role in it, was evil, he dedicated his life to righting that wrong. He was ordained an Anglican minister in 1764, writing "Amazing Grace" eight years later. He went on to write 280 hymns—though none would eclipse this painful plea for his redemption as a slave trader.[440]

As a pastor, he dedicated his life to abolishing slavery, to the point of directing a student of divinity, William Wilberforce, to forgo a career as a fellow minister and focus instead on politics. Wilberforce became an independent member of the British Parliament and with Newton as his spiritual adviser and wordsmith, achieved his mentor's goal. In 1807, England abolished slavery. Almost sixty years later, in the United States, President Abraham Lincoln issued the Emancipation Proclamation in 1863—setting the ground for the American Civil and, with the North's victory over the South, the abolition of slavery.

Today, Newton would have been called woke. The first dictionary definition of the word from *Merriam-Webster*: "aware of and actively attentive to important societal facts and issues (especially issues of racial and social justice)."[441]

Newton's first verse, fourth line phrase, "was blind, but now I see," 250 years prior, is a more poetic interpretation of the word woke. Likely, he would have worn the brand woke proudly. But a trick of the producers in the Theater of Lies, to extend a legal notion, is that everything you say can and *will* be used against you. Hence the emergence of the opposite word: anti-woke.

I remember being dismayed to the point of a headshake when I first heard the term *anti-woke* used, especially as a force for good (I could not understand how term that literally stood for being unaware could be stated with pride), rather than shame. But let's first take a brief look at how the word woke emerged.

Originally, it was a Black slang term, as more of a goal to achieve, as in "stay woke."[442] The term arose in the 1940s as a prompt to be aware of social issues, especially racial issues. In 1962, the *New York Times* published an opinion article titled *If You're Woke You Dig It* by William Melvin Kelly.[443] He was a Black novelist (and in 2018, referred to as the Lost Giant of American Literature[444] by *The New Yorker*). In the early twenty-first century, the term took on the broader meaning of all social issues, including race, gender identity, and immigration issues.

But by the 2010s, the term went beyond the notion of social injustice. It became used to suggest that someone is "being pretentious and insincere about how much they care about an issue," writes British journalist Natalie Morris.[445] I peg that change to the Theater of Lies.

Pastor/Captain John Newton would be shocked at that change in definition. He was hardly insincere. Yet, changing the intent of a word is a late-stage strategy in the Theater, the goal being to re-bake truth to make it as unpalatable as possible. To wit, US entrepreneur Elon Musk said, "At its heart, wokeness is divisive, exclusionary, and hateful. It basically gives mean people a reason—it gives them a shield to be mean and cruel armored in false virtue."[446]

Or, as a corollary to Newton, what once was found is now lost. The Theater of Lies has killed the word woke, perhaps irrevocably. In 2021, Kate Ng of Britain's *Independent* newspaper wrote:

People who actually identify as "woke" no longer use the word to describe themselves, preferring to use more complex language such as "empaths" or "social justice" instead of "woke" due to its current negative connotations.[447]

Looking to the notion of truth and gender issues, in the United States, the gender debate rages on. In the so-called *Don't Say Gay Bill* that passed in the 2022 Florida legislature (in which the word "gay" is not in the bill), proponents said, "[I]t would give parents greater control over their children's education, vindicating their 'parental authority.'"[448] Opponents of the bill said, "[I]t would unfairly target the LGBTQ community—particularly gay and trans students."[449]

Worldwide, Hungary, with a government many conservative opinion leaders seek to emulate, has voted to eliminate all teaching related to homosexuality and gender change, associating LGBTQ+ rights with "pedophilia and totalitarian cultural politics."[450] Similar legislation and resolutions have passed in Denmark, Romania, Poland, and Turkey.[451]

That's a global legislative movement based on parental authority and child protection on one side, and personal freedoms on the other. Yet only 8 percent of the world's population identifies as LGBQ+ (with 80 percent identifying as heterosexual and 12 percent not responding).[452] While data sources on gender identity are only now becoming far easier to find (the most credible aggregator of this data is the Williams Institute at the University of Southern California's School of Law), issues such as transgender identity are what I would refer to as fighting-above-their-weight. The Williams Institute, for example, finds that only 1.4% of Americans identify themselves as transgender.[453] But more alarmingly (for people opposed to what they referred to as the

LGBT agenda), the UCLA department found that fifty-six countries saw an increase in social acceptance of this so-called agenda.[454]

Such a battlefield is a ripe environment for the Theater of Lies. This issue has broadened into a larger bucket of popcorn. Whereas *woke* was originally 1960s Black slang advising fellow Black people to be self-aware of the dangers in their lives, followed by the word's growth into the popular vernacular as meaning being aware of the wrongs imposed by others in all areas (race, religion, and gender, for example), the producers of lies and misinformation created the term *anti-woke* to encapsulate the message "we'll have none that talk here." Talk being any laws or education on topics such as CRT and comprehensive sexual education (CSE). For the producers of lies, silencing these conversations has the power, in their opinion, of burying an issue—and that can be as powerful as changing minds.

The State of Florida has attempted to capture this notion through legislation in what has become known as its "Anti-Woke Law."[455]

> The law prohibits teaching or business practices that contend members of one ethnic group are inherently racist and should feel guilt for past actions committed by others. It also bars the notion that a person's status as privileged or oppressed is necessarily determined by their race or gender, or that discrimination is acceptable to achieve diversity.[456]

Woke versus *anti-woke* is, in my opinion, a direct consequence of the Theater of Lies.[11] The creation of the latter term was to manipulate

---

11   In Act Three, will we examine woke v. anti-woke as part of the barriers and opportunities that binary thinking create.

rather than debate the benefits and deficiencies of the former. As a result, the debate within the Theater of Lies is not about the underlying issues of gender, racism, and social justice, but one's ownership of one's individual *wokeness* or *anti-wokeness*. Now, rather than its base root of justice and action, *Merriam-Webster* has added a second definition: "disapproving: politically liberal (as in matters of racial and social justice) especially in a way that is considered unreasonable or extreme."[457]

It is evidence of the most recent evolution of the propagandist message of *don't listen to anyone but me*. And the people who do not believe what you believe—they are the enemy, and we must do everything we can . . . in law. . . in education . . . in how we raise our children . . . to protect ourselves from their nefarious plans. Because a propagandist needs villains, and it is easier to create them than to truly fight the real ones (such as taking on an organization that has been proven to support, hide, and cover for pedophiles within their global chain of operations—the Roman Catholic Church—but no one is calling for laws barring priests from educating children).

I refer you back to the International Organization for the Family and the word "only" their mission—"the natural family as the only fundamental and sustainable unit of society." And then back to Jack Nicholson as Colonel Jessup in *A Few Good Men*—"You want the truth? You can't handle the truth!" The truth being, of course, that only about 8 percent of the world identifies themselves as outside the "only" family unit worth of so-called recognition. Yet, the battle against them rages on with book banning, no place students with questions to turn to for guidance in schools, a deep distrust of teachers, and words like *abomination* and *damnation* thrown around like rocks at a heretic's execution.

The manufacturing and distribution processes of Theater of Lies initiated a slow poisoning of any remaining any value for the word *woke*. Guardian columnist Rebecca Solnit confirmed this in 2021.

> [Woke's] illness and decline was kidnapped by old white conservatives. There were often angry at words, especially new words, most particularly words that disturbed their rest—awakened them, you could say—and Woke was such a word. . . Rather than kill woke, they turned into a Zombie mercenary sent out to sneer at those who were concerned about racism and injustices. This backfired and "woke" became a marker of the not-OK Boomer, a bilious word whose meaning was more in who said it than in what it meant or mocked.[458]

While I agree with much of Solnit's comments, the characterization that the actions of anti-woke proponents "backfired" is incorrect. This is another consequence of Theater of Lies. The audience's adoption of a new word is fickle and open to their own interpretations. This is not a mistake. The audience has taken the words of the opposition and used these against them. Instead of *Merriam-Webster*'s first definition, woke's more contemporary meaning has fallen to the second: admonition of the perceived overstatement and action of left-wing values over the right.

In 2023, Thomas Chatterson Williams, a culture critic and professor of humanities at Bard College, confirmed the final stake in woke's heart. For him, it no longer has any value for the right to bash away at the left, either: "The word is not a viable descriptor for anyone who is critical of the many serious excesses of the left yet remains invested in reaching beyond their own echo chamber."

But he offers a good suggestion: clarity of thought and purpose.

> Perhaps we can all agree, at bare minimum, to set ourselves the task of limiting our reliance on in-group shorthand, and embracing clear, honest, precise, and original thought and communication. If we want to persuade anyone not already convinced of what we believe, we are going to have to figure out how to say what we really mean.[459]

As a professional communicator, I cheer this message and hope my colleagues – in business, government, and non-profits can rise to meet this inherent challenge.

On both sides of the woke world—or and against—truth has become lost in labeling, what Williams refers to as *in-group shorthand* (more jargon, which, as communicators, we strive to eliminate). "Speaking your truth," as Oprah Winfrey has demanded of us, has only emboldened both sides in what has now become a culture war—a war of beliefs and ideas, not facts.

This opinion, of course, may keep this book off Oprah's Book Club recommendations. Nonetheless, the remainder of this book examines ways we can create a world that better protects ourselves from the manipulations of lies, misinformation, and propaganda—by becoming better audiences and rebuilding trust.

We must create a world—personally, professionally, and politically—that limits the ability of lies to find a comfortable home in our psyches. As long as lies remain the most effective way to manipulate individuals and societies—then their strength as the world's most powerful weapons will remain.

As I look at my three grandsons, just a few years old, I wonder how they can thrive in a world where not everything they see or read is what it appears to be. And they and billions of other children are inheriting our world. We have forced them into the Theater of Lies with us. It is up to us to show them the way out of it—even if it means they must leave us behind.

We must start at the first teachable moment available: sunrise. We must point to the rising sun and tell our children that while it looks as if the sun is rising, what we are seeing is not that. What is happening is that our place on the earth is rotating toward the sun so that the sun only appears to rise.

Seems simple. But it's not. Television talk show host and comedian, Chelsea Handler (one of the cadres of entertainment celebrities who, as discussed in a previous chapter, the public looks to for truthful commentary), has admitted she "didn't know until [she] was 40 years old that the sun and the moon were not the same thing."[460] She must have had real trouble understanding a solar eclipse.

The producers of lies have taken advantage of us for thousands of years. But now, the Theater is so pervasive and persuasive that there is *no* walking out of the movie. As its audience, we are captive. If we hope to end the violence and mistrust these lies foster, we need a new strategy. As we live in a Theater of Lies, we must create an escape plan.

Indeed, the Theater of Lies is not just a metaphor for the producers' use of entertainment techniques to engage their audiences. The theater is now also theater of war. And a very effective one. If that war to manipulate our minds is successful (and as we've seen, in many instances, it has)—then the next consequence will be the Rule of Lies.

Around the globe, this has already happened. We call them autocracies and in 2022, they represented at least 60 of the 176 recognized nations in the world.[461]

Seven years after Edgar Welch armed himself and walked into a Washington, DC, pizzeria in search of a secret cabal of Democrats he believed were pedophiles—US Member of Congress Marjorie Taylor Greene repeated the trope on an internationally televised broadcast of CBS's *60 Minutes* newsmagazine: "Democrats support . . . children being sexualized, having transgender surgeries. Sexualizing children is what pedophiles do to children . . . They support grooming children."[462] What was once only talked about (falsely) in the conspiratorial terms of a few, was now a mainstream message of evil about a national political party. The Theater of Lies never stops, and like a good marketing professional, if its message is getting results, it will keep repeating it.

But let me remind you that the producers in the Theater of Lies are not collaborators. They are not a conspiracy network, no more than the sum of all the advertising agencies, public relations firms, and marketing departments of consumer goods companies using proven techniques to motivate your buying decisions. The difference is purpose. The producers in the Theater of Lies want you to make decisions that are better for them than you.

Lies work. We must work harder. And we must work fast, as we live in times when the Theater of Lies is at its persuasive best. That is not good news for anyone.

*More democracies are declining, and even sliding into autocracy,
today than at any point in the last century. This trend, continuing
for over a decade, appears to be accelerating, data shows, affecting
established and fragile democracies alike across the globe.*[463]

– MAX FISHER, JOURNALIST, NY TIMES

....

11

2024: THE THEATER PUTS LIBERAL DEMOCRACY ON TRIAL.

One of my earliest explorations into persuasion, as I discussed earlier, was at a sales training course by one of the greatest salesmen in the world (self-declared, but accurate), Zig Ziglar. He told those us just entering the business of persuading people to buy things—any things—that the only difference between a con man and a professional salesman[12] was the quality of goods they were selling and if they were in the best interests of the buyer should they decide to purchase. The sales techniques, he told us, were the same. The only difference was the

....

12   Apologies for the specific gender terms "con man" and "salesman"—but that those were terms of the time when my sales training occurred (late 1970s).

goal—in the best interest of the salesman (that's the con man) or the buyer (that's the professional salesman).

I took it as gospel at the time, but my years of research into lies and misinformation now inform me that Ziglar was wrong. Using these tactics to persuade people that the chocolate bar they are buying is *sustainably sourced* while the cocoa farmer doesn't make enough money to feed his family—that's not right. Nor is it right to bait and switch the consumer using the term *fair trade* to identify any cocoa the industry has purchased at a price that provides farmers with a *living wage* (the fair-trade cocoa's share of the global cocoa market is 0.5 percent).[464] That's just putting the burden on your customers rather than on yourself.

If you can't sell your products or idea based on its bona fides, leaning heavily on lies and misinformation is wrong. But what is of more concern to me than chocolate and other consumer products that rely on misinformation tactics is the way an emerging and relatively new global conservative movement has embraced these tactics to persuade people that it may be in their best interest to accept much limited forms of democracy, up to and including autocracy. Part of their strategy is what conservative writer and Notre Dame University professor, Patrick Deneen, refers to as the need for "Machiavellian means towards Aristotelian ends."[465]

To be clear, the new global conservative movement is not lying about its ambitions. While it may lean heavily on multisyllabic terms more commonly found in faculty lounges rather than barbeques, its goals are clear. However, it's using lies and misinformation to achieve them. Organizations such as the Edmund Burke Foundation[466] and the Alliance for Responsible Citizenship (ARC)[467] publicly embrace and promote an emerging coalition of these specific right-wing ambitions, each captured under phrases such as *national conservatism* and *common-good governance*—all of which have congealed in opposition to what these organizations refer to as "threats to moral order and the loss of moral bearing due to liberalism's relativism"[468] (translation, flexible perspectives). ARC's cofounder, UK House of Lords member Baroness Phillipa Stroud, has called for this movement to create a "better story"; that is (in my words), better productions from the Theater of Lies. She writes on the ARC website:

> Our lack of a common narrative has left us disillusioned and disempowered in a time when humanity is more prosperous, healthy, and resourced than at any point in history. We need a better story, one that provides an alternative to the myth that decline is inevitable. I believe that the new "Alliance for Responsible Citizenship" (ARC) represents a unique opportunity to formulate and tell that story.[469]

The baroness is joined by Canadian intellectual Jordan Peterson, if overwrought in his prose. He cites (among other right-wing opinion leaders) that the cause of all the world's ills is our loss of faith—which began in the late 1600s through to late 1700s (a period called *The Age of Enlightenment*). It was during this time Europeans began to question the role of religious institutions and monarchies and their roles as controlling forces in their lives (of note—it was also a time of rapid advancements in chemistry, biology, astronomy, and physics).[470]

Peterson's opinion is that we must return to pre-Enlightenment-Age thinking if our world has any hope of overcoming the left's "continual onslaught of ominous, demoralizing messages, most particularly in the form of environmental catastrophism." [471]

> [Despite] undeniable progress, a shadow has emerged . . . God is dead, so the story goes, and the future is uncertain. Five centuries of ascendant reductionist Enlightenment rationality have revealed that his starkly objective world lacks all intrinsic meaning. A century and a half or more of corrosive cultural criticism has undermined our understanding of and faith in the traditions necessary to unite and guide us . . . In the midst of this existential chaos, the false idol of apocalyptic ideology inevitably beckons.[472]

ARC held its first annual conference in late 2023 for "more than a thousand high-level leaders from politics, culture, business and academia across three days in London."[473] The group created the event as a philosophical alternative to the decades-old World Economic Forum. National conservative thinkers feel the Davos Switzerland event seeks to impose foreign agendas on national governments.

As Canadian Conservative Party leader Pierre Poilievre told his supporters in a 2023 fundraising letter, "It's far past time we rejected the globalist Davos elites and bring home the common sense of the common people."[474] In a media interview a month earlier, he said "freedom is making our own decisions here at home and that means banning our federal ministers from attending the World Economic Forum."[475] If you can't decipher the code, that's thought-police language.

The rising tide of national conservatism is making clear its goals. That means liberals should be asking themselves questions: *why now, and for what purpose?*

Because, in 2024, the US will see a wrecking ball tear through its constitution and sense of itself as a nation. That wrecking ball is, has been, and will be Donald Trump—empowered by four criminal indictments (federal and state) representing ninety-one charges regarding, mostly, his orchestration of lies and misinformation about the 2020 presidential election, the mishandling of confidential documents, and business fraud.

In the US, 2024 will experience an explosion of productions from the Theater of Lies as Donald Trump becomes the first person in history to go through several criminal trials while at the same time campaigning to be his party's candidate for president (and if successful there competing in the general election against the incumbent, Joe Biden). Lies, misinformation, and hyperbole have never had such powerful platforms from which to achieve their primary goals—division. And in this case, the most powerful nation on earth, already seriously divided on partisan basis, should expect a World War III attack from the Theater of Lies.

The criminal charges against Trump, while dampening general US voter enthusiasm for his 2024 presidential run (an August 2023 poll found that 53 percent of Americans say they would not support Trump),[476] three of four Republican voters plan to vote for him in 2024 presidential election (though at the time of the poll, Trump was still one of eleven candidates for the Republican Party's nomination).

The search of a smoking gun in the Theater of Lies—that is, any producer of lies speaking plainly about the use of lies and misinformation to manipulate opinion and achieve their goals—that's generally hard to find. Especially in politics. Until 2023, when Patrick Deneen published his book, *Regime Change—Toward a Postliberal Future*. There, he first referenced the need for "Machiavellian means to achieve Aristotelian ends—the use of powerful political resistance by the populace against the natural advantages of the elite."[477] He proposed what he and others call "common-good conservatism,"[478] a political philosophy that integrates Christian faith into government.

Charles King, a professor of international affairs at Georgetown University, reviewed Deneen's book, and those of two other conservative authors in *Foreign Affairs Magazine*. He zeroed in on language showing that, for conservative elites, democracy is not a requirement for their vision of "nature, community, and divinity . . . to work as one indivisible whole."[479] By community, Deneen means, people of similar backgrounds and values.

In *Conservatism Rediscovered* (one of the other books King reviewed), author Yoram Hazony challenges conservatives to move past the notion of *conservative government* and into the *practice of conservatism*, including the practice of being a *conservative person* and leading a *conservative life*.[480] Such a life, Hazony states, requires that "suffering individual has only one honorable way out of this decadence . . . he must find his way to one of the traditional paths through the wilderness."[481]

King refers to these and the similar thoughts of other conservative thought leaders as "code for their disapproval of the existence of gay and transgender people."[482] I call it a short step from theocracy—government of a state by immediate divine guidance or by officials who are regarded as divinely guided.[483]

King quotes the work of legal scholar Adrian Vermeule (professor, Constitutional Law, Harvard) who claims in his book, *Common Good Constitutionalism*, that democracy and elections have no special claim to delivering a common-good society such as he and other conservative thinkers propose. "A range of regime-types can be ordered to the common good or not",[484] Vermeule writes. And "if [government] structures produce outcomes contrary to the common good, they will have to be dismantled."[485] Vermeule adds that this political philosophy will be "difficult for the liberal mind to process."[486]

Difficult, indeed, for anyone to process. But that's nothing a decade or two of lies and misinformation might be able to fix. The phrase "Machiavellian means to achieve Aristotelian ends" is a central theme in Deneen's book (it is identified seven times in the book's index). A reminder of the psychological definition of *Machiavellian* is important here:

> A personality trait marked by a calculating attitude toward human relationships and a belief that ends justify means, however ruthless. A Machiavellian is one who views other people more or less as objects to be manipulated in pursuit of his or her goals, if necessary, through deliberate deception.[487]

If this doesn't sound like tactics of some producers in the Theater of Lies, I don't know what does. In practice, noise about the need for America to become governed as a Christian nation have been shouted out by such Republican members of Congress as Colorado's Lauren Boebert:

> "I believe that there have been two nations that have been created to glorify God. Israel, whom we bless, and the United States of America. And this nation will

glorify God. [I am] tired of this separation of church and state junk."[488]

Philip Gorski is a sociologist and co-director of Yale's Center for Comparative Research. Commenting on Boebert and the Christian national movement, he told *The Denver Post,*

> This is new and worrisome . . .There's an increasing number of people saying 'We're in this battle for the soul of America. We're on the side of good and maybe democracy is getting in the way. Maybe we need to take power and if that means minority rule in order to impose our vision on everybody else then that's what we're going to do.'[489]

Lies and misinformation are a Machiavellian weapon that, in this case, takes lessons from the so-called *Aristotelian ends* they seek to gain (by definition, a philosophical meaning virtues of the highest order). Beyond the real dangers of minority and autocratic leadership, of interest to me is the powerful use of pathos to persuade, as originally identified by that same fourth-century-BCE philosopher, Aristotle.

As we've discussed, *pathos* is about passion and deep concern for one's argument, over and above the facts of the matter. As the audience in the Theater of Lies, we are witnessing the overwhelming power of *pathos* for persuasion and the limited role facts, or *logos*, have in the process. Indeed, lies—delivered with a *pathos*, (or emotional resonance) from a speaker the audience highly regards—are Herculean in their force.

The Theater of Lies loves this. The storyteller driver of raising stakes ever higher, putting the victims at every greater threat . . . all this establishes the need for heroes to arrive and save the day. In 2024, a plain-language version of the dangers of liberal democracy will, in part, be presented as the need for faith-based governance to be one of those heroes.

That rhetoric will foster passion in both speakers and their audiences—solidifying the platform for the highly articulate delivery of *pathos*.

In July 2023, veteran journalist Judy Woodruff held a series of focus groups with right-leaning voters in Iowa. Her goal was to investigate the "divisions in America."[490] One of the questions she asked was, "Can a person be a liberal and still be a Christian?"

Here's how one woman, named Pat, answered:

> You can't. Life is, well, very important. And if you're a liberal, then you are pro-choice, and then you believe its OK to kill a baby. And I don't think you can believe that and be a real Christian.[491]

Another member of the focus group, named Peter, responded this way:

> God is more of a God of just love. He's a God of right and wrong. He's a God of truth. He's a God of righteousness. I mean, you can't be a liberal and be far left of beliefs and say, oh, I am a Christian. Well, you can say it. That's the worst thing. People do say it.[492]

The transfer of trust from institutions and government to new institutions and a government guided by Judeo-Christian principles is the next step in the process for national conservative leaders.

In his book, Deneen describes his solution to the ills of liberal democracy as *aristopopulism*—a regime headed by a new elite of what he refers to as trained *aristoi* (and if you consider that few elites understand words like *aristoi*, you'd be right. Especially as the very word itself, from the Greek, meaning the best in terms of birth, rank, and nobility, but also usually possessing the connotation of also being the morally best).[493]

These trained elites, says Deneen, will be people who:

> Understand that their main role and purpose in the social order is to secure the foundational goods that make human flourishing possible for ordinary people: the central goods of family, community, good work, a culture that encourages order and continuity, and support for religious belief and institutions.[494]

The villains, in Deneen's position, reflecting the words of Jordan Peterson, are "liberals [who] have purposely eroded the basic forums of social solidarity including family, neighborhood, association, church, and religious community."[495] He also calls for a celebration of the America's "Christian roots" and a cabinet position in the White House to encourage marriage and pregnancy in a similar way as can be found today in Hungary[13] and its president, Viktor Orban.[496]

As I have stated clearly before in this book, I have no problem with people following their faiths. I have no problem with them expressing their faith and urging others to join them. My concern and the focus of this book is the use of lies and misinformation to, in this very critical case, as a battering ram to persuade people to support massive change in government, up to and including attacks on the democratic process.

In my opinion, the emerging coalition of national conservatives are using Donald Trump as their Machiavellian means. Win or lose—his court cases and/or his presidential ambitions—Trump will prove to be the bull in America's constitutional china shop. He will become the proof point that American is broken and only massive change, led by conservative governments (municipal, state, and federal), can solve the program (in storytelling, this is called *enter-the-hero*).

Canada Conservative Party leader, Pierre Poilievre, has spoken regularly about my country "being broken."[497] And, a 2023 poll by Leger indicated that 67 percent of Canadians agree with that statement.[498] Respondents to the poll also "feel angry about the way Canada is being run." The Canadian government is already discussing, in private, how to react if America becomes a nation with a far-right government.[499]

....

13 Paul Hockenos, in *Foreign Policy* magazine, writes, "Hungarian conservatism is defiantly old-school: extoling of the conjugal family, anti-LGBT, and uncritical of the blemishes on Hungary's historical record, including its antisemitism. Hungary isn't Germany or the Netherlands, Orban proclaims—and it doesn't want to be." Paul Hockenos, "The Secrets to Viktor Orban's Success in Hungary," in *Foreign Policy*, April 1, 2022, https://foreignpolicy.com/2022/04/01/viktor-orbans-hungary-populism-election-nationalism/.

Such is power of the Theater of Lies and, in the case of some right-wing populists, used to erode trust in government and institutions to such a bottom-scratching low that constitutional change is possible. For them, Donald Trump may fit what the very definition of the term *useful idiot*—a naive or credulous person who can be manipulated or exploited to advance a cause or political agenda.[500]

While some may consider the use of lies and misinformation to set up a situation for constitutional change in the US as a conspiracy theory, I disagree. The consistent application of lies and misinformation by so many is not, in my opinion, a coordinated strategy. It is what in business we'd call *a best practice*. As others see the strategy work, they use it themselves.

The conservative base of academics is relatively clear about their biases and objectives (though their language is obtuse). The next stage in persuading others of those objectives gets muddier, and the use of lies, misinformation, and such language becomes even more voluminous.

Regarding the global perspective of conservative and liberal political thought, lies and misinformation have become the primary tools of division. In my lifetime, people from both conservative and liberal perspectives were able to debate, get along, and move steadily to governments in their names. Now, the Theater of Lies is coming very close to making this impossible. Conservatives and liberals, globally, are no longer political adversaries; they have become enemies. And enemies hate each other. They wave angry fists at each other; anger that provides powerful platforms for rhetoric, the refusal to listen to opposing facts, and the embrace of lies and misinformation as righteous proof of their positions.

In the US, 84 percent of people in an NPR-IBM Watson Health poll stated they were angrier today than a generation ago, with 42 percent of people growing angrier in 2019 than every before.[501] In 2021, the *Christian Science Monitor* reported that a poll conducted by SSRS in the US found that American felt much the same way as Canadians, with three out of four responding that "they felt at least somewhat angry at the way things are going in the country today."[502]

For the producers in the Theater of Lies, this is an Oscar-worthy achievement.

The national, or common-good conservative movement, is using the combined nuclear forces of Donald Trump, his criminal charges and court appearances, the US Republican primaries, and the US 2024 presidential election - as a launch platform.

I take no issue with the vision of national conservatives. They have a right to make their policy preferences known and to promote them. But supporting the use of the lies and misinformation of others to foster an environment where these policies have a better change of support is where I draw the line.

Because of this support (overt or covert), 2024 will be the year that the Theater of Lies becomes as a clear and present danger in America and around the world. It is not Donald Trump on trial. He is only the proxy. The Theater of Lies is putting liberal democracy on trial—not to see if it is guilty of crimes (that, they have already determined), but in the hope liberal democracy crumbles under the weight of righteous anger pressed upon it.

There is a chance (or at least a hope), that in the post-2024 world, liberal democracy will have come through the Trump trials/candidacy/election period unscathed. But I doubt it. For while mainstream media will focus on the day-to-day details and the expert opinions of lawyers, former judges, and political pundits, the Theater of Lies will be putting liberal democracy on trial, not Donald Trump. His win, loss, or draw in the real world are only pivot points in the court of public opinion; this is where the Theater of Lies conducts its business.

No matter the result, lies, misinformation and hyperbole in our world will continue to grow and gain even more traction. Divisions will go, unless we act as individuals, groups, and societies to protect ourselves.

Act Three, next, proposes solutions.

··········· ACT THREE: ···········

HOW WE CAN GET OUT
(ME, YOU, AND EVERYONE)

"It's not just conspiracy theorists and marginalized, angry people online. It's state actors, too, using disinformation, propaganda, and cyberwarfare to harm our economies, our democracies, and undermine people's faith in the principles that hold us together."

- JUSTIN TRUDEAU, PRIME MINISTER OF CANADA, SPEAKING AT THE HAGUE, OCTOBER 29, 2021.

1

THE SOLUTION
LIES WITHIN US.

Growing up in the Toronto area in the 1970s, Buffalo television was a staple. It was our source of US news, entertainment, and commercial advertising. There was a particular ad from a men's wear retailer in Buffalo, Syms, that has always stuck in my mind. The price labels on these suits, shirts, and other details for dapper gentlemen had four price levels. The first week—full price. If the item was still on the rack a second week, 10 percent off; third week, 33 percent off; and after four weeks, final sale at 50 percent off. His advertising slogan was "an educated consumer is our best customer."[503]

In the Theater of Lies in which we live, for the producers, the opposite is true. Their best customers are the uneducated (and here, I do not mean they did not go to school and are not intelligent)—as in uneducated in the ways, as an audience, people are being manipulated. The solution to protecting ourselves from their influence is to become educated consumers of information, thereby becoming the Theater's least malleable audience.

In Act Three we examine how to achieve this, first as individuals, then as a society. Organizations – both for profit and not –also have to ask themselves if they are part of the problem, the solution, or both, and we'll do so here. The most basic response to those living in the Theater of Lies is to become cynical, by definition, more and more distrustful of society and people's motivations. And that's where a lot of us have landed. 2019 research by Pew Research Center found that "fully 71% think interpersonal confidence has worsened in the past 20 years. And about half (49%) think a major weight dragging down such trust is that Americans are not as reliable as they used to be."[504] So it's not just governments, businesses, and media we distrust. More and more, we are distrusting each other.

For me, the stakes are too high for that response as it does nothing to resolve the situation. A world full of cynics would be as terrible a place as a world full of blind followers (of anything for any reason). And in that statement lies a key part of an effective response. We need to move beyond binary thinking. When we attempt to understand most any issue as binary—as a choice between one thing and another—we not only do ourselves a disservice, but we also plow the field for the producers of lies and misinformation.

"Binary thinking is the path of least resistance for human perceiving, thinking, and for linguistic structures," says University of

Massachusetts at Amherst Professor Peter Elbow in his essay, "The Uses of Binary Thinking."[505] As such, it is hardwired into our psyches. If the sun goes up, it must come down. As Elbow reminds us, "binary thinking almost always builds in dominance or privilege—sometimes overtly and sometimes covertly."[506] In simpler terms, inherent in our processing through this thinking structure, there seems to be a right and wrong.

This is what the producers in the Theater of Lies exploit. And while there is value in binary thinking, it does us a disservice when used incorrectly (more on that later). For binary thinking, like any tool, can be used well or poorly. Unfortunately, we tend to use it to make decisions with the precision of a sledgehammer dividing an apple. Efficient, yes. But you are going to make a mess of it and the end product would be worthless.

Whenever you are being pushed into binary choices—black or white . . . male or female . . . good or evil . . . socialist or capitalist . . . win or lose—and any time that you are being forced into a decision through the offer of two, and only two choices, you are being manipulated.

That is why, after the embrace of the word "woke" as shorthand for awareness of issues, the need to change was immediately fought with its binary opposite: "anti-woke." As if there is no space in the middle for alternate opinions, decisions, and actions.

Binary discussions, as best evidenced in the woke versus anti-woke debate, create two barriers to truth and trust—that is, one, the loss of understanding of what we really mean, to ourselves and others; and two, an inability to convince others of the value of our opinions. As we know, *ethos* (or reputation) is a powerful driver of persuasion, and a lack of trust crumbles the foundation of that *ethos*.

That would be complicated—and in the Theater of Lies—there can be no complicated thoughts.

This was one of the first lessons taught to me in sales training courses decades ago. A good salesperson will divide all decisions into two choices—neither of which is *not* to buy whatever you are selling (a car salesperson will ask if you are looking for a car or an SUV, a black one or a green one, four doors or two, all-wheel drive or two-wheel drive, etc.). Never, if they can avoid it, will a salesperson ask *yes* or *no* to the purchase (unless they are already sure of the answer).

By its very nature, binary thinking limits options. But it also has that joy-filling ability to make you believe you understand something when you actually don't. But the producers in the Theater of Lies do not want you to understand. They want you to believe what they want you to believe—like the car salesperson who needs you to buy the extended warranty to pad their commission.

In the Theater of Lies, binary thinking is pushed to the edges in what psychologists call *splitting*, defined as:

> A mental mechanism or pattern of thinking that is characterized by interpreting complex or overwhelming situations in oversimplified, either/or terms. This tendency often provides a narrow perspective that can exclude important details. In general, it's a limiting way of thinking that can cause issues with one's relationships, mental health, or other areas of life.[507]

The key in the above definition is its use in complex or overwhelming situations. This the environment in which the Theater of Lies thrives and, as such, promotes issues and conflicts that maintain it.

As a psychological principle, it reflects the need to polarize everything in life. Below is a list of tendencies that reflect splitting, the most dangerous and widespread form of binary thinking in our world. You see that, while splitting is a psychological construct, the Theater of Lies pushes its audience, us, to believe that this disordered thinking is perfectly normal.

> Your thinking is psychologically split if you:
>
> Think in absolutes or dividing concepts into two opposing camps. Believe that everyone is either good or bad with no room for ambiguity or imperfections. Believe that someone with a different point of view is against you. Easily turn on your best friend, and/or make fun of those who think differently than you do.[508]

If you didn't hear the end result of the Theater of Lies within that definition, read it again. The goal of the producers is a psychosis level of binary thinking that blindly follows their lead. However, we cannot completely stop thinking on a binary level, but we can learn to better use it while adding other structures to our repertoire of thinking processes.[14]

However, relative to the Theater of Lies, part of my recommended defense strategy *is* binary—in this case, a choice between two targets. The first target is the producers—by creating limits on what messages

....

14   I make declaration here (hand over heart, head down in shame) that I have used this technique throughout this book, as it is a work of persuasion. But as I learned from top salesman Zig Ziglar and identified previously, the tools of the con man and the professional salesperson can be the same. The only difference in the goal. So, I have used some of the techniques of the liars, such as binary messages, for my higher goal: to engage, educate, and encourage readers to take action to protect themselves in the Theater of Lies.

they can send. And the second is the audience—by improving our ability to withstand the attacks of those same producers.

The problem with the first choice is that its very nature requires the implementation of censorship. This is how autocracies like Russia and China have attacked truth in their nation. In nations with free speech cultures—like the US, Canada, and so many others—this heavy-handedness would not only be unwelcome, it also would fail. Just look at the US government's attempt to create the *Disinformation Governance Board* as it fell victim to the binary thinking of good v. bad, free speech v. censorship, and oversight v. overreach.

John Cohen, the former head of the US Homeland Security's Intelligence branch, attempted to frame the board as more of a think tank than an organization oriented on action. "It looks at policy issues," he said. "It looks at best practices, it looks at academic research relating to how disinformation influences the threat environment." That research would be provided to other government departments and agencies.[509]

The board died three weeks after it was born in April 2022. Its proponents and managers could not overcome the objections of politicos and media commentators about its so-called attack on free speech.[510] Republicans painted the board as Orwellian, calling it a *Ministry of Truth* to police people's thoughts.[511]

So, the Theater of Lies successfully killed the board in its cradle (in a May 1, 2022, op-ed, two professors stated that the initials of the *Disinformation Governance Board* were only "one letter off from KGB").[512]

I believe that the best course of action is the second choice—focus on the audience. This is the subject matter of Act 3: creating personal, professional, and organizational tools to defend ourselves.

Our defense from the Theater of Lies will come from three places: as individuals, as organizations, and as societies. We are each our own generals in this war, both soldiers and commanders. Our combined energy as individuals will pave the way for societal changes—changes that will require our votes and purchasing power to make real. Our organizations—institutional, corporate, and media—are the infrastructure we used to lean on to give form to the world we live in. These too must also up their game.

Each has witnessed the new reality. Truth has been reduced to a janitorial service sweeping the halls after the destructive power of lies has wrecked havoc on its targets. Truth will never influence opinions if the audience is unwilling to hear it. It will never change minds if the biases of those minds are already set against it. Truth can pound at the door like a police officer begging you to escape a fast-moving forest fire. But if you cannot see the smoke, you may pass off the warning as fearmongering. Or use it as proof of something entirely different (such as the smoke is coming from too many people using fireplaces).

Truth may now be better equated with the quote, "The arc of the moral universe is long, but it bends toward justice."[513] But as a weapon, relying on truth "to set you free" (carved into the stone of the US Central Intelligence Agency's headquarters)[514] is like bringing a garden hose to a five-alarm fire. It won't protect you. It won't protect others. It will only give you a false sense of security that with truth in hand you will one day be able to rebuild the destroyed edifices (or the visions that built them). If you believe, like me, that hope is not a strategy, then false hope is a delusion.

Truth has become best suited to a court of law, where complex issues can be debated, evidence presented, and time for deliberation is imbued in the process (remembering that, even there, we often get it wrong).

The real world moves too quickly for that. Lies are produced to be more quickly digested and adopted as the truths they presume to replace. Lies are both efficient and effective (a rare and powerful cocktail).

So much of twenty-first-century thinking has been focused on efficiency: more efficient supply chains, more efficient education, more efficient healthcare and social services, and more efficient governments. Effective, though important, has become secondary. It is not just that it's too hard to measure (though it can be); it just takes too long. Effective has become a horse-out-of-the-barn measurement that looks backward for information and ideas (and will discard the notion of looking to the past, at times, as a distraction from the very goal of the agenda-driven effectiveness).

Yes, there is value in the examination. But as noted business adviser Peter Drucker has repeatedly told us, "Culture eats strategy for breakfast."[515] This is where the Theater of Lies has led the fight—not about truth, not even about trust. It is now about culture. Across the globe, cultural wars are being waged, and the primary weapons are lies and misinformation—their purpose, power and profit.

I do not want my grandchildren to grow up in a world where they are told what to think and manipulated to entrench those thoughts in their minds. Instead, I want them to grow up in a world where they are taught and supported on a long-term journey and independent thought—encouraged at each step by a community committed to these ideals. We must go beyond teaching what to think and move, with purpose, with a focus on how.

Let's go back to sunrise, sunset. Again, a binary option when the truth is not binary all—our place on the earth constantly rotates toward or away from the sun. So why do we continue this lie? It reflects our need for simple, binary solutions. It has become ingrained in our culture.

So, while this final section of the book will give you some suggestions to become a less amenable target for lies and thoughts on how society can better defend itself—success will come through a culture change. And, as Gandhi said, "If we could change ourselves, the tendencies in the world would also change"[516] (inaccurately quoted most often as *be the change you wish to see in the world*).

That culture cannot be based on cynicism. It needs to be based around an infrastructure of people who are curious, who will ask questions, and who will respect public debate as a process, not a winner-take-all event.

Our ability to defend ourselves must become more than a series of fact-checking exercises (already tried and making little, if any, impact). The marketplace of ideas is full of suggestions on how to decipher lies and misinformation, but these do nothing to address the root cause.

You have to care.

We already know that if you believe the lies you are hearing and are repeating them to others, you don't care if those lies are true or not. They fit into your belief system without so much as a smidgeon of self-awareness that your belief system, too, has been manipulated through centuries of never-ending performances in our world, the Theater of Lies.

So, in this final Act of the book, you will not find a list of fact-checking tools (you can Google that). You will not find strategies for dealing with deep fake videos and the use of artificial intelligence (AI) to create words, pictures, and music that will only improve its ability to trick us. The Pandora's box of tools for the producers in the Theater of Lies has not only been opened; its flow is volcanic.

What I hope to persuade you of is the need for cultural change. We need to evolve our minds as a species to thrive in a world of massive information shared massively and repeated as massively, all with bias of intent.

The tools of this evolution are:

Care—you have to care (for this issue affects all of us), but it helps if you can find a personal connection (for me, it's my grandchildren).

Curiosity—you need to be curious enough to explore and foster knowledge and understanding.

Courage—some of the pathways you explore may, at first, be uncomfortable, and the knowledge you gain may be challenged by those around you.

With respect, Oprah Winfrey, I propose that *care, curiosity*, and *courage* are the most powerful tools we all have. These are our super-powers. Only then can the power of truth be employed and expected to be effective.

The sum of these, I want to call the Right to Bear Thoughts, modeled after the America's Second Amendment.

A well-informed population, being necessary to the security and prosperity of a free State, the right to bear thoughts and acquire knowledge, shall not be infringed.

Even though the producers in the Theater of Lies bear significant responsibility for the culture in which we now live, governments, politicians, and media must stop blaming others for the public's diminished trust. For while you can blame the soldier who fired the bullet that wounded you, healing that wound is a personal and institutional responsibility. In fact, the two go hand-in-hand, as Pew Research demonstrated:

> People's views on personal trust are strongly associated with their views on issues related to institutional trust. On virtually every survey question about institutions . . . high trusters have significantly more confidence in institutions than low trusters, whether it is the military, police officers, business executives or religious leaders.[517]

Act Three will also look at some of the ways that, in the end, we can use to rebuild the trust the Theater of Lies has so effectively eroded. We will examine how we, as individuals, as organizations, and as societies can defend ourselves and perhaps even thrive.

As individuals, we need to go beyond binary thinking—that requires a change in culture. As institutions, we need to rebuild trust. As a better-informed audience, the Theater of Lies will have far less influence over us.

"Be curious, not judgmental."[518]

– WALT WHITMAN, AMERICAN POET AND ESSAYIST.

....

2

NURTURING OUR SUPERPOWERS.

Previously, I introduced you to Professor Alex Edmans of the London School of Business and his debate between facts, evidence, and data. He has lamented that rather than living in a post-truth world, "we should consider that we are living in post-data world,"[519] because fewer of us are looking to data for answers—and if we are, we're only really looking for the answers we want. As you know, I would call this world not post-data, not post-truth, but post-trust.

But Edmans' statement does point to the widening gap between how decisions are being made by businesses and governments, on the one hand, and the public, on the other. Indeed, in 2021, the data analytics industry was estimated to be worth close to $32 billion a year and expected to grow to 330 billion by 2030 (that's about 30 percent a year).[520] So, while business takes deeper and deeper dives into the data pool for its decisions. The public turns to Google (and looks no further than the first or second response it finds).[521]

More large businesses and governments are embracing AI, mass data storage, and complex data analysis to provide themselves the information to improve their efficiencies, operational methods, and marketing operations, all with the goal of more efficiency. In the business world, accuracy equals efficiency. In terms of the old cliché, "I know that half my advertising dollars are wasted; I just don't know which half," combined with the massive storage capacity of cloud-based computing, modern data management and analysis can now provide an answer to that cliché without relying on the traditional solution of a coin flip.

But people don't think like machines, nor do they want to. So, what is the best pathway to decision-making without access to massive loads of data and the ability to process and analyze it? For some, it means becoming skeptical of most things they see and hear. But skepticism has come to have a negative connotation. Skepticism, for some, is the first step down the slippery slope toward its more negative cousin, cynicism. That's because few people truly understand the neutral connotation of the word.

The practice of skepticism is growing to the point that it is now being taught as a subject in more general interest university courses. Indiana's Notre Dame offers a micro-course in "Truth and Skepticism," where students "grapple with the fundamental philosophical question of how we should decide what to believe."[522] The late US President Ronald Reagan unknowingly provided us with the best and most positive definition of skepticism when he coopted an old Russian proverb in his discussion of nuclear arms negotiations with the Soviet Union. He said to "trust but verify"[523]: which is nice, assuming the facts you are verifying are not themselves, as Kellyanne Conway might have called them, "alternative facts." And, as we have seen, facts are not evidence.

As in the case of the COVID-19 debate, when we back into arguments of "my science" versus "your science," there's often some third party yelling, "It's all a conspiracy!" When this happens, natural skepticism quickly evolves into cynicism—and quite frankly, the propagandists win. Understanding reality becomes so hard that it becomes easier to revert to fantasy. The propagandists need not burn any books that run counter to their preaching—we no longer want to read them.

Scientists, academics, philosophers, and theologians have all studied the decision-making processes of us mere humans. Most of the models this broad-spectrum group have created are complicated to the point of putting more emphasis on process than the validity of any decision that might arise from them. Since the 1950s, visual models have become popular under various versions of what academics have referred to as "design rationale." But the benefit of most of these models is for large groups of people who need to influence a decision. It is what might be called *a logic tree* that some of us may have been taught in school. The basis of them all is critical thinking. Translating such processes to a personal level is challenging, hence our preference for search engines over visits to our local library (efficiency over effectiveness, again).

In fact, even you want to learn critical thinking, from my research, it seems that it is only in university settings that the process is taught (which, to me, seem a little late in the learning curve). The example below comes from Monash University in Australia (named after Sir John Monash whose motto was *Ancora Imparo* ("I am still learning").[524]

> Critical thinking is most commonly associated with arguments. You might be asked to think critically

about other people's arguments or create your own. To become a better critical thinker, you therefore need to learn how to:

1. Clarify your thinking purpose and context.
2. Question your sources of information.
3. Identify arguments.
4. Analyze sources and arguments.
5. Evaluate the arguments of others; and,
6. Create or synthesize your own arguments.[525]

The challenge with the above, or any critical thinking model, is that while it is effective, it can be a burdensome process and, as such, inefficient.

Let's examine the findings of a few experts in how we think.

Nobel laureate Daniel Kahneman has written extensively about what he and others consider our basic thinking systems: System 1 and System 2. Or, as he characterizes them, Fast and Slow (and at other times, lazy or deliberate).[526]

System 1 is what we use when we drive; it is automatic, effortless, and avoids too much analysis or too many choices. System 2 is more rational, deliberate, and logical. Neither is inherently better than the other; we use both of them. Kahneman claims that there is too much going on in our lives for System 2 to analyze everything. So, System 2 has to pick its moments with care and is "lazy" out of necessity.[527]

Matt Grawitch, PhD, is a professor at St. Louis University. His favorite course to teach is Ethical, Evidence-Based Decision Making.[528] For him, System 1 is heuristic-based decision-making and is not inherently bad or lazy: it can be very effective if, he says, one can "learn to better calibrate one's confidence in the heuristic response (i.e., to develop more refined meta-thinking skills) and one is willing to expand search strategies in lower-confidence situations or based on novel information."[529]

If you're like me, once someone begins talking about meta-thinking, you quickly run for the exit (just so you know, meta-thinking is thinking about thinking, about as deep a rabbit hole, I think, as you could possibly fall into). So, while I appreciate the thinking that the thinking about thinking professionals have done (and will continue to do), as it relates to living in the Theater of Lies, I prefer to weave critical thinking into its inherent motivation: curiosity.

For those who demand such a structure, you will not find one here. Like fact-checking sites, the internet is chock-full of models for critical thinking. If you wish to apply any of them to the lies that come your way daily, in my opinion, you will be driven madder by the process than the lies themselves. You will also become quite boring at dinner parties. Your partner may leave you. You may come to the truth of many matters, but I don't think you will find much joy in your life.

Whatever process you choose to follow is your business. This would be the same as if you told me you wanted to learn music and I took away any choice you had in what instrument you wanted to play or which teacher you wanted to learn from. Decision-making and critical-thinking models are only as effective as the people who use them. Beneath that is the motivator—you need to care.

From there, you can tap your superpower: *curiosity.* Plug into it and it will power your critical thinking like it was the electrical socket firing up your computer.

Children are naturally curious. It's how they discover their world. They also learn a second element, though: respect for authority. Directions from parents, children quickly learn, are very important. Don't touch the stove. Look both ways when you cross the street. Don't talk to strangers. Curiosity and respect for authority are two natural thinking processes that compete in children's minds for dominance. The competition begins at birth and continues into daycare settings, kindergarten, and full-time schooling. At each step in the process, we add more and more authority figures.

The authority figures we provide our children teach facts—the *what*—but it is only curiosity that allows our children to understand the *why*. Yet, through the process of education, we take away opportunities for curiosity, allowing it only in higher education, such as in a master's thesis or PhD dissertation. And then, that curiosity had better be supported by facts. Beyond this, it is only from artists—painters, writers, poets, sculptors, musicians—that we demand curiosity. Even in music, curiosity and exploration are welcome only at the highest levels—unless, of course, one is a prodigy; then, we all sit back in awe and applaud as though a monkey had taught itself to speak. It is only with curiosity that we encourage exploration, which drives so much of science.

There is value in skepticism, but it seeks to determine whether something is wrong or right. Curiosity is more neutral. Curiosity is the condition of being interested: pondering, being prepared to jab around and make sense of something. Skepticism may lead you to understand that what you're seeing or hearing, what someone is trying to make you believe, is untrue. Curiosity will take you a step further. Being curious demands that you ask the *next* question, like: if what this person is trying to convince me of is false, why are they trying to get me to believe it? Curiosity helps you determine not only the truth of the message but also the motivations of the sender. And that is the best defense against the pervasive and persuasive influence of the Theater of Lies.

For a real-life example, let's look at how one man's curiosity was the tipping point for the toppling seventy-five years of communism in the USSR.

In 1989, Boris Yeltsin was able to step out of the Soviet Union's Theater of Lies in way few of us can. At the time, he was a rising figure of opposition in the Gorbachev era and a proponent of two foundational changes in government policy: *glasnost* (openness) and *perestroika* (restructuring). Frustrated at the slow pace of these reforms, Yeltsin became the first-ever member of the Soviet Union's central governing committee, the Politburo, to resign voluntarily. Despite pleas from President Gorbachev, Yeltsin refused to return to the governing party in its current form. He would later become the chief architect of the Communist Party's demise and of the Soviet Union as we knew it. Why? Because he refused to continue to believe the lies he'd lived with all his life. How? Because he was curious.

Yeltsin, a massive man with a full head of white hair, was visiting the Johnson Space Center in Houston, Texas. He had come to see the early stages of the International Space Station as it was being constructed. On the way back to the Houston Airport, he requested a stop at a local supermarket, *Randall's*. As one of his aides later reported, after Yeltsin completed his tour of the supermarket, "the last vestiges of Bolshevism collapsed within his boss."[530]

Yeltsin said, "If Soviet people, who much often wait in line for most goods, saw the conditions of US supermarkets, there would be a revolution. Even the Politburo doesn't have this choice. Not even Mr. Gorbachev."

Within two years, he would officially leave the Soviet Communist Party, eventually becoming the first president of the new Russian Federation.

According to *Houston Chronicle* writer Craig Hlavaty, for Yeltsin's epiphany, "you can blame those frozen Jell-O Pudding pops."[531] In his autobiography, Yeltsin confirmed it:

> When I saw those shelves crammed with hundreds, thousands of cans, cartons, and goods of every possible sort, for the first time I felt quite frankly sick with despair for the Soviet people. That such a potentially super-rich country as ours has been brought to a state of such poverty! It is terrible to think of it.[532]

As a society, we've stacked the deck against curiosity. Even the dictionary defines it "as in inquisitiveness, an eager desire to find out about things that are often none of one's business."[533]

Really? None of one's business?

Our attitude reminds me of the matriarch's dinner table admonishment in Act Two concerning an open discussion on the facts of an argument, *we'll have none of that, here*. And, of course, we even have a highly memorable proverb as a warning against it: *curiosity killed the cat*. Its source lies in Shakespeare's time, and the word *curiosity* was originally *care*; its propagandist evolution came at the turn of the nineteenth century. A clearer warning against inquisitiveness has never been written.

And clear connection to care being the motivator to defend ourselves in the Theater of Lies.

A psychologist will tell you that curiosity is propelled by the "desire and freedom to ask questions" and "is a clear foundation for a more creative life". [534]

Well, I cannot say if curiosity has ever killed a cat. But I can tell you with a high degree of certainty, however, what kills curiosity. The first is from others: direction from authority figures that curiosity is not tolerated (it is a challenge to the status quo and, therefore, must be stopped and punished as an example to others). The second comes from yourself: your belief system, the sum of your biases. Put these two powerful forces together, and, any notion of curiosity will be stillborn.

My wife, Carol, sometimes tells the story of how, as a young girl, she watched Neil Armstrong walk on the moon. It was July 1969. With her was her Lithuanian grandmother, Carol on the floor staring at the black-and-white television images of the Apollo 11 astronauts beaming back from the landing site on the Sea of Tranquility. Her grandmother was knitting and shaking her head. "It is all fake," she told her granddaughter. "They are making this up."

For a person born in Lithuania in the late 1800s, who had immigrated to America to escape the crumbling Russian Empire and the rise of communism, landing on the moon was beyond her grandmother's ability to comprehend. She didn't have the opportunity that Boris Yeltsin would have years later, experiencing that metaphorical grocery store, firsthand.

Yeltsin's belief in communism was certainly waning prior to visiting Randall's market. But the experience of seeing the true impact of fully stocked shelves and multiple produce choices, of holding the "pudding pops" in his hands, killed off his long-held belief system. He was already throwing off the shackles of authority—by his nature and his request to stop at the American supermarket.

My wife's grandmother couldn't go to the moon to experience it for herself. Many of us, in any situation, cannot experience things for ourselves that would counter our long-held beliefs. We must accomplish these feats with our minds (such as trusting the reason we can only see along the horizon for so far is because the world is round).

In the next chapter, we will examine the first task in preparing our defense from the Theater of Lies—addressing our biases. For it's not the world we need to be skeptical of; it is ourselves.

"The easy, casual lies—those are a very dangerous thing. They open up the path to the bigger lies, in more important places, where the consequences aren't so harmless."[535]

— JAMES COMEY, FORMER FBI DIRECTOR

....

3

CUM GRANO SALIS (WITH A GRAIN OF SALT).

It was 2019 when, on opposite sides of the planet, two people stood up in the Theater of Lies and said, *that's enough.*

One of them, Catherine Hughes of Perth, West Australia, was appointed to the government of Australia's Sharing Knowledge About Immunization (SKAI) project. The other? An eighteen-year-old student from Ohio, Ethan Lindenberger. He was testifying before the United States Senate Committee on Health, Education, Labor, and Pensions on why he chose to go against his parents' wishes and get vaccinated. For such independent thoughts, the Theater of Lies attacked both. Hughes and Lindenberger would demonstrate that in addition to curiosity and critical thinking, protecting ourselves in the Theater of Lies requires another *c*-word: *courage.*

Hughes's son Riley was just four weeks old when he died from complications of whooping cough, one of the world's most dangerous and preventable infections. If the world has a ground zero in the anti-vaccination conspiracy, it is on the island so large it is considered a continent.

Vaccination rates in some Australian communities are over 90 percent, but in others, just over 50. When Riley died, his parents were at first labeled anti-vaxxers (even though the whooping cough vaccine is not administered until a child is six weeks old). Later, they were relabeled as pro-vaxxers. as Catherine Hughes and her husband went on to publicly tell the story that if others had been vaccinated, their son would still be alive.

The couple were pilloried on social media. Catherine, however, had the courage to stand her ground, at one point writing,

> To all the strangers sending me Facebook messages and asking why my son wasn't vaccinated. He was 4 weeks old!!! Too young to be vaccinated! Go learn something about immunization and stop bothering me. Our whole family was vaccinated but we live in the state with the worst vaccine rates and sometimes family vaccination just isn't enough to protect our babies.[536]

The Hughes family learned the hard way that when you try to stand up and leave the Theater of Lies, it fights back. Part of its strategy is to make it personal. It will set upon the unruliest members of its audience and use them to advance its own propaganda.

After Catherine Hughes was appointed to SKAI, an anonymous healthcare professional with a hate-on for so-called big pharma, posted:

> "Hughes's connection with disreputable groups, and her public derision of parents who hold concerns about the safety and effectiveness of vaccines, raises obvious questions about her suitability for appointment on character grounds alone."[537]

Six years after Riley Hughes's death, thousands of people joined marches in major Australian cities to protest vaccination plans for COVID-19. In Melbourne, the march turned violent when protesters stormed a Saturday cricket match.[538] At the same time, Facebook participation on anti-vaxx pages rose 300 percent.[539] Members of the group Make Australia Healthy Again[540] frequently shared links, photos, videos, and statuses with false and misleading information about the pandemic, with common topics being claims about the danger and inefficacy of vaccines and the threats posed to civil liberties and personal freedoms by lockdowns and mandatory vaccination programs.[541]

The Theater of Lies went into high production mode as it exploited the COVID-19 pandemic to focus the anger of anti-vaxxers. Chris Cooper, who leads Reset Australia, a digital advocacy group, said,

> Public Facebook groups are the tip of the iceberg when it comes to track and tracing anti-vax and COVID-19 misinformation. The real danger of rampant vaccine hesitancy and scientific skepticism is tucked away in algorithm-created bubbles of Facebook, YouTube, and

Twitter, where ideas fester and spread, unseen and unchecked by mainstream conversation.[542]

On the other side of the planet, at about the same time that Catherine Hughes joined SKAI, an eighteen-year-old American high school student from Ohio was challenging everything his parents had brought him up to believe. Ethan Lindenberger looked beyond his age in a white shirt, polka-dot tie, and blue blazer, rarely taking his eyes off the members of the US Senate Committee on Health, Education, Labor and Pensions. As he spoke to them, unlike the series of experts who had preceded him, he didn't refer to notes or speak in obscure scientific or legal language. He was the boy who defied his parents and went out and got vaccinated. In March of 2019, he had come to Washington, D.C. at the request of the committee to tell them how and why he had done such a thing.

"My mother would turn to social media groups and not to factual sources like the Centers for Disease Control and Prevention," said Lindenberger. "It is with love and respect that I disagree with my mom. As I approached high school and began to critically think for myself, I saw that the information in defense of vaccines outweighed the concerns heavily."[543]

Earlier that year, he had posted a question on the information-sharing site Reddit. There, he sounded more like the questioning teenager he was than the blue-blazered young man in front of the United States Senate Committee. His post went,

> "My parents are kind of stupid and don't believe in vaccines. Now that I'm 18, where do I go to get vaccinated? Can I get vaccinated at my age?"[544]

There were over twenty-one thousand views and comments on the post, and much of the advice he received was to go see his doctor. He did. In response, he told the Reddit forum,

"Thanks, my friends have been really supportive which helped when my mom put me down and told me how disappointed she was I was wanting to get my vaccines."[545]

In the US, Lindenberger told the Senate Committee he first learned how to find "truth in a world of misleading facts and false views" when he had joined his high school's debate club.[546] In addition to Reddit, he said he also consulted information from the Centers for Disease Control and Prevention, the WHO, and various scientific journals. When he confronted his mother with information from the CDC, which states in large, bold lettering that "there is no link between vaccines and autism," Lindenberger told the Senate Committee his mother responded, "That's what they want you to think."[547]

Lindenberger's mother, Jill Wheeler, is part of the global anti-vaccination movement. The movement calls the safety and necessity of immunizations into question for "religious reasons, personal beliefs or philosophical reasons, safety concerns, and a desire for more information from healthcare providers."[548] At the hearing, she told reporters,

He's a great kid. I love him very much, but I feel what he's representing is wrong. It's taken away our freedom of speech, and my question is, what is going to be next?[549]

Lindenberger's mother was using a common propaganda mind trick: when you are losing on one battlefield (vaccinations), change the battlefield (in this case, to freedom of speech). It's such smooth trick that most people don't even notice, like a magician pulling a coin out from behind your ear.

We can assume that Wheeler had taught her son not to believe everything he heard. However, she also taught him that vaccines were dangerous, which is what *she* had heard. I don't believe Wheeler wasn't trying to be a good parent, but she let her biases get in the way. What we need in this world is a billion children like Ethan, the curious. Children who are feel free to ask questions . . . about anything. That teaching begins at home—as it did with Ethan (accepting the risk, of course, that we might not like the questions nor the answers).

However, before we can teach our children to understand that not everything they see is as it appears, we need to understand how we ourselves come to understand things. In fact, our children, like Ethan, can teach us as much about this as we can teach them.

Even if we wanted to, we are not likely to ever eliminate our biases. Lies, in many instances, fall into the category of free speech, constitutionally enshrined in the US and elsewhere (such as several African nations), though less so in most other countries, including Canada and the United Kingdom (where what's called *freedom of expression* establishes barriers to hate speech, for example). Of course, in countries such as China and others with authoritarian regimes, free speech is forbidden by law or in practice (such as by arresting or killing journalists), and misinformation abounds as the product of the regimes and media they control.

Complete free speech is not the answer, though, as the US has proven. While, as president, Donald Trump would have chosen to lessen the freedom of the press if he could have, there is an anti-political-correctness backlash spreading that is pushing more freedom of speech, not less. In 2014, the *Reform Section 5* campaign in the UK, better known by its slogan, "Feel free to insult me," gained enough support to remove as crimes "insulting words and behavior." As comedian and actor Rowan Atkinson (of Mr. Bean fame) said, "If we want a robust society, we need more robust dialogue, and that must include the right to insult or to offend. Because, as someone once said, the freedom to be inoffensive is no freedom at all."[550]

Cancel culture is the binary opposite of free speech. It is, in my opinion, the natural push back in the Theater of Lies from people fighting against the message of free speech, because that freedom has become weaponized. We want to fight it, and the only way we know is to eliminate those whose words offend from our lives. There are better solutions than that. We must find ways for people to say what they want, but in turn, the people listening must be free to debate and ask questions, without consequences.

An informed diabetic understands how their body reacts to sugar and manages it accordingly through diet, exercise, and drugs. The first step in managing our intake of lies, likewise, is to understand what it does to the decision-making process wired into our brains. Our bodies have evolved to need sugar. And while our minds have not evolved to need *lies*, they *have* evolved to seek answers - quickly—because long ago, our lives depended on it. This means we often decide what we are going to do before we've understood why we're going to do it.

The way we make thousands of little decisions every day is based on something called *heuristics*. These are the mental shortcuts we take to process information quickly. It's how we quickly organize the massive volume of information in our lives. Gerd Gigerenzer and

Wolfgang Gaissmaier, a pair of German psychologists defines them as "a strategy that ignores part of the information, with the goal of making decisions more quickly, frugally, and/or accurately than more complex methods."[551]

We all use them unconsciously in every aspect of our lives. Yet, they can be problematic, as researchers Amos Tversky and Daniel Kahneman identified 50 years ago. "Heuristics," they wrote, "are highly economical and usually effective, but they lead to systematic and predicator errors."[552]

The Harvard Business School has taken a deep dive into how heuristics foster bad executive decision-making. In short, heuristics establish biases in our thinking—which are what producers in the Theater of Lies use to manipulate what we believe and how we act. If I know what your biases are, I can feed you information that reflects them.

The most well-known type of bias is *cognitive bias*, but there are many others, such as *anchoring*, in which, when considering a decision, the mind gives disproportionate weight to the *first* information it receives. Initial impressions, estimates, or data anchor subsequent thoughts and judgments. That's why advertisers fight for your attention—and why those first few years of your life were so important.

As a child, you had no ability to deflect any fictions your parents might have told you. You were born looking to your parents not only for love but for critical information (don't touch the stove, rat poison is not good for you, and so on). I'll leave it to the mental health professionals to debate how to best repair any harmful biases you may have retained from your family, but in terms of dealing with the lies of today, understanding how you have come to your opinions is valuable. Without this, you can make some bad decisions—and very likely will.

Another bias to fight is *status quo*. Unfortunately, our minds are constructed to protect our egos from being damaged. Breaking from the status quo means action, and when we take action, we demonstrate responsibility. This opens us up to criticism, regret, and damage to our egos, like young Mr. Lindenberger. (Keynote here, the attacks on Lindenberger from the Theater of Lies were not really meant for him. The attacks were a message to others—keep in line or this will happen to you).

Sticking with the status quo represents the safer course, because it puts us at less psychological risk. In a business situation, the *Harvard Business Review* reported, "sins of commission (doing something) tend to be punished much more severely than sins of omission (doing nothing), [so] the status quo holds a particularly strong attraction."[553] It can also hold true at the family dinner table and the board room.

Another natural bias is our tendency to accept any information that supports our decisions and reject any that doesn't. This is the bias that created the power of Fox News and the media fallacy that fact-checking makes a difference (and convinces us of that same belief). The *confirming evidence trap*, as *HBR* called it:

> Leads us to seek out information that supports our existing instinct or point of view while avoiding information that contradicts it. [It] affects where we go to collect evidence but also how we interpret the evidence we do receive, leading us to give too much weight to supporting information and too little to conflicting information.[554]

Yet as we have seen, facts are not evidence, especially if they can also be used to support other ideas. Quite often, facts are even not data—only *some points* of *some* data. This why you feel the urge to share things on social media that support things staying the same. Anything else is disruption.

Brit Hume, a senior reporter at Fox News, demonstrated this when he tweeted a link to a *National Review* article, "Stats Hold a Surprise: Lockdowns May Have Had Little Effect on COVID-19 Spread."[555] The headline alone (all most people ever read) is evidence of the biases of Hume, his colleagues at Fox News, and most of their audience. But a careful review of the article showed that the study was done only in the US, where shutdowns were sporadic and poorly managed. If evidence from other countries had also been used, the results of the study would have been quite different. Nonetheless, opponents to any economic shutdowns were no doubt waving the article around as evidence of their now supposedly well-researched opinions.

As this effect relates to beliefs about climate change, it has a broader scope. One might be surprised that one of the largest US government agencies that studies climate change is NASA, more familiar to most for the exploration of space. But the earth, too, is a planet, and NASA has many satellites in orbit. So, part of what NASA explores has become the causes and impacts of climate change. To that end, it should not surprise you that NASA has stated:

> Multiple studies published in peer-reviewed scientific journals show that 97 percent or more of actively publishing climate scientists agree: climate-warming trends over the past century are extremely likely due to human activities. In addition, most of the leading scientific organizations worldwide have issued public statements endorsing this position.[556]

Despite this scientific consensus, though, just one in five Americans agrees that climate change is real and caused by humans.[557] The others prefer the claim, often presented by the fossil fuel industry, that, as Sterling Burnett, Managing Editor, Environment & Climate News at The Heartland Institute has stated:

> The evidence suggests human greenhouse-gas emissions are having a limited impact on global climate, with virtually all the alarmists' model predictions routinely failing to match reality.[558]

Part of the evidence used by climate change deniers is a 2019 research paper by the Potsdam Institute for Climate Impact Research (an academic institution funded by the German government) It shows that three million years ago, the earth had the same CO2 levels as it does now.[559] According to climate change opponents, this proves human activities have nothing to do with global warming as no humans were on the planet at time. *There. See?*

So, NASA, who sent men to the moon and have working for them some of the finest scientific minds on the planet, has told us, "We have more evidence that human activity is responsible for climate change than we do that smoking cigarettes cause cancer."[560] This is coming from a government agency funded solely by taxpayer money, without the influence of any industry or think tank aligned with the generation of greenhouse gases. Yet only one in five Americans agree with the scientific consensus that climate change is human caused (in Canada, it is three out of four).[561]

For humans to survive, evolution and our social constructs have wired us up with many biases. Some are even helpful at times. Others, not so much—such as *outcome bias*, where only results matter, which is especially dangerous when you've been lucky rather than smart. It's a *trust-my-gut-bias*. An extension of that is *overconfidence bias*, which stock markets, sports, and gamblers are especially prone to. In this bias, the ego is the enemy.

There is also the *ostrich bias*, whereby we ignore any negative information, sometimes to the point where we stop looking for information at all. There is the *bandwagon bias*, most prominently followed by stock market investors and organizations, which creates *groupthink*, the antithesis of independent thought. One of my favorites is *selective perception*, whereby one's frame of reference is biased based on a need to be positive or negative (as found in a lot of self-help books).

Australian fundamentalist Christian, Ken Ham, has provided us with the most persuasive statement on the power of bias: "It is not a matter of whether one is biased or not. It is really a question of which bias is the best bias with which to be biased."[562] George Orwell would have been proud of this contemporary example of doublespeak, then promptly and rhetorically throttled the life out of him.

All of this tells me that the first opinion you should doubt is your own.

While you may have heard *take with a grain of salt* about any information about others, I recommend the term as the starting point for yourself. It is a self-acknowledgment that you have biases and that like grains of salt, they can be swept away or at least placed aside for the moment.

The path to creating a prophylactic against your own biases will be long and hard, but worth it. It begins with finding ways to park them. The advice of a bias management expert like Candy Khan, from Alberta, is a good place to start. In *Folio*, the University of Alberta's news journal, she has provided four tips on how to manage your own bias.[563] They are as follows.

Acknowledge you have them.

"If you're human, you have unconscious biases," said Khan. "We acquire them through socialization, our upbringing, media, and education."[564]

Learn what your biases are.

Recognizing your unconscious biases is hard, and perhaps the hardest part of the journey. Khan has recommended Harvard University's Implicit Association Test.[565] She has also advocated for exposing yourself to "the other." Quick, easy ways of doing that include attending a cultural festival that's new to you, reading a book about a different religion, or consuming media from a different cultural tradition. You can also seek out an IDI—an Intercultural Development Inventory,[566] which assesses people's cultural sensitivity and competence—the ability to adapt their perspectives and behaviors to other cultures.

Ease into new waters.

The next step after awareness, Khan recommends, is to expose yourself to the subject of your bias—but to do so gradually. For instance, if someone has a fear of heights, they don't overcome that fear by bungee jumping—they look at pictures, watch videos, or maybe visit a second-story balcony. Spending time with people you may have a bias against—gays, people of color, people with

AIDS, people with disabilities, immigrants, etc.—in my experience, starts best with conversations. I recommend coffee shops.

Use tact when talking about biases with others.

Once you've uncovered some of your own biases, you may be tempted to point out unconscious biases in others. Like a new non-smoker admonishing the smoking habits others, we know how that goes. That can be constructive if broached tactfully, says Khan, but it's important to strike the right tone by emphasizing the benefits of eliminating unconscious bias rather than accusing someone of bigotry.

Khan explains: "The way I approach it is to ask people, who is at the table? Who are we missing? Chances are you've skipped some valuable perspectives. There's your unconscious bias."[567]

Ultimately, any personal insights need to be driven by simple curiosity, combined with a little courage. If you are not curious about your own biases, or if you fear them, you will not take any steps to discover and understand them. Your protection from the Theater of Lies will be weakened before it even begins.

Ethan Lindenberger took teenage curiosity to examine the bias of his mother's beliefs, and instead went to sources based on the most current, peer-reviewed scientific literature and recommendations to make up his own mind about vaccinations. Compare that course to that of NFL quarterback Aaron Rodgers, who focused on information that supported his own bias against vaccination and, for reasons of his own, chose to distrust the recommendations of the Center for Disease Control and Protection (CDC) and the WHO. We need more

Ethans, fewer Aarons, or we are end up with what we are already seeing - more Edgars.

In the next chapter, we examine ways to foster your curiosity in ways that are relevant to the Theater of Lies. You will read some good advice from a Nobel Prize-winning theoretical physicist, who reminds us, "the first principle is that you must not fool yourself, and you are the easiest person to fool."[568] *Accipe te cum grano salis.* Take yourself with a grain of salt. It is the first step in the process of going beyond binary thinking.

With that reminded, let's look examine the freedom and joy of discovery that curiosity can bring you, and how it can be your primary defense in the Theater of Lies.

"Imagination is more important than knowledge. For knowledge is limited to all we now know and understand, while imagination embraces the entire world, and all there ever will be to know and understand."[569]

- ALBERT EINSTEIN, PHYSICIST.

4

WELL, IMAGINE THAT.

Though Richard Feynman died in 1988, his contributions to the scientific community will live on for centuries. Yet it is not his groundbreaking work on quantum electromagnetism that interests me, nor is it his work on the Manhattan Project (which gave birth to nuclear fission). No, for me, whose understanding of physics involves little more than the ability to use a light switch, Feynman's real contribution to the world was his thinking process—a process that disregarded the fictions and assumptions of our lives, treating them exactly as one should.

Microsoft founder Bill Gates called Feynman "the greatest teacher [he] ever had," because of his thinking process, too (not because he had had any influence on computer software design). "Because he had pushed himself to have such a deep understanding, his ability to take you through the path of the different possibilities--was incredible," said Gates. "He's taking something that is a little mysterious to most people and using very simple concepts to explain how it works."[570] Feynman was able to use the propagandist's tactic of simplifying things to better manipulate people but used it instead to help people find truth. He's also on my list of dead people I'd like to have dinner with.

Feynman founded his thinking on the difference between knowledge and understanding (knowing a fact and the ability to discuss, debate, and even teach it). He told a story about not being able to name a particular bird he once saw on a walk with his father. His father told him the name of the bird, a brown thrush, then told him about the same name in Chinese, German, and French. Then his father said, "Now you know the name of the bird in all these languages, but you know nothing about the bird."[571] He didn't know how the bird's plumage came to be, what the bird ate, its mating habits, and so on. Many of us experience the same every day: we think we know something but do not truly understand it.

Understanding, Feynman told us, comes from looking at things from a different perspective. He called this "thinking like a Martian."[572] This process of assuming one knows *nothing* about a question or situation combines two superpowers, curiosity and critical thinking. An example Feynman used centered on sleep. *Why does everyone on the planet become unconscious for eight hours a day?* Ask yourself this question as a Martian, from the perspective of an alien being whose species does not sleep. Feynman's genius was his ability to distill the complicated process of considering alternative points of view and make this easy to repeat.

An example of my own is the process of identifying every point in the process of making a good golf swing. It can be done, but if you are busy thinking about the process while doing it, you will never make a successful swing. Again, the difference here is knowledge versus understanding. Knowing the steps in a complicated process is very different from being able to accomplish it.

The focus on knowledge over understanding is a problem in our education system. American journalist and Harvard professor Chris Hedges once commented on the students he taught at the university: "They may have known the plot and salient details of Joseph Conrad's *Heart of Darkness*, but they were unable to tell you why the story was important."[573] The corporate world, too, has this problem, with so-called "knowledge transfer" being framed as a process of passing information from one person to another as though they were both computers. All that is missing is a data port, as in *The Matrix*, where the avatars of the real-life protagonists can instantly learn to fly attack helicopters or know the best route through a building. People become parrots. They know the right word but have no idea what it means. And the people they speak to are impressed by the parroting, too! This might be amusing, but like junk food, in the long run, it doesn't satisfy our needs.

At a more fundamental level, I see this same issue in our understanding of World War II, even though we and our children have likely seen most every movie produced about it. We know Hitler was evil, that he was responsible for killing millions of Jews, and that the Nazis lost. But without understanding the details of the development of Hitler's National Socialism movement and his government's use of propaganda, how can we know not only why defeating the Nazis was important then, but why these ideas need to be defeated again, today?

As Hedges explains:

> Elite universities have banished self-criticism. They refuse to question a self-justifying system. Organization, technology, self-advancement, and information systems are the only things that matter. They disdain honest intellectual inquiry, which is by its nature distrustful of authority, fiercely independent, and often subversive.[574]

Efficiency over effectiveness, again. In the case of universities, it is delivered as steamrolling curiosity.

We may believe that universities by nature are bastions of freethinking (think back to the protest movements of the 1960s and the pressure it created for civil rights, the resistance to the Vietnam War, and nuclear arms). However, in practice today, they are not. To me, it is ironic that a model for critical thinking, curiosity, and understanding comes not from the humanities, but from a nuclear physicist.

Feynman had a simple process for learning. He used it repeatedly to learn as much as he could about anything that interested him. It's a great process for learning a subject well enough to not get baffled by any lies thrown your way. It's called the *Feynman Technique*.[575]

Step 1: Teach it to a child.

Take out a blank sheet of paper. At the top, write the subject you want to learn. Now, write out everything you know about the subject you want to understand as though you were teaching it to a twelve-year-old who had just enough vocabulary and attention span to understand its basic concepts and relationships.

This step overcomes the use of jargon or academic language, language too thick to understand, as impressive as it may seem when used at a cocktail party. When you write out an idea from start to finish in language a child can understand, you force yourself to grasp the concept at a deeper level. You strengthen your ability to simplify relationships and connect ideas.

Step 2: Review better and learn more.

When you find you can't explain what you want to learn or pieces of what you want to learn to a twelve-year-old, dig into some original research on the matter. Keep doing this until you break the illusion of your knowledge on the topic. This reveals the bounds of your knowledge. It shows that your learning process, your process of truly understanding, never ends. It keeps you open to new facts and ideas. It keeps you fresh.

Step 3: Organize and simplify.

Completing the above steps will create a lot of notes—in Feynman's case, binders full of them. If you're really serious about things, you'll need to organize your notes into a simple narrative that you can recount. Read it out loud. This will reveal your own level of understanding. If the explanation sounds confusing, that's a good indication your understanding in that area still needs some work. Take the notes out a couple times a year and review them.

Step 4: Transmit.

Explain what you know to somebody else as though they were a twelve-year-old (and maybe they are!). If they understand it, you do too. If they don't, you don't. The process also works well in the opposite direction. When someone tells you something you really don't understand, ask them to explain it to you as though *you* were a twelve-year-old. It will get them thinking and communicating more clearly and will keep you better engaged with what they have to say.

All that said, you may be thinking, hey . . . only a theoretical physicist could take something as simple a notion as curiosity and turn into a critical thinking process that, of course, makes it a whole more complicated process (as simple as "think like a Martian" sounds). Feynman kept binders full of notes on every subject that interested him, but let me offer a simpler way to foster your own curiosity process. The basis of this comes from *Fast Company*'s Shiv Singh (the writer who coined the term *post-truth era*).

He recommends confronting any information with the notion "consider if the opposite is true." He says, "Before believing something outright, always consider the alternative viewpoint and potential outcomes."[576]

Both Feynman's detailed *Martian-thinking* process and Singh's simpler *take-the-opposite-position* approach have the same foundation for effective curiosity in the Theater of Lives: the need for imagination.

That's why I lean to curiosity as more powerful than critical thinking (though also important). Critical thinking requires no imagination. Curiosity demands it. And it improves our thinking in many ways.

For example, imagination can even prevent disaster (or could have). Take the case of Apollo 1 (not a typo for the much-better-known Apollo 11—the historic NASA mission that landed three men on the moon in 1969).

On January 27, 1967, the crew (Virgil Grissom, Edward White, and Roger Chaffee) of the first scheduled Apollo mission, were conducting what was called a "plugs-out" test. That is, fully suited up and in the capsule, they unplugged Apollo 1 from the umbilical power cord attached to the launch platform. The result was a horrific fire inside the capsule that killed all three men.[577]

During US Senate hearings investigating the accident, Frank Borman (who would later command Apollo 8 on a journey around the moon and back in 1968), when asked why the fire occurred, answered "a failure of imagination—we couldn't imagine a ground test could be hazardous."[578]

No doubt the NASA engineers were masters in critical thinking, but without being curious enough to imagining all the possibilities, for the Apollo 1 crew, they fell short. Using your imagination is now standard procedure at NASA.[579]

How is this relevant to living in the Theater of Lies? Because it takes imagination to be curious. Especially when it concerns examining the motives of those producing the lies. It also takes imagination to imagine the opposite and look for information to support that polar position. It also means taking the time to imagine.

"Sometimes it is easier to see clearly into the liar than into the man who tells the truth. Truth, like light, blinds. Falsehood, on the contrary, is a beautiful twilight that enhances every object."[580]

– ALBERT CAMUS, FRENCH PHILOSOPHER.

....

5

EMBRACE THE LIAR'S GREATEST GIFT.

The liar's greatest gift, ironically, is the truth. You just have to work hard to find it. Like bashing a pinata horse, it takes time, but the truth, like the candy, will spill out. The liar's gift to you is the opportunity to find out who they truly are and discover the agenda they wish to push on you.

The Republican Party's promotion of the latest Big Lie in America is a case in point. Donald Trump and his followers have pursued the Big Lie that election fraud was the cause of the former president's loss in the 2020 election to Joe Biden. And while one could concede that Trump's narcissism was the driver of this delusion, the real question is why rank-and-file Republicans would support it so much. Indeed, consistent polling results demonstrated that in 2021, month after month, about one in three Americans believed that election fraud had brought Joe Biden into the White House.[581] Perhaps worse, these same polls showed that only one in three believed the audits done to discover voting irregularities were legitimate.

The truth of the matter lies not in the cause but the effect. While the cause may seem to be Trump's election loss, that is not the case. In every other presidential election, in most all elections in the US, the loser concedes to the winner. Why not here? It's too easy to assign the reason as Trump's ego. That's a red herring the size of a sturgeon. And the effect of Republicans' promotion and repetition of the Big Lie, without any evidence, was not to bring Trump back into office, nor really was it to position the Biden administration as illegitimate. Those are some obvious effects, but the truth lies deeper.

A March 2021 Monmouth poll showed that concern about voter fraud being a major problem has increased among Republicans since 2012 (from 51 percent) while it has declined by the same amount among Democrats (from 23 percent). The Big Lie is pushing mainstream Republicans to support enhancing election security laws across many states. (And how, at first glance, can demanding more secure elections not seem a good idea?) This is the most significant effect of the Big Lie and where the truth of the Republican Party's ambitions lies.

As early as 2016, *The Wall Street Journal* identified a report by three political think tanks (the liberal Center for American Progress, the more centrist Brookings Institution, and the conservative American Enterprise Institute) demonstrating that the demographic profiles of US voters were becoming more and more favorable to Democrats. As source material, they examined demographic change projections by race, age, and states' voter turnout rates and party preferences for the

2004, 2008, and 2012 elections. They concluded "the voting population [is being] transformed by an influx of young minorities and the aging of baby boomers."[582]

In 2017, the Pew Research Center confirmed these projections—and went deeper. While 37 percent of registered voters identified themselves as Independents (alongside 33 percent as Democrats and 26 percent as Republicans), when the partisan leanings of the Independents was examined, 50 percent of all registered voters leaned toward the Democratic Party, versus 42 percent identifying with the Republicans. [583] Digging even deeper, Pew Research found that Black, Hispanic, and Asian voters would vote overwhelmingly Democrat, while white voters tended more and more to vote Republican.[584]

The political strategists of the Republican Party have taken this information and applied it to the projected demographics of the US's future population. The US Census Department's *Demographic Turning Points for the United States: Population Projections for 2020 to 2060* predicts that 2030 will be a watershed year for the nation, when immigration will overtake the birth rate as the primary driver of population growth. The percentage of the population that is white but non-Hispanic will shrink, though, as the America becomes "more racially and ethnically pluralistic, they will still be the largest single racial group in the country until 2060."[585] Understanding this, in 2021, seventeen Republican-controlled state legislatures passed twenty-eight laws that effectively made it harder for Blacks, Latinos, and younger Americans to vote. In addition, fourteen states passed legislation to all partisan officials to control oversight of the election process.[586]

The truth of the Big Lie is that its purpose is to provide what political strategists call "air cover" for the "ground war" occurring in state legislatures. Republicans believe they cannot defeat these predicted demographic changes in America. So, rather than address changes in their policies and leadership, they've chosen to limit the access of the emerging tide of non-white voters to polling booths. As a few percentage points can determine election results, the Big Lie is an election strategy for the survival of the Republican Party's power.

You can find the same motivations behind the GOP's new anti-woke platforms. With Florida as its test case and other Republic-governed states following suit, legislation is being passed to limit and, in many cases, eliminate teachings on the history of slavery and its impact on contemporary society in America (awkwardly named critical race theory), book banning in public and school libraries (some of which I have cited in this book, such as Abram X. Kendi's *Stamped from the Beginning*), and allowing no in-school discussions about gender issues. Why? For me, it's a get-out-the-vote strategy, doing whatever the party leaders can to engage their ever-smaller voter base of white conservatives. Remember, a standard tactic in the Theater of Lies is promotion of one binary solution over another. We drink those messages like parched soldiers after a desert march. Binary options are a political prize package. Binary options are the wedge used to clearly define them versus us.

The rise of the issue of gender dysphoria, the role of schools, and the right of parents to determine what their children are taught is another example. It came not from a rising concern of parents on the issue, but the need to find a single issue that would engage American conservations in the way same-sex marriage had a decade before. After losing that battle at a state and judicial level, organizations like the American People Project (APP), used the old fashioned business technique of brainstorming to find something new.

"We knew we needed to find an issue that the candidates were comfortable talking about," said Terry Schilling, APP president. "And we threw everything at the wall."[587]

What stuck was transgenderism. They implemented the campaign around the leading edge of the transgender issue in 2021—the participation of transgender girls in school sports. They convinced a few Republican lawmakers to advance legislation barring transgender participation in sports. Not only stepping their conservation toes into school policy on the issue, but also stepping into one that had a broad spectrum of media interest.

And, let's remember that the focus on issues of gender, beginning specifically with people identifying as transgender, was a strategic election decision directed by leading conservative opinion leaders.

As the *New York Times* reported in 2023, "The appeal played on the same resentments and cultural schisms that have animated Mr. Trump's political movement: invocations against so-called 'wokeness,' skepticism about science, parental discontent with public schools after the Covid-19 pandemic shutdowns and anti-elitism."[588]

The strategy worked so well it was as if it had been laid on a trail of gasoline. The match lit, the push to ban healthcare for youth with gender dysphoria fired up legislation in twelve states by end of March 2023, with another nineteen states considering similarly restrictive bills.[589] Legislatures in Europe are not seeing this same degree of restrictions proposed; however, opposition is gaining momentum in many countries.[590]

In the US, as Democratic Party policymakers fought back against the tidal wave of legislation and right-wing media converge, Congresswoman Margorie Taylor Greene began calling Democrats, on mass, as "pedophiles" and "grooming children for sex"[591]—reminiscent of the Edgar Welch armed attack on a Washington, DC, pizzeria eight years prior.

As awful as lies about pedophilia are, and as dangerous as misinformation is about a small percentage of children who may have gender dysphoria, examining these messages is a power defense in the Theater of Lies. They are how liars provide us with the gift of the truth.

The truth lies in the *effect* of their lies and the *motivations* behind them. The real truth to discover is not the facts, but the why. That *why* regarding transgender issues was to find a single message to rally both Republican voters and their elected officials.

Lies tend to work because they are distractions. In the Theater of Lies, liars take their cues from magicians, the original masters of misdirection, to conceal their true intentions. But the truth is out there. You just have to dig hard to find it.

This, again, is where curiosity and imagination are critical for not only discovering facts but going beyond this into motivations. As we seen, the challenge with facts and truth is that both sides on an issue can use them to prove their points. Asking the curious question—*why would they do this?*—is a power tool for living in the Theater of Lies. With enough time and effort, asking this question over and over again will turn it into a jackhammer that can bust you out of the Theater's walls of the mind.

Imagination is also a tool, however, of the producers of lies, misinformation, and propaganda. So, we need also set our defenses against their powerful expression of imagination delivered to is, their audiences. That is storytelling.

"We have, as human beings, a storytelling problem. We're a bit too quick to come up with explanations for things we don't really have an explanation for."[592]

– MALCOLM GLADWELL, CANADIAN JOURNALIST AND AUTHOR.

....

6

BEWARE THE LIAR'S
TWO GREATEST POWERS.

For a couple hundred dollars, sometimes a few thousand, you can take a course on how to become a better storyteller. These courses are not for writers but for businesspeople. The goal is to teach you how to integrate the art of telling a story into the marketing of your business or organization. Why? Because stories are more persuasive than mere facts. Stories foster the emotional resonance component of the persuasion equation. Stories *work*.

Effective propagandists could teach such a course. Storytelling is one of their two most powerful weapons. Why? Because stories are easily repeated. Like the Australian woman, Belle Gibson, who told her false tale about a cancer cure, stories played out before the audience are most effective when the audiences hear, embrace, and then repeat them to others. Stories—the really good ones—transform the audience into actors and bring them up on stage, like a magician drawing volunteers from those in the seats of the auditorium. These powerful stories have a hypnotic quality, too. The audience-turned-actors have no idea that they have been identified, recruited, and directed to repeat what they've been told. Stories create Edgars.

Conspiracy theories are another of a favorite version of storytelling, as they engage us as victims against evil. The audience eats them up. As Alan Moore, author of the graphic novel *Watchmen* and others has said, "Conspiracy theorists believe in a conspiracy because that is more comforting. . . The truth is frightening. Nobody is in control. The world is rudderless."[593] Moore is recognized by his peers as one of the best comic book writers in the world. Perhaps it takes such a writer, working both within the mainstream media and outside it, to tell us the truth of the matter.

As humans, we are wired to search for truth. The propagandists abuse that fundamental nature with stories that reflect their needs (not ours). In almost any situation, we want to know who's behind the plan, who the evil one is, and who is plotting every nefarious step along the way. Somebody *must* be in charge. Whether it is American Democratic Party leaders, as part of a cabal of pedophiles or involved in stealing a presidential election; whether it is a supernatural being that created the earth and humanity; whether the COVID-19 pandemic was planned to change our DNA or it was wireless cellphone towers that created and spread the virus worldwide. We become engaged first by the mystery, then the solution. Finding that solution makes us feel *smarter*. Yet, the impact is the opposite—we close our minds to other possibilities and snap the lid closed on our critical thinking.

As a public relations professional who has worked both within government and outside of it, in business and other sectors, while individual organizations may conspire (or plan) to make something happen; organizations and their leaders have trouble enough agreeing on the *lunch menu*, let alone a collective strategy. Our nature wants us to believe that there is not only someone behind the curtain, off stage and controlling every action, but that they are secretly working against our interests.

But little, if anything, in the real world, happens in complete secrecy. This is the failure in traditional conspiracy theory narratives. No conspiracy theory—such as that of pharmaceutical companies colluding to vaccinate us to control the population or a "deep state" controlling the US government—has ever had any evidence. But as stories, they sure *sound* good. This is where the internet and social media have enabled so much of it . . . good stories attract clicks, emoticons, and shares.

What are often used as evidence of conspiracy are the day-to-day strategies and tactics of business and governments, repackaged to appear evil. Under the ominous heading "*TIME* Admits 'Conspiracy' of a 'Cabal of Powerful People' Heavily Influenced Last Election," the self-professed right-wing website *Lifesitenews.com* took a *TIME* magazine story with the headline "The Secret History of the Shadow Campaign That Saved the 2020 Election" and attempted to position the Biden campaign's strategy to get out the vote as conspiratorial. In it, Patrick Delany comments on *TIME* writer Molly Ball's story:

> She described these groups who worked together for many months before the election as a well-funded cabal of powerful people, ranging across industries and ideologies, working together behind the scenes to influence

perceptions, change rules and laws, steer media coverage and control the flow of information. Their work touched every aspect of the election. They got states to change voting systems and laws and helped secure hundreds of millions in public and private funding.

They fended off voter suppression lawsuits, recruited armies of poll workers and got millions of people to vote by mail for the first time. They successfully pressured social media companies to take a harder line against disinformation and used data-driven strategies to fight viral smears.

They executed national public-awareness campaigns that helped Americans understand how the vote count would unfold over days or weeks, preventing Trump's conspiracy theories and false claims of victory from getting more traction.

And, after election day, they monitored every pressure point to ensure that Trump could not overturn the result.[594]

Then, Delaney adds, "Ian Bassin, who is identified in the column as the cofounder of Protect Democracy, is quoted as basically affirming Giuliani's assertion, stating 'it's massively important for the country to understand that it didn't happen accidentally.'"[595]

Having been involved in dozens of political campaigns, I can state emphatically that very little in these campaigns happens accidentally, or even without publicity. But that does not mean it is conspiratorial (unless you believe every management meeting in your workplace is also conspiratorial rather than just a planning session). To be a conspiracy, the meetings have to held in secret and the intent of those meetings and the actions taken from them has to be harmful to others and illegal.

Note that what Ball writes about, such as fending-off voter suppression lawsuits, a national public-awareness campaign, and convincing social media companies to take a hard line against misinformation—all these actions were taken to counter the Big Lie in the 2020 US presidential election. All these actions are standard practice, not conspiratorial.

The same facts are used to create a different story. This the power of propagandists.

After the storytelling power of conspiracy theories, what is the *second* most powerful tool of liars? Making you feel crazy and less valuable as an individual if you don't believe them. The term for it is "gaslighting."

The phrase comes from real-world theater—a 1938 British play called *Gas Light*, where the protagonist, a wife, is manipulated into believing a false narrative by her husband. As a tactic, gaslighting might mean telling the audience what they remember to have happened *never did*. If done effectively, the targets of gaslighting begin to question their reality. The goal of the gaslighter is to erode the trust of their target in others and themselves to the point that they believe only what the gaslighter tells them. This tool is powerful when used by members of the audience in the Theater of Lies to demean and discredit fellow audience members who don't believe the lies being presented.

"Stick with us. Don't believe the crap you see from these people, the fake news. . .. What you're seeing and what you're reading is not what's happening,"[596] said Trump during a 2018 speech at the Veterans of Foreign Wars (VFW) Convention. He and others pushed back on political correctness (and everything else they don't like), claiming such standards as unreasonable and threatening to the right of free speech. The message becomes, *if you don't like what I am doing, that's your problem.* This tactic also includes defending name-calling and other forms of baiting, upon confrontation, as mere "jokes." Trump's repeated message that January 6, 2021, was a "beautiful day"[597] is his well-practiced expression of gaslighting—as if people didn't die, laws weren't broken, and dozens of the leaders of the attack on the US Congress have not been charged, convicted, and some sentenced to prison.

The US Republican party has followed his lead. Six months after the event, Fox News host Maria Bartiromo said, "They continue to call this an armed insurrection, and yet no guns were seized."[598] On June 2, 2021, dozens of American right-wing sites published the same story, "Insurrection Debunked, New Video Shows Completely Peaceful Protest Inside US Capitol on Jan 06."[599] This story is gaslighting, telling us not to believe the live coverage from the mainstream news, and it continued months later when the Republic Party took over the majority in the US House of Representatives.[15]

Gaslighting is harmful. It divides families and nations. It is especially hard on children, who look to adults for truth. Of the hundreds of thousands of children around the world who were abused by Catholic

....

15   Almost two years after this story was disseminated on right -wing sites, and three months after the conclusion of the "House Select Committee to Investigate the January 6th Attack on the United States Capitol," Republican House Leader Kevin McCarthy released 41,000 hours of security footage, exclusively, to then-FOX News Opinion host Tucker Carlson, who falsely depicted the January 6 riot as a peaceful gathering. See Sahil Kapur, "Tucker Carlson, with Video Provided by Speaker McCarthy, Falsely Depicts Jan. 6 Riot as a Peaceful Gathering, *NBC News*, March 6, 2023,https://www.nbcnews.com/politics/justice-department/tucker-carlson-new-video-provided-speaker-mccarthy-falsely-depicts-jan-rcna73673.

Church priests—just in the twentieth century—how many of them were told the abuse never happened? That they were wrong about the cleric's intentions or had made up the incident in their minds?

The only good news about gaslighting is this: if the liars are gaslighting you, *you must be close to the truth.* This takes us to what we can learn about the producers in our Theater of Lies simply by listening to them.

The world will throw up a lot of barriers between truth, lies, misinformation, and even informed beliefs. The next chapter will provide you with a tipsheet to avoid them.

"The test of a first-rate intelligence is the ability to hold two opposed ideas in the mind at the same time, and still retain the ability to function."[600]

– F. SCOTT FITZGERALD, AMERICAN WRITER AND AUTHOR.

7

A TIP SHEET FOR SELF-DEFENSE.

You can never leave the Theater of Lies. The doors are locked, and you're strapped in a comfortable seat as though in a planetarium, the lies spinning all around you looking as real as the night sky at dusk. The secret to surviving in the Theater is your awareness of it—curiosity—to become a more critical member of the audience. To wrap up this section on what we can do as individuals to both protect ourselves and also thrive, I provide a tip sheet.

My persuasion model is informative here, as it is not only a mathematical encapsulation of the formula propagandists use to produce lies and misinformation – but understanding this equation from the perspective of the one being persuaded is important.

$$f \quad \text{THE} \atop \text{ARGUMENT}^n \left(\text{REPUTATION}^x + {\text{EMOTIONAL}^y \atop \text{RESONANCE}} \right) + {\text{PROOF} \atop \text{POINTS}}$$

The formula demonstrates the weakness of proof points as factors in persuasion. Their role, whether truth or lies are used, is better assigned to confirming the decisions that have been made prior to proof points being fully deployed. This is why the push for social media outlets to fact check and correct misinformation will not lessen the ability of lies to influence us. While that process is necessary, we cannot fool ourselves into believing that government and corporate actions in this area are the answer. Like proof points themselves, fact checking *is part* of the answer, but only a small part. The best defense will come from our own efforts, not others.

The driving engine of persuasion is the structure of the argument, then the added power of high octane of the emotional resonance created between the speaker and the audience (or more accurately, the target of persuasion).

So most of these self-protection tips come from the place of limiting the ability of the producers of lies and misinformation from reaching that point of unity of thought, resonance) between them and you. These tips may be challenging for you, as all of us have our biases. But like any new habit, they become easier to adopt the more times you attempt it.

Here are some ways you can limit the creation of emotional resonance between you and the producers of lies and misinformation.

Avoid ideology.

Ideology is the most powerful curiosity-killer of all time. It is the sum of all biases shared within one group with a management structure specifically designed to enforce and entrench those beliefs. Belief in a specific shared ideology is the litmus test for being considered a true member of a group (remember, for example, Judy Woodruff's focus group with Republican voters who stated clearly that one could not consider oneself a Christian if one supported legalizing abortion).

If ideology informs your thinking (religious, political, or moral), you examine most everything you see, read, and hear from that perspective. If you cannot wholly abandon your ideology (and frankly, few of us can), then learn how to park it. Perhaps you've been in those interminable meetings where a thousand thoughts are being debated, when a skilled facilitator flipped their whiteboard and on it, wrote "parking lot." This is for ideas that won't be discussed at that time. You need to create your own mental parking lot, where you corral your biases and ideologies just long enough to entertain different perspectives.

It can be in your mind, or you can write down what your ideology tells you, like "I believe abortion is wrong," "I believe the 2020 election was stolen from Donald Trump," or "Human activities are not responsible for climate change." Then, go ahead and research other opinions, seeking out conflicting facts, asking questions. Don't worry. Your ideologies are nice and safe on the page you wrote them. No one is trying to take them away from you. You can be partisan. Just be an educated, well-informed partisan, open to debate.

Explore the motivations of the producers.

One of the best questions to ask yourself is why someone wants you to believe something and what they will stand to achieve if you do. If it is not *you* they need to believe, why would they need whoever their audience is to do so? What is in it for them? Manipulators always have a goal. Discover how they benefit. French philosopher Jean-Paul Sartre said, "the worst part about being lied to is knowing you weren't worth the truth."[601] But once you realize we all live in the Theater of Lies, you learn to treat being lied to as an invitation, because each lie hides a truth—and behind that truth lies the treasure—*the why of the lie.*

Encourage debate.

Always listen to the other side of an argument, even from people you may not like. They have something to teach you. You need to understand them as much as yourself. Be neutral in your attitude about them, even sympathetic. Remember, they have biases, too, and this does not make them bad people. Being misinformed without intent is not evil. If there is intent, that is a problem that must be addressed.

The harder the producers of lies fight you, the more powerful you are. They may call you crazy or attack your reputation. This only provides a stronger stage for your debate and avenues for your curiosity.

Beware the facts-as-evidence paradox.

From television shows like *Perry Mason* in the sixties to *Law and Order*'s ongoing run of more than three decades, many of us have taken entertainment and comfort from the plotline, *crime committed, crime investigated, evidence found, criminal arrested and prosecuted.* That plotline is the foundation for almost every mystery novel in almost every language in the world. But what the Theater of Lies often places before us are not crimes. They are ideas. As we learned through Aristotle and in more modern per-suasion models like mine, facts are not the most persuasive tool when someone is trying to win someone over to their ideas—yet we latch onto them as though they were life-preserving vests in a turbulent sea of misinformation.

"How can you believe the ramblings of the defense," a prosecutor might say to their assembled audience, "that the earth not only travels around the sun, each day spinning upon itself like a child's toy or a ballerina, when each and every one of us has seen the rise of the sun each morning, watched its journey across the sky, and marveled each night as it went around the other side of the planet to return to repeat this miracle of nature?"

Don't be tricked into believing that the Theater of Lies has estab-lished procedures and rules of evidence. The only rule in this theater is the one they do not tell you: *caveat emptor.*

Hyperbole foreshadows danger.

In Donald Trump's *Art of the Deal*, his ghostwriter told at least this much truth:

> "The . . . key to the way I promote is bravado. I play
> to people's fantasies. People may not always think big
> themselves, but they can still get very excited by those

who do. That's why a little hyperbole never hurts. People want to believe that something is the biggest and the greatest and the most spectacular. I call it truthful hyperbole. It's an innocent form of exaggeration—and a very effective form of promotion."[602]

But let's go back to the dictionary again. *Dictionary.com* defines hyperbole as "an extravagant statement or figure of speech not intended to be taken literally." In this, hyperbole might fall into the same category as the Bible: are the statements literal or metaphorical? Trump had the temerity to put the word "truthful" in front of it.

Hyperbole and its kin—exaggerations, overstatements, embellishments, and the like—if they are not lies, themselves, all foreshadow lies to come. They should be trigger words for you, indicating attempts at emotional resonance between you and the speaker.

Encourage curiosity in others.

Encouraging curiosity can take time, and you always risk failure, but that's OK. The best way to do so is to demonstrate the value of curiosity, enjoying the process while you do. You can do this through a life devoted to learning, encouraging others to live the same. It begins with asking yourself and others *what if?*

Beware the "everyone agrees" statement, even if it is true.

It's a curtain-closer on critical thinking, curiosity, and imagination—and the Theater of Lies loves it. There was an ancient Jewish law under which a person could not be convicted of a capital crime if all the jurors agreed on his guilt. The University of Adelaide in South Australia found that when all the jurors agree in criminal cases, there's a greater chance of collusion or bias in forming their verdict.

Watch for changes in terminology.

Though this might not always indicate a lie, a softening or a change in a term might make you feel less threatened by it. The public relations profession, of which I am practically a charter member, is the most artful practitioner of such terms. Sewage sludge has been changed to "biosolids" (more technically, a processed form of sludge). Garbage dumps have become landfills—and here's one that's coming; in some municipalities, wastewater treatment is becoming known as "water recycling."

The phrase for what the facility the nuclear industry plans for burying all the radioactive waste will be called a "deep geological repository," completely avoiding the words *nuclear*, or *waste*, or the industry's own term—*spent fuel*.

In Canada, we've had quite the terminology change regarding the status of the Province of Quebec and the desire of many of its residents to become their own nation. Whereas the people who wanted their own separate country of Quebec called themselves *separatists* and those who wanted the province to remain in Canada, *nationalists*—after the failed referendum on same, the terms evolved. After that, separatists referred to themselves as *nationalists* and those that wanted to remain, *federalists*. (As a further conflagration of terms—in Northern Ireland, those who wish to join Ireland as an independent state are called *nationalists* and those who wish to remain part of the United Kingdom and the leadership of Great Britain are called *unionists*). Word use by professional misinformation producer often challenges your ability to understand their goals, and that is their goal.

Comedian and satirist George Carlin has been warning the world about this self-soothing process since the 1960s. It was then that he attacked what he called "euphemisms." In his stand-up act, he reminded audiences that in World War I, we had "shellshock," which, in World War II, became "battle fatigue." By the time the Korean War came around, the term had morphed into something called "operational exhaustion." Finally, after Vietnam, the term changed once again, and has remained in its clinically safe iteration for decades as "post-traumatic stress disorder."[603] The changes through time reframed the horrible process of permanently damaging the psyches of the soldiers who go to war for us as *clinical* rather than *personal*. It made it seem less harmful and more common. This is the propagandist's stock-in-trade. Changing terminology makes the unacceptable acceptable. This is what is happening in Quebec, as we watch, in real time, the process of it separating itself from Canada not by proclamation, but by stealth.[604]

If you find yourself being gaslighted or given binary choices (one choice, the right one, the other choice, the wrong one)—heads up—you are being manipulated like you were a hockey puck being stickhandled from one end of the ice rink to the other.

Focus on the effect.

In the battle of cause versus effect, focus first on effect. Many have been quick to blame the Chinese government for the COVID-19 pandemic, and its early denials of the virus did little to help. However, *cause* is a euphemism for *blame*, and our instinct to lay blame often blinds us to the *effect* of something. Effect is where we will find the nuggets of truth. While anti-vaxxers blame pharmaceutical companies for their hesitancy to vaccinate themselves or their children, the effects of vaccinations have saved millions of lives. The effect of vaccine hesitancy has allowed measles to flourish in certain regions. Once you have a true understanding of the impacts of something, you can focus on its cause.

Improve your imagination and curiosity skills.

You must be able to ask yourself a lot of "what ifs"—what if this is true? What if this is false? What if this happens? Etc. It will help you on the journey of discovery to your most important find, *the whys of lies.*

The best place to hone those skills, in my opinion, is the regular practice of reading fiction (and I don't think genre or style is that important). Fiction creates people, places, and situations in front of you that you know are false, but with the skills of the writer, our brains suspend disbelief and enjoy them for what they are: engaged, perhaps entertained, and the ability to take different thoughts as worthy of exploration—without the binary need to either accept them as truth or lies, fact or fiction—just as they are.

This is part of the mirrored process of protecting ourselves in the Theater of Lies, allowing you to explore the messages without outright adoption or rejection. Imagination puts you in charge, not the producers.

Use binary thinking, effectively.

The efficient use of binary thinking is what we do every moment of every day—hot or cold, win or lose, right or wrong. Effective binary thinking is much different. The short definition of that is following up one binary answer with a second binary question. A good example of this is what physicians call *differential diagnosis*—a process where your doctor differentiates between two or more possible conditions behind your symptoms. It's a good model to try, as the process focuses on the worst possible outcome (indigestion, for example, as a sign of a heart attack), examines it, and if that is not the case, then goes on from the most life-threatening, to the second most life-threatening, all the way to the least (in the case of indigestion, perhaps recommending a couple of Tums).

The producers of the Theater of Lies most often want you to believe the worst possible outcome, rather than the least; socialism will destroy capital markets and governments, COVID-19 vaccinations will kill you, or immigrants will cause crime, take your jobs, and be a plague on the country. The same goes for their most positive messages on their solutions, that the world and your life will be better if . . . you buy their product, vote for their policies, or commit to their religions. It is the very foundation of Trump's *Make America Great Again*—presupposing that the country was great before, is not now, and can, under Trump, become so again. (As a communicator, I can tell you the phrase is *brilliant* in its division of binary options and even its poetry).

Differential diagnosis allows you to walk through all the options and ask the question, of yourself, if what they say is true, what is the evidence that supports it? If the evidence is not strong enough, perhaps a less positive or negative outcome is likely. What would be the evidence of that? Work your way through the options, positive and negative, until you find the best evidence . . . in medical terms . . . the best diagnosis, treatment, and prognosis . . . for the situation the message wants you to agree with. It's a great way to examine a situation or issue from a binary perspective, yet it also allows for a progression of inquiry that follows logic, curiosity, and imagination.

The next chapters will go beyond what we can do as individuals to protect ourselves and examine the opportunities for institutions and societies to establish broader defenses. If we want to embrace the Right to Bear Thoughts, we will need cultural changes.

"Education without values, as useful as it is, seems rather to make man a more clever devil."[605]

– C. S. LEWIS, IRISH NOVELIST.

....

8

FROM THE INFORMATION AGE TO THE KNOWLEDGE AGE.

I define the path to fully understanding something, anything, to go from seeing a single point of data to a large set of data (let's call this information), to knowledge (information in context with experience), then wisdom (the complete ability to understand something and communicate this understanding to others). Since the mid-twentieth century, the developed world has lived in what we call *the Information Age*—and while this period has seen the invention and embrace of information technologies, fiber optics, satellite transmissions, and computers from the elemental to ever-faster silicon chips to process all this information—this has also enabled us to not just find the information we might be looking for, information now bombards us. While we used to read newspapers in the morning, watch television news at the supper hour, or search libraries to find information, information now searches for us (and through ever sophisticated algorithms, we are found).

Our challenge is no longer about information. It is understanding it—and that takes another step along the path toward understanding: knowledge. The education system of developed nations, however, is not based on this. It's just catching up to the Information Age. Yet, while education professionals have embraced it, their goal remains the same: workplace preparation.

As the Government of Ontario's Education Minister, Stephen Lecce noted in 2023 in an announcement of a new requirement for high school students to earn at least one credit in technology education to graduate, the message was clear. Lecce said, "I am proud to announce another step forward to ensure all students learn the critical skills necessary to succeed and get a good paying job."[606] This focus ignores the obvious: our children need life skills as much as or more than they need job skills. Moreover, our children need to learn and develop thinking skills.

I am not a teacher, nor have I studied education. But this much I do know - our education system needs to catch up to the digital production world in the Theater of Lies. As humans, we are not hardwired to protect ourselves from it. As I have enumerated, the consequences of this are far reaching.

We not only need to teach ourselves self-defense from lies and misinformation, but also our children. It's more important than teaching ourselves as, if we don't, we will raise a generation of cynics. But just as it's challenging for most of us to understand the math homework our children bring home, we need to have our own passable knowledge. And especially in terms of the Theater of Lies, we need to not create barriers for children to establish their own defenses. This may be hardest lesson of all. Yet, as I write, in the US, PEN America (a 100-year-old non-profit group focused on free expression) has found that a state level, there are 400 bills aimed at limiting teaching of subject matter concerning race or gender issues all under the catch-all banner of *parental rights*.[607]

So, I will carefully wade into the need for education reform. It is a political minefield, not just in the US, but in most of the developed world (and the Theater of Lies likes it that way, as part of the common-good conservative agenda to erode trust in government institutions—and as institutions go, education is bedrock).

That bedrock is deep. The foundations of our current education structure were established in Prussia (later Germany) in the early eighteenth century. The Prussian system instituted compulsory attendance, specific training for teachers, national testing for all students (used to classify children for potential job training), a national curriculum set for each grade, and mandatory kindergarten.[608] German philosopher Johann Gottlieb Fichte summarized the purpose of the Prussian system, saying, "The schools must fashion the person, and fashion him in such a way that he simply cannot will otherwise than what you wish him to will."[609] For many, this purpose remains, and it is the cinder block barrier to developing citizens to care about issues, to be curious enough to learn more, and to have the courage to do so.

American educator, Horace Mann, traveled to Prussia in the mid-1850s. He came back with a mission to model the American system after it—beginning in Massachusetts and then New York State. By 1929, all fifty US states had mandated compulsory, state-funded and directed, education.[610] (In Canada, Egerton Ryerson is regarded as the most influential driver of what he, as Minister of Education in 1846, drafted the Common School Act, like Horace Mann's model, though with religious divisions for Protestant and Catholic children). [16]

As Joel Rose wrote in *The Atlantic*:

> Mann's vision also made sense for the Industrial Age in which he lived. The factory line was simply the most efficient way to scale production in general, and the analog factory-model classroom was the most sensible way to rapidly scale a system of schools. Factories weren't designed to support personalization. Neither were schools.[611]

Propagandists know this system is one of the most powerful and sustainable ways to indoctrinate a nation into thinking the way you want is to embed your messages into school curricula, having your lies taught as dogma in the classroom. You may have heard it referred to as *patriotic education.*

After the Tiananmen Square protests in 1989, the Chinese Communist Party launched its patriotic education campaign to instill national pride and build a generation loyal to the country's leadership. In addition to curricula that promoted hatred for all China's enemies (current and past), each school day was made to begin with the following pledge of allegiance:

....

16 Egerton Ryerson made such an imprint on Canadian education at the time that his opinion leaned heavily into the establishment of the residential school system for Indigenous children. To address this legacy, Ryerson University changed its name to Toronto Metropolitan University in April 2022.

No matter where I was born, the blood of my motherland is always flowing inside me. No matter if I am alive or dead, this will never change. For all this, I commit to love my motherland.[612]

America is taking this same course. In late August 2020, Donald Trump announced that America had to restore patriotic education in schools as a way to calm unrest in cities and counter lies about racism in the US. "Many young Americans have been fed lies about America being a wicked nation plagued by racism," Trump said.[613] He blamed violent protests in Portland, Oregon, and other cities on "left-wing indoctrination" in schools and universities. After his 2020 election loss, many Republican state legislatures carried on with the agenda with bans on teaching critical race theory.

Brazil's government, too, under the leadership of its populist president, Jair Bolsonaro, is rewriting school textbooks to "de-emphasize" the atrocities committed by the military dictatorship that held power between 1964 and 1985. According to Brian Winter, editor-in-chief of *Americas Quarterly*, the country's National Truth Commission, which identified 337 agents of the former dictatorship who had participated in arbitrary imprisonment, disappearances, torture, and the deaths of political opponents has largely been forgotten. 2023 Russia was no different, as it introduced a propaganda curriculum, where students were "issued with new textbooks teaching them about the *special military operation* [invasion of Ukraine] and taught how to handle Kalashnikovs, grenades and drones."[614]

The US is another outlier of the cliché that "history is written by the victors," as a woman named Mildred Rutherford almost single-handedly changed the school curriculum in America's South to present a pro-Confederacy view of the American Civil War. Her goal was to purge textbooks of any Yankee sentiment, and she may have been the originator of one of America's biggest lies.

Born into a slave-owning family in 1851, Rutherford was an early and active member of the United Daughters of the Confederacy, becoming its historian general in 1911. Slaves, according to Rutherford, were the happiest set of people on the face of the globe, free from care or thought of food, clothes, or home. Miss Millie, as Rutherford became known, sent hundreds of women into classrooms and school offices with instructions to reject any book that:

> Calls the Confederate soldier a traitor or rebel, and the war a rebellion . . . that says the South fought to hold her slaves . . . that speaks of the slaveholder of the South as cruel and unjust to his slaves.[615]

She remains a symbol held in high regard today. In 1939, the University of Georgia named a student residence hall after her. Rutherford Hall dormitory was redesigned in 2013, but the name has remained despite the controversy associated with it.

Eighty-five years later, Florida Governor Ron DeSantis reintroduced Miss Millie's teachings when he spoke in 2023 about new education standards in his state. He said the new curriculum would show "how slaves developed skills which, in some instances, could be applied for their personal benefit."[616]

Unfortunately, both the political left and the political right see education as both necessary and evil at the same time. It is cognitive dissonance on a scale I have never seen before.

Canadian psychologist and right-wing firebrand, Jordan Peterson, is developing an online university to "knock enrollment down in post-modern, neo-Marxist cult classes by 75% across the West. Our plan, initially, is to cut off the supply to the people who are running the so-called indoctrination cults."[617] In 2023, he launched it.[618]

So, another person's use of the education for indoctrination is bad, while if that same person is doing it themselves, is good. Education as indoctrination rather than learning is, unfortunately, alive and well in the twenty-first century. Climate change deniers are even using the education system to influence children that carbon is not really a bad thing. It feeds cats. Very cuddly cats.

In March 2023, a group called the CO2 Coalition handed out 700 comic books to teachers at the National Science Teaching Association's convention in Atlanta before being evicted from their trade show booth. The comic book, *Simon: The Solar-Powered Cat,* uses a friendly scientist to tell the story of how carbon is "a miracle molecule that fueled all life on earth by helping plants turn sunlight into food." The cuddly cat is solar powered, of course, because he eats such food—so all this talk about reducing carbon in the world will only harm the cat.[619] Now, there's a way to manipulate children—tell then we need carbon or the cats will die.

Lesson learned. If we want to manage the influence of the Theater of Lies on our children, we need to take a page from the propagandists' playbook. Yes, education will always be a form of indoctrination, so let's make it neutral and use it to indoctrinate our children into better thinking habits and let *them* decide what they want to believe.

We need to rethink education so the development of critical thinking skills is integrated into the everyday lives of students. This will allow them to judge for themselves the validity of the information they are taught as well as learn to follow pathways for more information: first the formal pathways, then later, how to use curiosity and imagination to create new ones.

I am not talking about rewriting textbooks. I am talking about learning from Feynman how to teach our children the difference between information, knowledge, and understanding. What I am talking about is critical and creative thinking, not as an optional course for students, but as a method integrated into the whole pedagogy of the education system. In short, we need to teach our children *how* to think, not *what* to think. And if the political powers pulling the strings of education policy push back on such a notion, then, like the promoters of *Simon the Cat,* that education might have to be delivered from outside the state-funded systems.

Education's primary focus on preparing students to enter the workforce has left a wide hole in the system, top to bottom. And as we learned in science class, nature abhors a vacuum. Propaganda, misinformation, lies—whatever you want to call it—has filled that void. The proof can be found even in how teachers who are supposed to be promoting good thinking skills through the humanities (English, history, art, philosophy, music, and so on) are packaging their subject matter through this same narrow lens.

Dr. Carol Geary Schneider is president emerita of the Association of American Colleges and Universities (AAC&U), an association that espouses so-called liberal education, its mission being "to advance the vitality and public standing of liberal education by making quality and equity the foundations for excellence in undergraduate education in service to democracy."[620]

I am not sure what that really means (as it's written in the bafflegab prose of an academic trying to make a political point). When it comes to the importance of teaching the humanities, however, Schneider is clearer:

> What does this matter when students are looking to college to prepare them for the first job or their next job? Because in today's economy, the name of the game is to be able to keep adapting our services and our products to a very fast-changing world. [The humanities] teach us all the questions that need to be part of working decision making, thinking, and judgement. Employers are the first to say, do not send us graduates who are locked into mental cubicles. They will be left behind. We are changing fast. If they can't change with us, they simply won't have a future in our industry.[621]

With that statement, the top American spokesperson for the value of the humanities in education regurgitated the lie that education exists primarily for workplace preparation. Yet, as Chris Hedges has written, that focus is precisely the reason for the "bankruptcy of our economic and political systems,"[622] a bankruptcy that is directly related to "the assault against the humanities."[623] The AAC&U's strategy, it would seem, is capitulation—force-fitting the humanities into the worker/patriot/soldier model of the Prussian structure, when that is the opposite of what needs to be done.

Of the elite students of Harvard, Yale, the University of Toronto, and McGill, among others, Hedges further writes,

> [They] are not capable of asking the broad, universal questions . . . which challenge the deepest assumptions

of a culture and examine the harsh realities of political and economic power. They have forgotten, because they have not been taught that human nature is mixture of good and evil. They do not have the capacity for human reflection. They do not understand that for every answer there arises another question.[624]

In his book *Empire of Illusion: The End of Literacy and the Triumph of Spectacle*, Hedges warned "those who suffer from historical amnesia, the belief that we are unique in history and have nothing to learn from the past, remain children. They live in illusion."[625] Amnesia, of course, assumes that you knew something you've since forgotten. As the physicist Richard Feynman once said, however, I'd argue that it is not only highly likely that people don't know some things in the first place—on many subjects and specific details—but that even if we do know something, we often do not understand it. As a criticism of the system and not the teachers, the education process at present seems more like an information dump than any attempt to build better thinkers.

The world we end up with is one where lies and fictions reign. As Grammy-winning singer and actor Lady Gaga put it, "We need fantasy to survive because reality is too difficult."[626] By contrast, University of Regina professor Gordon Pennycook believes "it's mostly a lazy thinking problem."[627] Fantasy, I guess, is easier. But it also highlights a large problem. Our school systems are designed to build better workers, not better thinkers and as such, are ill equipment to deliver solutions that will protect our children from the influence of lies, misinformation, and propaganda. The Theater of Lies programs itself to take advantage of this fatal flaw and has done so for generations.

Perhaps this was okay during the Industrial Age. But the Information Age has now overwhelmed it. Educators, with all the best intentions, are being forced to apply nineteenth-century solutions to address twenty-first-century problems (some, with their hands tied by legislation that includes threats of criminal prosecution).[628] Political leaders still can't resist the electoral power of ideology-friendly curriculum disruption, up to and including complete bans on some subject matter. Schools have become arenas to control information as much as teaching it.

The solution lies moving past the *Information Age* and into the *Knowledge Age*. We need to acknowledge that while we will always have to teach our children how houses are built, we need to go beyond that to *why houses are built*. We need to teach our children, and ourselves, the pathway to discovery is not in the information provided, but in the lessons on how to use it.

We need perspectives that will both protect us from misinformation and empower our children and their children to develop solutions to the challenges of the third millennium and the opportunities these solutions will foster. If we limit our intent to, as the Ontario Government states "developing skills today for tomorrow's jobs"—we've ignored the need to provide our children with the tools to thrive in world where information is as much suspect as it is embraced.

The Right to Bear Thoughts will be a cornerstone of the Knowledge Age. With it, education, within the system or outside of it, can become a place that nurture creative thinking. While I do not think we will ever evolve past the *more and better workers* foundations of education, we can expand its reach. How involves embracing a bit of science fiction (or at least the thoughts of one of its masters).

"How can teachers cultivate in students a love for learning that lasts forever, when they are forced to teach a one-size fits-all curriculum that rewards grades and standards over creativity and choice?"[629]

— ANA LORENA FÁBREGA, AMERICAN TEACHER AND ENTREPRENEUR.

9

THE STAR WARS DEFENSE INITIATIVE.

In the 1980s, America was deep into the Cold War with the Soviet Union. The threat of nuclear missile strikes was very real. The 1983 movie *War Games*, starring Matthew Broderick, attracted large audiences, as it told the story of a computer that was about to unleash all of America's nuclear warheads against a fake Soviet attack. It followed in the footsteps of 1960s classics like *Dr. Strangelove*, *The Manchurian Candidate*, and *Fail Safe*, and predated another Cold War thriller, *The Hunt for Red October*, in 1990. Fear of missile attacks was a fundamental feature of the zeitgeist of that era.

In 1983, US President Ronald Reagan gave a televised speech in which he labeled the Soviet Union an "evil empire." To set up that position, he quoted British author, C. S. Lewis:

> "The greatest evil is not done in those sordid dens of evil that Dickens loved to paint, but is conceived and ordered (moved, seconded, carried, and minuted) in clear, carpeted, warmed, well-lighted offices, by quiet men with white collars and cut fingernails and smooth-shaven cheeks, who do not need to raise their voices."[630]

Soon after that speech, Reagan announced what he referred to as the Strategic Defense Initiative (SDI). He challenged American scientists to create a space-based shield that could defend the US against any nuclear attack:

> What if free people could live secure in the knowledge that their security did not rest upon the threat of instant US retaliation to deter a Soviet attack, that we could intercept and destroy strategic ballistic missiles before they reached our own soil or that of our allies. I call upon the scientific community in our country, those who gave us nuclear weapons, to turn their great talents now to the cause of mankind and world peace, to give us the means of rendering these nuclear weapons impotent and obsolete.[631]

For me, two thoughts collide at this moment. One, few people today could quote C. S. Lewis, if they even know who he was or the influence he had on Western thought (evidence of the need for a broader scope of teaching, I think). Two, the impact of lies on the world is more real today that nuclear weapons were in the previous century. Nuclear war, also called mutual assured destruction (MAD), was a threat. But it never happened. The impact of lies on our behaviors and our beliefs, however, is a real and present danger. The Theater of Lies has become our threat of MAD.

For society, the most significant impact of the Theater of Lies is division. It divides nations, governments, families, and religions. It divides our worlds. Lies and misinformation have prevented our society from effectively addressing critical issues like the COVID-19 virus, climate change, racism, voters' rights, poverty, and hundreds of others because, with regards to the F. Scott Fitzgerald, we are unable as a society to function with opposing thoughts; they paralyze us and demand as a solution that one dominates the other. This is the fundamental goal of the producers of propaganda: they want their thinking to dominate yours.

As attacks by the Theater of Lies are societal, as society, how do we deal with this?

The answer lies in how we foster broader and better thinking in our children. It is here that I believe the greatest long-term achievements can be made in our defense against the ongoing onslaught of lies. To paraphrase Reagan, we need a means of rendering the Theater of Lies impotent and obsolete. We need to build an education system, with the system and outside of it, that teaches us how to have two opposing thoughts and remain functional.

At the time of Reagan's announcement, US Senator Edward Kennedy—an opposition Democrat and once-candidate for president himself—dismissed the idea as a *"Star Wars* scheme"[632] (referencing the popular *Star Wars* movie franchise that was just emerging). The moniker stuck, and SDI became known as the *"Star Wars* Defense," despite President Reagan's repeated protests against the new title. (He felt it denigrated the effort that had gone into it, casting the initiative as science fiction rather than a possible reality).

The Right to Bear Thoughts strategy is a version of this *Star Wars-*style defense. Improving and maintaining our thinking processes are a shield against weaponized lies and misinformation. Part of that solution is personal. Another part is practical: an education system that fosters thinking processes beyond linear and binary.

Ironically, one of the people who can help educators and the people that influence them (government policy makers and taxpayers) is the person who brought us *Star Wars* in the first place, George Lucas. He took part of the wealth he earned from the sale of the movie franchise and turned it into an organization wholly focused on improving the education system, the *George Lucas Educational Foundation.*

In the Industrial Age, from which most of our current system has grown, workers needed the rote skills of mathematics and basic language use to later learn the tools of their trade and be productive. With AI, machine learning, and advanced automation, the future is the power and plasticity of the mind, not the skills of the laborer. The education system I propose would be purpose-built to make us better thinkers, less influenced by misinformation and lies.

This will also have a much-intended additional benefit: as it is difficult, if not impossible, to teach our children today the knowledge they will need ten to fifteen years later—when they enter their independent, work-based lives. Learning how to become better thinkers will prepare them to acquire that knowledge more easily themselves in the future. Our broad education goal should be to nurture and develop the thinking abilities of our children so that they are far superior to our own.

From my lay perspective as one of the education system's products and a parent of more of its products, it seems today to be a vertical system. We begin with basic concepts, like adding two plus two, and keep adding more vertical complexity until some exit the system with PhDs in fractal geometry. It is same for our ABCs, reading, geology, biology, and almost every other subject matter. What is missing is a *horizontal* system to support the development of our minds to connect disparate thoughts *across* the subjects we are taught.

George Lucas refers to this kind of learning as "project-based." It is how such horizontal connections are made.:

> Anybody who's an adult, working in the adult world, realizes that your ability to encourage other people, form groups, and get the best out of everybody is the secret to success. One of the things we discovered is that the primary driving force for young people is curiosity: they naturally wonder how things work. And the other one is that they want to be adults. So, you give them adult projects like building a house, building a rocket ship, running a newspaper. You've got to give them an actual goal, and it has to be a goal they enjoy. Kids love to create things, and they'll learn if you let them create.[633]

I include the thoughts of Lucas not only for their validity in the development of better thinkers but as an example of how outside influence is needed, especially from experts in communications and engaging audiences. It reminds me of when NASA brought filmmaker James Cameron in to help them with their Mars missions. It was 2005, and Cameron told them, "They weren't going anywhere without the public's buy-in,"[634] and that NASA were lousy storytellers who "focused more on technology than people."

What I remember most, at the time, was Cameron telling NASA to send two rovers rather than one, so a camera mounted on one could capture images of the other—to bring the audience, represented by the second rover, into the images rather than just photos of Martian landscapes. (NASA took the advice, sort of, placing two cameras on one rover.)

How often, I wonder, has an education system asked a Hollywood director to help them engage students? Yet, I suspect much of what students know, will know, and remember about such topics as history, religion, and art comes not from the schools but movie screens. We know the propagandists have done this (referring back to John Ford's image of American culture expressed through films with John Wayne, guns, and bad guys thwarted by heroes).

Yes, our children need to learn more history, for there are lessons there, not in the recitation of facts, but in the knowledge of the mistakes that were made and challenges overcome. Our children need more religious education—of *all* religions. There are lessons to be learned from each and respect to be gained. Religion and history have many horizontal learning opportunities, as they are so connected with time, place, and the societies in which they operate. The same might be said of literature and art (how can you fully appreciate DaVinci's Last Supper if you know nothing of the religious story behind it?).

Each horizontal connection made strengthens the fabric of our defenses against the Theater of Lies. The links between the humanities and the sciences must be established and taught, not solely to better prepare students for the workforce, but to demonstrate how curiosity and critical thinking are what will help society flourish.

Science education is important, but as Harvard Education Professor Howard Gardner reminds us, the most powerful lesson is not in the facts of the science, but in the scientific method of their discovery:

> I actually don't care if a child studies physics, biology, geology, or astronomy before he goes to college. There's plenty of time to do that kind of detailed work. I think what's really important is to begin to learn to think scientifically. . .. You have to learn about it from doing many different kinds of experiments, seeing when the results are like what you predicted, seeing when they're different, and so on. But if you really focus on science in that kind of way by the time you go to college— or, if you don't go to college, by the time you go to the workplace—you'll know the difference between a statement that is simply a matter of opinion or prejudice and one for which there's solid evidence.[635]

Gardner preaches an educational gospel that strikes at the very foundation of how we currently teach children, calling it unfair.

> Once we realize that people have very different kinds of minds, different kinds of strengths—some people are good in thinking spatially, some in thinking language, others are very logical, other people need to be hands-on and explore actively and try things out—then

education, which treats everybody the same way, is actually the most unfair education.[636]

Gardner's solution is part of the Right to Bear Thoughts approach. He recommends using many of the same tools employed in the Theater of Lies to manipulate us:

> We can actually provide software, we can provide materials, we can provide resources that present material to a child in a way in which the child will find interesting and will be able to use his or her intelligences productively and, to the extent that the technology is interactive, the child will actually be able to show his or her understanding in a way that's comfortable to the child."[637]

In short, Gardner is telling us to move out of the eighteenth-century production mode of education and its read-a-textbook/hear-a-lecture style of learning and embrace the digital communications tools of the twenty-first century.

And let us fear not that such indoctrination on lateral thinking and creativity will undermine the study and development of science. At least, according to another Harvard professor, this one a chemist, Dudley Herschbach. In his words, "In science, you actually aren't concerned right off the bat about getting the right answer—nobody knows what it is. You're exploring a question we don't have answers to. That's the challenge, the adventure in it."[638]

Imagine for a moment the quality of thinking across societies that understand that science isn't about getting the right answer, right away.

While each building block in a new education strategy is important, one remains critical to defending society against lies and misinformation: ethics. The common denominator for all propagandists is an underlying philosophy that the ends justify the means. Whether it be placing a nuclear waste dump in a community, ensuring people with like minds have an easy path to the voting booth, selling cars with false emissions data, or reinforcing racial inequalities, the path of least resistance is to produce misinformation. We need not only to increase our resistance to these lies, but also to teach ethics to each new generation and integrate it into all subject matter. We need to teach that the ends do not justify the means, and beyond not cheating on tests. We need to remember that lies are not only efficient, but they are also effective. That, we need to sabotage.

It will take Gardner and everyone of his like to build this lie-shielding defense, but they need the permission of parents and governments to make it a reality. The results, however, will be astounding. It is time to stop nibbling away at the edge of our education system. We must build anew, using twenty-first-century tools and communications strategies. That is why we must use the power of the internet, the content skills of entertainment producers and educators, and the funding of people who see the value in delivering education in new ways; indeed, outside the system, if we have to.

In our school systems, we must allow for opposing ideas to be discussed. This would allow concepts such as critical race theory (CRT) to be introduced and the truths and concepts within it to be debated. Yet, so much of a line of thinking such as CRT threatens the status quo and its opponents . . . you may want to leap on them as wrongheaded. But why not allow CRT and its discussion to go through a "what if the other side is right about this?" process. If America doesn't have structural racism, then let that evidence be introduced. Let our children learn the value of opposition to ideas and what other people think bears debate, not condemnation.

In fact, debate programs in school, throughout elementary and secondary school, should become part of the curriculum. That process alone brought Ethan Lindenberger to his own opinions on vaccinations, rather than his parents. Though within that statement lies the fear . . . that parents lose control over their children's thinking.

The producers in the Theater of Lies depend upon compliant audiences on who they can pile their propaganda. The defense strategy would foster an audience that is more resilient, questioning, and able to access the tools necessary to defend themselves and each other. The lie producers understand this and have exploited it. But we do not have to fight them on their own terms. That would be a losing strategy. Allow teaching of conflicting ideas and foster debate.

My first instinct toward this solution was the integration of creativity into all aspects of the education system. I discovered I was wrong. As you will see in the next chapter, the notion of creativity in education has been determined—as both accomplished and not accomplished (as seems to only occur in the binary world of the Theater of Lies).

What I learned in that the real solution is much simpler, less disruptive to the current structure of our education systems, and relatively inexpensive. It is a solution that I believe will be both efficient and effective. It is centered on the idea of the school bus.

"Can the education system as a whole, the most traditional, conservative, rigid, bureaucratic institution of our time . . . come to grips with the real problems of modern life? Or, will it be shackled by the tremendous social pressures for conformity and retrogression, added to its own traditionalism."[639]

– CARL ROGERS, AMERICAN PSYCHOLOGIST.

....

10

THE SCHOOL BUS PROPOSITION.

When I was working for Canada's largest public relations firm, the owners asked me to develop a creative thinking process for our consultants that could foster better ideas to serve our clients. While developing the model, I learned that creative thinking is not an isolated thinking process. Which, of course, makes sense. Our brains are not wired as individual blocks of thinking material, so why should creativity be any different.

What did surprise me then, but not now (ten years later), is that within my large group of colleagues or the small team I gathered to support the effort, there was a wide difference of opinion on what creativity actually was. Working in a PR firm, some thought that creativity was the purview of advertising agencies and, on a small scale, our own graphic design and digital departments. Others thought it was ideas, in the general sense, or the stroke-of-genius moment when an idea came to you. This, some thought, couldn't be trained or learned. Creativity was ephemeral. You either had or didn't have, like being tall, smart, or finding that math comes easier to you than others.

Early in our lives, we had all been creative (just give a child a pot of paint, their fingers, a large piece of paper, and watch) but to some degree, each of us had been educated out of it. True creativity, many of my colleagues believed, was the stuff of artists, writers (some), dancers, and musicians. Today, we even have a work class for such people. They are called *creatives* (who, according to *Fast Company* are "typically more neurotic, more antisocial, and less conscientious than others." [640] (*Yikes!*)

Edward de Bono was a twentieth-century Maltese physician who later committed his life to improving the way people thought. He wrote and published extensively on the subject. Many workers, including me, took at least one of his courses, most commonly his *Six Thinking Hats* process. He too had a problem defining creativity—so much so he divided the term into four subsets.

The first, mini-c level creativity, happens anytime you attempt a new task. For de Bono, it was inherent in all learning. The second, little-c level creativity, is growth from that first level to something that may be of value. Pro-c level was his third level, where creativity is taken into a professional setting (like the advertising agencies my colleagues identified), and the final level, Big-c creativity, is the sum of career achievements that are at the top of your artform (in any subject or professional area).[641]

Much of the teaching profession uses this model at some level – and like so many fundamentals, we have a tendency to complicate the simple, rather than the opposite.

At time I began my own investigation into thinking creatively and expanding its practice, I had not conceived of creative thinking as a defensive mechanism for the belief in lies and misinformation. That came later. Perhaps it is why we've looked to the comedians and other artists in our world as one of our preferred sources for truth, all in the hope they will fight our battles for us.

But in the Theater of Lies (indeed, a theater of war), we need to empower our societies to fight the battle for themselves, like a well-armed militia during a bullets and bombs war. That's the origin of my recommended strategy, *the Right to Bear Thoughts*: a well-informed population, being necessary to the security and prosperity of a free state, the right bear thoughts and acquire knowledge shall not be infringed. That right, empowered, will allow us to hold two or more opposing ideas in our mind at once, which may become the bane of the producers of lies and misinformation.

The tools to entrench the right to bear thoughts are: caring—you have to care about the issue; curiosity—you need to be curious enough to explore and foster knowledge, and explore different pathways to this knowledge; and, finally, courage—as some of the pathways you explore may be at first uncomfortable and the knowledge you gain challenged by those around you.

In this chapter, I want to explore enabling the curiosity and courage required to enable this right to thrive, the foundation of which must be nurtured through our education systems. As it concerns caring, that should be an outcome of the process. As for courage, that too (though my own might be challenged in recommending any of this as I expect opposition to them). So, I decided to first examine the potential for a focus on creative thinking to make this happen (full disclosure, one of my biases).

I began with a review of the policy of integrating creativity in education. It seems governments around the world are ahead of the game. In 2010, Professor Robina Shaheen from the UK's University of Birmingham conducted a review of relevant government policies around the world from a wide range of sources. She concluded, "the inclusion of creative into education documents is evidence of the fact that the focus on creativity is not merely of paying lip service to the concept but rather action is being taken" and "practical steps are being taken to make creativity part of the educational agenda."[642]

Shaheen cites the 1999 work of O'Donnel and Micklewaite, who reviewed the primary and secondary school curriculum of sixteen countries (American, European, and East Asian). They found that "creativity was included at various education levels, at least from early years through primary education for most countries and beyond, up to higher education for some."[643]

She also cites her own research into the creative education policies of these countries: Australia, Canada, South Korea, Sweden, France, Germany, the Netherlands, Japan, Singapore, China (including separately, Hong Kong), Turkey, Ireland, and—not surprising, given her workplace—the United Kingdom (including, separately, Scotland), as well as the US states of Florida and Kentucky.[644]

I would summarize her findings as overwhelmingly positive (even in Turkey, she says, the "concept of creativity is being discussed more and more, however attempts to enhance it through education are limited").[645]

This all sounded promising.

The reason for all this integration of creativity into education policies, according to Shaleen, is best encapsulated in former British Prime Minister Tony Blair who, she says, "couples creativity in education to the future needs of the national economy."

Yes, we are back to the Prussian strategy that education is the foundation for better workers, so creativity needs to fit into that paradigm. Fortunately, it can. (See de Bono's creativity subsets and their focus on production.) Unfortunately, people who have spent their careers focused on creative thinking strategies disagree with Shaleen's promising conclusions.

At the same time Shaleen was publishing her work, a professor of creativity at the University of Connecticut, Ronald Beghetto, found that teachers did not regard teaching creativity as part of their job, and "where creativity is managed from above, it tends to be just another chore to be endured."[646]

That same year, in the *Cambridge Handbook of Creativity*, writers James Kaufmann and Robert Stemberg found that "creativity is simply not part of the forefront of the education debate."[647] And, they added, US laws such the *No Child Left Behind Act* (2001) that legislated schools be setting high standards and goals and be held accountable for their performance on standardized tests had "sucked all the air out of educators who support creativity."[648] The invasion of the business perspective—if it can't be measured, it has no value—also meant the teachers who valued creativity, in turn, were not valued as educators.

There seems to be a difference of opinion between the people who make education policy and both the people whose teaching methods extend from those policies and experts in the development of creative thinking.

This reminds of a blank stare moment between me and the president of a large international marine shipping company, when he told me there were no drugs or alcohol on their merchant marine ships, as there was a policy in place against it. At the time, one of my sons was serving on one of those ships, and my brother-in-law had served on another for over thirty years. From their boots-in-the-engine-room perspective, substance use (and for some, abuse) was as common as the diesel fuel in the engines.

Managers and political leaders can sometimes use policy as both legal shields for denial and demonstrations that they are addressing current issues, yet not act on them. In the case of education policy and creativity, creativity looks like it has fallen into the trap that George Orwell called *meaningless words*. Like democracy, freedom, and rights, they not only mean different things to different people, but in political language, they become the plaster covering real cracks in the wall.

The term *creativity*, as a thought process, is best now assigned to the arts and humanities. In education policy and as a tool for defending ourselves from lies and misinformation, it's dead on arrival. There's even research from the universities of Harvard and Duke demonstrating that creativity has a dark side: "original thinkers can be more dishonest."[649] *Yikes again* for creative types (with apologies to my friends who are).

In light of all this, I propose a thinking process that is more neutral and less politically compromised, based on lateral thinking. Ironically, it was Edward de Bono who first coined that that term in his book in 1967.[650] It took him another decade to publish his more famous

Six Thinking Hats in which he attempted, I think, to both trademark and profit from a training style program using the same notion (in that book he also added conflict resolution training to address what I believe is the courage part of the process).

In the end, I think de Bono is only guilty of overthinking improved thinking. Simpler solutions have broader appeal (part of the reason we know lies are some easily accepted).

Let's go back to school.

At its foundation, the education system is based on linear thinking—a logical progression of one point to another until the solution is found: think kindergarten, grades 1 through 12, bachelor, masters, doctorate. A linear progression from student to worker (with, at the end of the progression, the choice to go back and teach others through the same system).

In and of itself, lateral thinking is about rejecting the status quo of ideas and conceiving entirely new ways of looking at a problem. But I think it can and does go beyond that, and as such, is vital for the preparation of our children in their defense from the Theater of Lies.

Here's why.

Linear thinking, as inherently taught in our schools, takes a step-by-step approach to not only learning, but also problem solving. It makes sense and it works—for traditional problems. But we've seen it fail in helping our children (and us) in detecting lies and misinformation. It was never intended for this new world, and our schooling platform of *listen to authorities* (your teacher, your parents, your boss), by its nature, shuns such thoughts as those that lies from people in authority can even exist.

Linear thinkers thrive in environments where there is one answer to a problem. When there may be multiple answers (or multiple problems creating a situation), linear thinkers often fail. Solutions deemed either right or wrong (binary options) satisfy the needs of linear thinkers. But in the social sciences and those places where science meets social acceptance, linear thinking fails.

Lateral thinking can provide a neutral, safe, and nurturing place to engage in such thoughts and do so throughout our education system. The danger, as de Bono himself demonstrated by outputs such as the four c levels of creativity, *Six Thinking Hats*, and the myriad of thinking improvement "systems" that others have developed (and mostly sold into the corporate training world) is that these processes are complicated, expensive, and frankly highly intellectual (you have to have a high level of thinking in order to improve your thinking).

We teach higher levels of thinking like higher levels of locomotion, as in you have to be able to walk before you can run. Yet, we know that curiosity and even that much-confused word, creativity, exist in our infancy. Our education system unteaches it, rather than nurturing it.

We need to find ways to broaden the thinking of our children while remaining within the traditional linear structure of the education system. This system, after all, is a process of inputs and outputs. We need not change that, nor should we.

A form of lateral thinking can be fostered in every grade level of our education system and in almost every course taught along the way. Therein lies the solution, and I think I have discovered a way to do so. For just as teachers do not announce, "Today, we are learning linear thinking"—they continually demonstrate it—the teaching of lateral thinking must be done the same way: by living it.

I call it *the School Bus Proposition*, and it can be the enabler of *the Right to Bear Thoughts* throughout life.

The simple school bus is something students at all levels recognize as both a tangible object and an enabler of learning directly associated with their education. It is a tool that, for many, takes them from home to school and back again. It is, for all, a tool that takes them outside the school environment for other places of learning—from field trips to transportation for extra-curricular activities (such as sports events and competitions). It is also a presence, a symbol, and an experience that maintains itself throughout their schooling (and beyond, as they will see them throughout the rest of their lives and one day may place their own children in them).

We can integrate some lateral thinking in our children's education by using the school bus as a place to regularly return to for what's missing in so much of the information teaching we dump on our children: *relevant context.*

For example: for a kindergarten student, the school bus is an introduction to the color yellow (What else is yellow? What other colors can buses be?) It can also be used for counting (How many buses?) and other simple mathematics. It can also be used as a launch pad for talking about the people in the bus and where the bus goes. All are lateral thoughts from the simple notion of the school bus.

In later grades, the school bus can be used to discuss locomotion, more complex areas of mathematics (area, volume, weight, and mass), as well as what it is made from (steel, glass, wiring, rubber, chrome, etc.) Those discussions can lead to the chemistry of each material in the bus, and the principles of physics in real life (acceleration, sudden impacts, direction, and velocity). In secondary schools, business concepts such as risk management, insurance, rules of the road, the civics of road building and transportation policy, and almost all other topics can be discussed. All through lateral thinking and its never-ending power source: curiosity.

The School Bus Proposition proposes that our education system challenges itself to make the school bus relevant to every course in every grade. In this way, we have created a continuous thread that will carry through a student's entire education. It can be a decades-long demonstration that enables the curiosity and courage to apply lateral thinking to all aspects of that student's education and indeed, their life.

Integrated into the natural linear thinking of our education system—that is, "a school bus is a vehicle that transports student to a from a place of education"—to that we add, "a school bus can be representative of almost everything we need to learn," as if the answers were circular, not straight ahead.

A school bus is yellow. A lemon is also yellow. It is often harvested when it's green. As it ripens, the green chlorophyll breaks down, then revealing the carotenoid pigments that make lemons yellow. They were brought from North Africa to Europe in the Middle Ages, another gift from the Moors. Columbus brought lemon seeds with him, beginning the citrus industry in the Americas. Lemons are coated in wax to extend their shelf live.

All these thoughts can arise from the discussion of the familiar to the unfamiliar (from the school bus to other subjects and possibilities): from kindergarten, to history, to chemistry, and to business and marketing. Lateral thinking can be ingrained horizontally through the image of school bus in every classroom, as a teaching tool for the message that everything is interesting, worthy of exploration, and through curiosity, you can learn more about anything over your entire life. It will also challenge teachers to think more laterally about subjects they teach yet provide them with easily followed road map.

In the many intellectual debates about thinking processes, the School Bus Proposition may be thought of as a process with many different names: lateral, non-linear, creative, critical, left-brained, circular, or even spherical (such is the nature of these debates – and another example of how we complicate the simple). However one defines it, its power in terms of our societal defense in the Theater of Lies is that it puts any issue as the center point of a discussion, rather than at the beginning or the end. It allows all options to be discussed, even if only in one's own mind.

The School Bus Proposition is a shield that allows everyone to think widely rather than narrowly. It is this shield that will protect the next generations from the Theater of Lies as curiosity improves the thinking processes of its audience.

The shortest version of this idea to digest was given to me by a boss of mine almost forty years ago. Her advice on changing your perspective was this: *you just have to change your seat on the bus.* That advice stuck with me, as did she. A decade later, I married her.

"Teachers have a legitimate role to influence students – it is not only their right it is their obligation to do so."[651]

– ANTHONY R. PRATKANIS,
PROFESSOR EMERITUS OF PSYCHOLOGY, UNIVERSITY OF CALIFORNIA

....

11

BUS DRIVERS NEEDED.

It's one thing to have a school bus, but it won't go far without a driver. As a communications professional, I would be naive to think that re-tooling the education systems to integrate lateral, critical, and creative thinking will be easy. But, as I've written, the need to protect ourselves and our societies from the Theater of Lies is urgent, so necessary to our future, that the solutions must be both accessible and sustainable. We did not get to this place overnight, with our seats comfortably padded, sharing the misinformation produced for us. Nor can any of us act like the little Dutch boy from *Hans Brinker, or The Silver Skates*, and simply put our fingers in the breaking dam of information pouring over us and expect this to work (of note, that story is part of American folklore and is not a Dutch story).

When you pair the need for urgent education reform with the reality that, for the most part, it is a government-controlled process, then add the depth, scope, and debate of education professionals—pushing for change, making change happen, and having a real impact on students could be considered a pipe dream. As the US is experiencing, the push to limit education on several subjects (race and gender studies, notably) flies directly in the face of opening up education to neutral teaching processes that support curiosity.

More unfortunately, however, is that at least in the US, the entire education system is under attack. Under the guise of parental rights, the number of children who are homeschooled (rather than attending traditional schools) has grown to 3.7 million in 2023.[652] That's about 7 percent of all students. In Canada, the numbers are harder to track. (Ontario, for example, does not require homeschooled students to register as such.) The Canadian Centre of Home Education reports in 2021, 3 percent of students as homeschooled, their parents making this choice because of "dissatisfaction with the public-school culture or the progressive ideology in public schools."[653]

A US conservative Christian lawyer, Michael Farris, has been a decades-long advocate for homeschooling, campaigning on the theme that "public schools were indoctrinating children with a secular world-view that amounted to a godless religion."[654]

As *The Washington Post* reported in August 2023, Farris is working to gather sufficient political capital to "siphon billions of dollars from the public schools" and "take down the education system as we know it."[655] America's education is becoming ground zero for the national conservative movement's goal of creating a governing structure that holds the Christian faith as the values-base for decision-making and operations. *Parental Rights* are the rallying cry across state legislatures,

Donald Trump's 2024 presidential campaign—a right, according to Farris, "which comes from God."[656]

Michael Farris has been a driver of educational change for decades. As we've seen, the Theater of Lies is happy to use people like Farris to deliver and propagate its messages. Farris's traction comes, in part, from being outside the traditional education (though, he owns a university that is focused wholly on the post-secondary education of homeschooled children).[657]

Yet again, we need to take a page from the propagandist's playbook. We need to recognize that parents who aren't represented by the rallying cry of parental rights need support. We also need to recognize that society has now moved past the school system as the only place to influence children. If we want to introduce the lateral, critical, and creative thinking process to our children through a concept like the School Bus Proposition, we need people outside the education system to drive it.

I am not against homeschooling nor the right of parents to choose religious education for their children. My only goal is to foster open-mindedness and provide our children and their children with the thinking tools and philosophies to support it. To protect children from the influence of lies and misinformation, we need to provide them with an environment that gives them full freedom of intellectual exploration; that is, the right to bear thoughts and acquire knowledge.

This can be accomplished through private donors, foundations, and corporate sponsors who see value in this goal. Outputs can vary, but these outputs should provide the tools to teachers who want (and can) embrace them, parents too, and of course, be accessible and support children in their personal paths to maintaining their fundamental nature as curious individuals. The goal of these *Bus Drivers*, as I will call them, will be to build bridges around the barriers close-minded governments, individuals, and ideological organizations continue to create.

Let us use the tools of the Theater of Lies for better purposes. Not to lie or misrepresent, but to provide pathways to accuracy and openness. Let us the tools to foster creativity and support children (and adults) on their paths past information and into knowledge. We need new John Fords to tell these stories and an internet/social media machine to share them. That, and opinion leaders to influence government decision-makers.

This, dear Oprah Winfrey, will be the most powerful weapon we have. Not truth, but enabling people to be curious, ask questions, and follow their own paths to their own decisions. Whereas the national conservatives do not trust people without faith in religion to make decisions, we must prove that *with or without such faith*, people are not only capable of such, but they can also thrive.

On a societal level, the greatest protection we can create to the divisive influence of the Theater of Lies is the promotion and support and personal pathways to knowledge. That, and looking at ourselves and our own organizations to see if we too are contributing to spread of lies and misinformation—and if we are, daring to be clear, transparent, and non-hyperbolic in our communications.

The next chapter examines how we can do this and rebuild the institutional trust that the Theater as been so successful in attacking. Because blaming others for any distrust that our audiences have in our institutions is a fool's game. All organizations must take responsibility for their reputations, earned or embellished.

"Building trust comes from giving people the agency to understand, challenge misconceptions, and recognize misinformation where it exists."[658]

– FARHAAN LADHANI, CEO, DIGITAL PUBLIC SQUARE.

....

12

ICH BIN EIN BERLINER (I AM A BERLINER).

John F. Kennedy, then president of the United States, stood in front of a wall that divided the city of Berlin in two—the Berlin of West Germany, democratic; and the Berlin of East Germany, communist, under the control of the German Democratic Republic, and wholly aligned with Soviet Union. On June 26, 1963, JFK uttered the words that would ring in history, "[A]ll free men, wherever they may live, are citizens of Berlin, and, therefore, as a free man, I take pride in the words 'Ich bin ein Berliner!'"[659] The statement is often referred to as "we are all Berliners," as Kennedy was speaking for all the free world, illuminating the 27-mile-long Berlin Wall as the dividing line not only between two cities that were once one, but also between all people living under democratic and autocratic rule.

That Berlin Wall—now fallen and the city whole again—was a tangible and dangerous symbol. The Theater of Lies is wholly virtual and as a danger, even more so. Yet, as Kennedy inspired, the free world needed to be engaged in the solutions that would eventually bring down that barrier. Today, we need no less inspiration to act on defending ourselves from lies and misinformation. And, as the Theater has attacked the credibility of our much-needed institutions, these institutions, too, have an important role to play.

There are four groups of large institutions that form the legs of what I would call the table of institutional trust. Over time and especially the last several decades, the Theater of Lies has steadily chipped away at reputations of three of these big four institutions: big government, big media, and big corporations. In the Western world, the fourth "big"—big religion—has been variously attacked or coddled, depending on the message needs of the producers.

Rebuilding trust in all four of these big institutional groups will play a key role in our society's defense against the manipulative power of the Theater of Lies, and yes, I include big religion in that structure (religion is too important for too many people to ignore, whatever one's personal beliefs are). With all four, rebuilding trust will be a challenge as, in my experience, the larger the size, scope, and history of an institution, the more small "c" conservative its thinking.

Change is hard, but not impossible. But just as I proposed the simplicity of a school bus to tie together disparate ideas across multiple school grades and courses, a focus on language that is plain and simple, rather than the convolutions of meaningless words, will be the solid base on which to rebuild institutional trust.

There have been so many books and papers published on the subject of trust that to do justice to the topic of rebuilding it in one chapter, over four large institutional sectors, is impossible. Nor do I think it is required. For the leaders of these institutions who want to seriously address trust, there is a deep well of professionals who can assist you. There are cadres of consulting firms willing to take on the work.

I will instead focus on three points of rebuilding trust that are relevant to our society's need to defend itself against not just the power of lies and misinformation, but the theater's ability to have empower its audience to believe and repeat those lies.

Public confidence in these institutions must be re-built and sustained. That will take actions some of these organizations will be uncomfortable with, such as acknowledging mistakes, taking responsibility for them, and providing their audiences with the time and space for trust to be regained. Building public confidence is an exercise in persuasion, and as I've demonstrated ... that comes from establishing emotional resonance more than facts. That's where acknowledge mistakes becomes paramount in the process.

Like individuals, institutions must park their biases. In the case of institutions, the bias of many leaders and their support teams is to keep to the status quo. Their position is often that any stakeholder trust issues are not their fault. These are just part of doing business. But just as I recommended for individuals to park their biases and explore their curiosity, for institution leaders, the former is a challenge, and the latter practically impossible. Nonetheless, it is critical.

To accomplish this, I offer these three solutions. The list could be much longer, but as it relates to lie and misinformation, these are the most important. In my experience, most large institutions get these actions wrong, if they undertake them at all.

Let me ask you a question. What is the purpose of your national government? What is its unique responsibility above all others? What is the same for your hospital, your school, your police force, and even the media you access? What is the unique purpose of each of these institutions? If you work for an institution, what is the purpose of yours?

Chances are that each person I ask will have a different answer: some similar, some longer, some using big words and complicated themes. And this is where the process to rebuild trust must begin.

That comes from a simple formula:

> *Tell people the purpose of your institution; and when its actions fail to live up to that purpose—own the error, correct it, and tell people how it won't make that mistake again.*

The first solution to rebuilding institutional trust is a shared definition as to the purpose of each institution in our lives. Without that shared definition, it is all too easy for the producers of lies and misinformation to exploit for their own gain. In politics, they call it defining your opponent before they get a chance to define themselves. Now, as government itself and so many of its institutions are also under fire, each of these organizations has let their opposition define them. That's like being in a poker game where your opponents have declared the rules.

Unfortunately, searching on a country-by-country basis, I could not find a single national government that clearly defines its purpose, including my own country and the Government of Canada. As a negative example, it is a good one. It shows what *not* to do, and it deals with the bedrock task of managing a government: how it spends taxpayer money.

The budget of every government is the most powerful statement about what that government does: how it raises money and how it spends it. Creating that budget is a complicated process involving hundreds of civil servants and elected officials across all government departments and agencies, as well as multiple layers of consultation. As far as tasks go, it's a whopper. In terms of impact, media, business, and advocacy groups eagerly await its announcement and pour over the details in the same way a physician studies *Gray's Anatomy*.

Here is how the Government of Canada titled its budget in 2023:

> *Budget 2023: A Made-in-Canada Plan—strong middle class, affordable economy, healthy future and statement and impacts report on gender, equality, diversity and quality of life.*[660]

Let's pass over the made-in-Canada part (where else would it be made, unless previously, the government was outsourcing the work?), and then there is a litany of vague words and phrases after that opening title.

Nowhere in the budget's 27-word title nor in its 388 pages does that document state what the purpose of the government is or what it does. It does not even provide the most basic information about the document itself—that is, what is the purpose of the document? The hidden message (or assumption) is *Yes, people, you are supposed to know all these things.* There may even be a bit of arrogance in this absence—as in, *If you have to ask, then you are too stupid to understand the answer.*

But this lack of defined purpose—of the government or its annual planning document—is not the only example.

Nowhere on the Canadian government's massive website—a website that covers every department and agency—is the unique responsibility of that government stated, or again, what it does. Again, it is left to you, the funder and user of the institution to already know this. I guess.

Yet, an Ipso Reid poll in 2008 (commissioned by the Dominion Institute) found that most Canadians did not have an accurate understanding of its government.[661] Seventy-five percent could not correctly name the country's head of state.[662] (Answer: The King of England.)

Responding to results, Marc Chalifoux, executive director of the Dominion Institute said, "Our school system needs to be doing a better job of training young people to be citizens."[663]

In 2011, the director of the Annenberg Public Policy Center responded to similar results in the United States ,where only 38 percent of people polled could name all three branches of the US government, and a further 33 percent of people polled could not even name one.[664] The Center's director, Kathleen Hall Jamieson, said, "[T]he nation should be troubled by the extent to which civic education is downplayed in its schools."[665]

There are two glaring errors here, though, in both Canada and the US, and likely other nations.

First—focusing on concern on the lack of knowledge of the structure of government is a red herring. It is peoples' understanding on the purpose of their government and its institutions that is missing. Structure comes after that, like understanding the purpose of the sum of the parts before understanding what each part is and does.

Second—blaming the school system is a deflection of responsibility. How many of us remember what we learned in Grade 10 (where civics and citizenship are taught in my home jurisdiction of Ontario, Canada)?[666] Regarding political systems, it would pass through our heads as soon as the test was over. Why? Just ask yourself this question: how relevant to your life was government to most of us when we were teenagers (other than perhaps getting a driver's license or becoming old enough to drink)? On the question of relevance, business gets is better.

I don't normally lean to the notion that institutions should be run more like businesses—but in the case of statements of purpose, they can be a beacon of clarity. McDonald's Restaurants is a great example. They made clear to the world that they are in the business of selling hamburgers. So much so that during the decades after their launch in most every market, their signs had a simple slogan. "Billions of Hamburgers Sold."[667]

McDonalds knew it was their responsibility to inform their customers. It is so, too, for our institutions. Each and every one of them, must constantly remind us as to their purpose in our lives and how they fulfill that purpose.

I hope this is a blinding glimpse of the obvious. It is not up to others to educate your audiences. A best practice in defending your institution from lies and misinformation is to always assume people know nothing about your institution, and worse, what they do know is probably incorrect.

By this, I do not mean vision, mission, and values statements. These were imposed upon many organizations in the latter twentieth century to align employees in common beliefs to increase productivity. In human resource jargon, they were team-building exercises and had no relationship to the consumer.

No, I have been in too many of those meetings and the outcomes, most often, were large, verbose documents, unwieldly PowerPoint presentations, and intranet sites that no one visited. All of these, once completed, quickly collected dust—while the consultants who sold and delivered such services just as quickly cashed their checks (on occasion, I confess, I was one of them).

So, how do we do this? How do we communicate the purpose of our institutions?

Let's take a page from Richard Feynman, the theoretical physicist I introduced you to earlier in this book. His learning technique began with the following concept, "Pretend to teach a concept you want to learn about to a student in the sixth grade."[668]

This requires two important things: one, you and your colleagues understand the purpose of your institution and can communicate it in a way that any twelve-year-old can understand. And two, as Feynman recommends, transmit that information to a real twelve-year-old and see if they do understand it. If they don't . . . the responsibility for understanding is not the twelve-year-old's, it's yours.

For this technique to work, you must first understand the purpose of your institution in this same basic, simple-language way. What makes it especially challenging is that your institution can only have one purpose.

McDonald's got it right. Twelve-year-olds know, understand, and can tell others that the restaurant sells burgers.

For the Government of Canada, I suggest,

To maintain and improve the quality of life
for the people who live in Canada today and in the future.

If that were its published purpose—repeated in every document and media release the government publishes—then everyone in the country could judge the government on its fulfillment of that purpose, as expressed by what it does and how it does it. As the producers in the Theater of Lies have shown us, repetition fosters acceptance.

This will be easier for some institutions than others, such as electricity distributors, hospitals, and telecommunications companies (in the private sector, including the need to be responsible to both their customers and their investors).

But the key to the effectiveness of this solution is the complete and utter avoidance of brand language (as trustworthy, persistent, and honest—brand language reflects what a business wants its customers to say about it, not necessarily what they *are saying* about it).

Let the brand language fly in your advertising and public relations. But, in statements of purpose and what you do to fulfill this purpose, it must be understandable to a twelve-year-old. Police departments have long had a clear purpose statement— "to serve and protect"—but I question the need for the word "serve." I don't think a sixth-grader will understand what that *really* means (nor do I).

The last part of these overlooked communications elements is: What does the institution do when it fails to achieve its stated purpose? When it messes up. This is the cement that holds the trust-building together.

Because every institution will fail, at times, to make good on its purpose. It makes mistakes and even, on occasion, does wrong things in pursuit of that purpose. But in my forty years of communications and public affairs experience, I have yet to find an organization that has a set-in-stone process for dealing with its failures (except where regulations mandate these plans, as in many utility sectors). Any failures are typically managed on a case-by-case basis. Yet, in the building and maintenance of trust, this is as critical as financial management is to the successful operation of any organization.

In addressing failures on an institutional scale, I can provide a positive example and a negative one.

First, the positive.

At the time, I was consulting to a very large electricity company that transmits power over the 400,000+ square miles of Ontario (by comparison, Texas is about 270,000 square miles). It also delivers this power directly to 1.5 million homes and, through a network of independent electricity distributors, to another 3 million. It's a huge public company, with almost half of its shares owned by the Province of Ontario.[669] The media follows almost every step the company takes. Especially when a team of tree trimmers decide to cut down a swath of hundred-year-old trees in a Toronto urban park.

The public's reaction was immediate—aggressively negative. The media coverage reflected it. The company decided to hold a community meeting to address the issue (this is where I came in, as a specialist in managing public meetings—especially angry ones).

At the board room table, the CEO was surrounded by his leadership team: communications, forestry management, transmission services, finance, legal, and operations. Plus, me. As the CEO went around the table, asking for advice, a common theme was emerging. Start the public meeting with statement about how much the company valued the environment, its practices that supported that commitment, and what the company was prepared to do to re-plant the trees. The communications lead handed out a draft press release, key messages, and speaking remarks.

The CEO shook his head through the advice-gathering process. I wasn't asked. I was there to manage and moderate what was expected to be a very tough event. Thankfully, the CEO and I were on the same page.

The CEO held up his hand and said, "Please, everyone. Just stop. The first thing out of my mouth better be: *We made a mistake. I am personally very sorry. This is something that should never have happened.*" Then, he told his team that after making that statement, he wanted to hear from the people in the meeting what the mistake meant to them and how they'd like the company to respond.

It was a genius move. Textbook. Don't offer a defense to people who don't want to hear it. Apologize, then listen. Only after all the angry people have had their platform do you respond. The public meeting started, of course, in front of a sea of sour faces. But the CEO's words took the heat out of the air, and the rest of the evening was an open conversation between a community and a leader who had the interest and ability to make things right.

Trust attacked, trust re-built.

Then there is the opposite of that—the Catholic Church's apology to Canada's Indigenous peoples for its leading role in the abuses and deaths within the Canadian residential school system (the last school closing in 1996, after operating since the late 1800s).

Pope Francis had, to his credit, taken a personal role in the apology process in 2022 when he visited Canada and asked for forgiveness from the living survivors of this abuse for what he referred to as genocide. That was a good step. But what Indigenous groups also called for was a public revocation of the Church's centuries-old *Doctrine of Discovery*—a papal bull (an official decree)—that authorized the Christian nations of Europe to legally acquire vast tracts of Indigenous land in the New World by simply making landfall and raising flags, planting crosses, or digging up some sod.[670]

Plant a cross, gain a million acres of land. Good deal. That papal bull spurred the exploration of the Americas (North and South) and the exploitation all the Indigenous peoples that had populated the area for at least 12,000 years.

Canada's Truth and Reconciliation Commission had demanded that revocation, in writing, in 2015. Eight years later, the press office of the Catholic Church responded with what it referred to as a *special bulletin* (rather than a more official papal bull, which would have replaced the one in question):

> In no uncertain terms, the Church's magisterium upholds the respect due to every human being. The Catholic Church therefore repudiates those concepts that fail to recognize the inherent human rights of indigenous peoples, including what has become known as the legal and political "doctrine of discovery".[671]

Sounds reasonable, if late. But the troubling part of the above statement (point 7 in the special bulletin) is what comes before it in Point 6.

> The "doctrine of discovery" is not part of the teaching of the Catholic Church. Historical research clearly demonstrates that the papal documents in question, written in a specific historical period and linked to political questions, have never been considered expressions of the Catholic faith . . . The Church is also aware that the contents of these documents were manipulated for political purposes

by competing colonial powers in order to justify immoral acts against Indigenous peoples that were carried out, at times, without opposition from ecclesiastical authorities.[672]

TRANSLATION: not part of the teaching of the Church. Manipulated for political purposes. We didn't protest it at the time. Yes, we are sorry, but even though our pope issued the said papal bull, it was not doctrine, not teaching, and it was misused by others. Not us.

The statement closes with:

> Pope Francis has urged: "Never again can the Christian community allow itself to be infected by the idea that one culture is superior to others, or that it is legitimate to employ ways of coercing others."[673]

TRANSLATION: As the current pope can only "urge" the words that followed (and not direct them, as in an order, or yet another unfortunate papal bull), the Church confirms that any statement from the Bishop of Rome is not the doctrine of the Catholic Church, should only be taken as, I guess, encouragement. *Go team.*

This is not how an institution should apologize. Equivocation does nothing to rebuild trust. In fact, it further diminishes it. And while my heart is heavy for the Indigenous peoples of Canada—in terms of lies and misinformation, the Catholic Church has only further plowed the field for the producers in the Theater of Lies.

This leads me to my third solution that institutions need to act on—examining their own role in the Theater of Lies.

If any institution is serious about the issue of lies and misinformation in the world, has it ever asked itself what role—if any—has the institution played in the manufacture and distribution of such lies and/or misinformation?

Chances are the knee-jerk reaction will be to say, *None*. Followed by the phrases, *Of course, what are you even thinking? That's impossible.* Exclamation marks would be employed . . . liberally. I know because when I've asked this question in person, I've sometimes been asked to leave. (*Who is this guy? Who hired him?*)

But unless you've done a careful, unbiased review of your institution's communications, that might not be so. Institutions need to make certain that they are not part of the problem; that they are not—perhaps unwittingly—producers in the Theater of Lies.

I will give you an example.

The global nuclear industry is, thankfully, taking steps to address the long-term storage of the waste products created using nuclear energy to generate electricity. The industry's term for this is *spent fuel* (as they avoid the use of the term *nuclear*, where possible). Most people refer to this as *nuclear waste*. In the case of the fuel used to generate electricity, it is actually called *high-level nuclear waste*—the really bad stuff that takes centuries to lose its powerful radioactive properties.

The industry's solution to the storage concern is called deep geological repositories (DGRs)—placing the spent fuel in special capsules and placing those capsules 500 meters or more below ground in geologically stable rock formations (once again, avoiding the word nuclear). The operation of the world's first DGR is expected in 2024 in Finland.[674]

Yet, when the Canadian organization assigned the role of developing and operating Canada's own DGR (the Nuclear Waste Management Organization) responded to a March 2021 story in the *Globe and Mail* questioning their DGR concept, the president of the NWMO, Lauri

Swami, said this, "The deep geological repository is safe and protects the environment."[675]

Sounds very good, but at the time she made the statement, there weren't any operating DGRs anywhere in the world. As of writing this book, not even the Finland DGR is operating. And the quote from the NWMO president remains on its website.

The nuclear industry's DGR concept may indeed be determined to be safe and to protect the environment when one and many more of them are operating. But to state in unequivocal terms that it *is safe and protects the environment*, in the present tense, as if it was operating at that time, is not just an overstatement. It is a false statement. Hopes are not facts.

And while I hope—as many others do—that the industry's DGR concepts will be safe and can assume that the industry will do everything in its power to ensure these operations will be safe—including regulatory oversight—that does not mean that today they are safe.

In that same response to the *Globe and Mail*, Swami also states that "deep geological storage is an international best practice," then further that it's "an area of scientific consensus."[676] The latter is correct. The former? False.

Let me go the dictionary on that. A best practice is "a procedure that has been shown by research and experience to produce optimal results and that is established or proposed as a standard suitable for widespread adoption."[677]

I may be accused of splitting hairs here. But when your role is to safely store the waste from the process of splitting atoms, I expect a high degree of precision in procedures and language. If not, the nuclear hatch opens for the Theater of Lies.

In my opinion, institutions cannot make statements like these and expect to foster trust with their stakeholders, the public. And statements such as these and their fallout (pun intended) diminish the credibility of the nuclear industry and the nascent organization assigned the responsibility of managing its waste. Further, such language as "is safe" rather than "will be safe" further entrenches the mistrust in institutions that the producers of lies and misinformation take advantage of.

In most instances, the public has no choice but to work with the institutions that the government assigned a specific task. This is called *government license.* But what institutions regularly fail at is respecting that the public has no choice. These institutions tend to operate from what I refer to as a we-know-better-than-you perspective, which is fundamentally harmful to the establishment and maintenance of trust.

I ask that institutions recognize their role to play in the larger world of reducing the impact of lies and misinformation. It is a key role they need to embrace, as so many already have with similar societal issues such as climate change, equity, work/life balance, and Indigenous reconciliation.

Institutions have three simple, but very challenging steps. (The challenges will come from organizational culture more than any external force)

One, know the purpose of your organization and be able to communicate it so clearly that twelve-year-old can understand it.

Two, acknowledge your mistakes, correct them, and let people know you've corrected them so these mistakes should not happen again.

And, three, examine your own organization's role as a producer—if an unwitting one—in the Theater of Lies. Are you expressing hopes as facts or misrepresenting them?

Our defense from the Theater of Lies will come from all of us, individually and as societies, taking responsibility for our dual roles: we are the audiences for lies and misinformation, and also its distributors.

John F. Kennedy inspired the world with "I am a Berliner." Today, we need to inspire ourselves with *"Ich bin im Theater"*—I am in the Theater.

"Learn from yesterday, live for today, hope for tomorrow. The important thing is not to stop questioning."[678]

— ALBERT EINSTEIN

....

13

FADE TO BLACK.

With the enabling power of the internet and its handheld offspring, social media, the Theater of Lies has become a theater of war. In some places, it is a hot war: shots fired, armies engaged, and death tolls in the thousands. In others, it is a cold war that is rapidly heating. And the producers of lies and misinformation are winning. They have successfully killed any debate on complex issues of race, language, gender, abortion, healthcare, gun control, climate change, education, free speech, and almost any other issue that requires nuanced discussion, into a single binary option. Woke v. unwoke—and woke, the once-simple notion of being aware of injustice and the need to address it—has lost. On that single but enormous scope of an issue, the Theater of Lies has demonstrated its power.

It is no longer possible, now, to be a conservative thinker who can openly discuss these issues. Liberal thinkers (my apologies for the binary division, here), are challenged as well, with their responses to what they see as oppressive conservative tactics and messaging and the imbalances of history—swinging too hard to the absolutes of political correctness and identity-based categorizations. Whereas conservative causes seem to lend themselves to Theater of Lies tactics, self-styled progressive causes tend to lean to the politics of exclusion—better known as cancel culture. Both are harmful.

By entrenching binary absolutes, debate is limited to self-serving echo chambers of social media and partisan media programming. People no longer talk to each other, only *at* each other. Words are bombs and media platforms their launch pads.

It is the *independent* thinkers who will foster change, not the bias-prone. It is a harder road to travel, but much more personally rewarding. Our goal must be to foster, grow, and engage this group.

In Matthew 5:5 NIV, the Bible misleads. It reads, "Blessed are the meek, for they will inherit the earth." Yet, word "meek" is defined as those who are quiet, gentle, and easily imposed upon—submissive: *just* the kind of audience the Theater of Lies wants.

Perhaps that is not what Matthew meant. But this I know: it is not the meek who will inherit the earth but the *curious* and those with the *courage* to act upon it.

Finally, there is yet another "c" word along this path. As many in the audience with us are angry, even righteously angry (especially those who rise up from the audience to join the producers in action), I urge you not to respond in kind. Instead, show compassion, for their anger—if not their facts—come from an honest place. And that is a good place to start.

Rather than fear the Tree of Knowledge, we must embrace it. We need to plant an entire forest of them and share their fruits far and wide. Beginning with ourselves.

Let us teach our children thinking habits that will enrich their lives, as we, together, move past our collective discomfort with thoughts and instead, embrace them.

THANK YOU.

FURTHER READING

....

Bad News, *How Woke Media is Undermining Democracy*, Batya Ungar-Sargon, Encounter Book, 2021

Calling Bullshit, *The Art of Skepticism in a Data-Driven World,* Carl T. Bergstrom and Jevin D. West, Random House, 2020

Common Good Constitutionalism, *Recovering the Classic Legal Tradition,* Adrian Vermuele, Polity Press, 2022

Conservatism, a Rediscovery, Yoram Hazony, Regnery Gateway (Salem Communications) 2022

Empire of Illusion, *The end of Literacy and the Triumph of Spectacle,* Chris Hedges, Random House and Nation Books, 2009

Fool Proof, *Why Misinformation infects our minds and how to build immunity,* Sander van der Linden, W. W. Norton & Company, 2023

How Democracies Die, Steven Levitsky and Daniel Ziblatt, Broadway Books, 2018

How to Stand Up to a Dictator, *The fight for our future,* Maria Ressa, Harper Collins, 2022

Knowledge Illusion, The, *Why we never think alone*, Steven Sloman and Philip Fernbach, Riverhead Books, 2017

Lie Machines, *How to save democracy from troll armies, deceitful robots, junk news operations, and political operatives,* Philip N. Howard, Yale University Press, 2020

Manufacturing Consent, *The political economy of the mass media*, Edward S. Herman and Noam Chomsky, Random House, 1988

Munitions of the mind, *A history of propaganda from the ancient world to present day,* Philip M. Taylor, Manchester University Press, 2003

Off the Edge, *Flat Earth, conspiracy culture, and why people will believe anything*, Kelly Weill, Algonquin Books of Chapel Hill, 2022

Politics of Obedience, The, *The discourse of voluntary servitude*, Étienne de La Boétie, reprinted by the Mises Institute, 2015

Postjournalism and the Death of Newspapers, *the media after Trump: manufacturing anger and polarization*, Andrey Mir, 2020

Propaganda and American Democracy, edited by Nancy Snow, Louisiana State University Press, 2014

Regime Change, *Toward a Postliberal Future*, Patrick J. Dineen, Penguin Random House, 2023

Savvy, Navigating Fake Companies, Fake Leaders, and Fake News in the Post-Trust Era, Shiv B. Singh and Rohini Luthra, Phd, Idea Press Publishing, 2019

Stamped from the Beginning, *The definitive history of racist ideas in America*, Ibram X. Kendi, Bold Type Books, 2016

The Life-Changing Science of Detecting Bullshit, John V. Petrocelli, St. Martins' Press, 2021

Weaponization of Everything, The, *A field guide to the new way of war,* Mark Galeotti, Yale University Press, 2022

ACKNOWLEDGEMENTS

This book is the result of my personal and professional exploration into the world in lies and misinformation in which we all live. Throughout this exploration, I have benefited from the guidance and inspiration of others along the way. I want to thank Rick Antonson, an old friend re-connected, who showed me how to raise my game as a non-fiction author, and Steven Bright, a long-time colleague who helped me to get my facts straight and language clear. To Barry Campbell, another valued colleague, I must thank for asking me the hard questions that guided many revisions, and Heather Bastedo, whose encouragement helped me balance vernacular prose with academic rigor. I also thank the editors and production specialists at Friesen Press who brought this 20th century author into the realities of 21st century publishing and the communications pros at Smith Publicity who have help get this important story to a wider audience. And, to Billy Murray, a special thanks for photographing the journey.

INDEX

Mann, Horace, 320,

Márquez, Gabriel Garcia, 7

Marx, Groucho, 19, 217

Maslow's Hierarchy, 179, 181

McConnell, Mitch, 64

McLuhan, Marshall, 103

McMaster University, Canada, 26

Mercer, Rick, 203

Milbank, Dana, Washington Post, 39

Mir, Andrey, 156

Moors, the, 58-62, 103, 348

Moyers, Bill, PBS, 104

Mudd, Roger, 84

Mueller, Robert, 38, 66-68

Murrow, Edward R., 105

Musk, Elon, 8, 227,

NASA, 32, 196, 281, 282-293

Naveed, Fakhar, 193

Nebiolo, Primo, 31, 33-34,

New Democratic Party of Canada, 132,

Nicot, Jean, 49-50

Nixon, Richard, 87

No Child Left Behind Act. 343

Obama, Barrack, 60

Olympic Games, 145

ENDNOTES

....

Preface – Why I Wrote This Book.

[1] Timothy Synder, "Ukraine Holds the Future," *Foreign Affairs Magazine* (September/October 2022): 137.

[2] "COVID – Coronavirus Statistics," *Worldometer*, April 13, 2023, https://www.worldometers.info/coronavirus/.

[3] "Bombing of Hiroshima and Nagasaki – Causes, Impact & Deaths," *History.com*, https://www.history.com/topics/world-war-ii/bombing-of-hiroshima-and-nagasaki.

[4] Carla Johnson, "A Year of COVID Vaccinations: Many Lives Saved, Many Needlessly Lost," *Chicago Sun-Times*, December 15, 2021. https://chicago.suntimes.com/2021/12/15/22836536/covid-vaccines-anniversary-one-year-lives-saved-needlessly-lost-coronavirus.

[5] Johnson, "A Year of COVID Vaccinations."

[6] Edouard Mathieu and Max Roser, "How Do Death Rates From COVID-19 Differ Between People Who Are Vaccinated and Those Who Are Not?" *World in Data*, November 23, 2021, https://ourworldindata.org/covid-deaths-by-vaccination.

7 James Ball, "Taking a Bite Out of Reality," *New Scientist Magazine* (July 22–28, 2023): 23.

Introduction - Welcome to the Theater of Lies

8 Garcia Marquez Gabriel, *The Autumn of the Patriarch* (London, UK: Picador Publisher, January 1, 1975).

9 "Pizzagate gunman recorded video for daughters, said he's standing up for children," *CBS News*, June 14, 2017, https://www.cbsnews.com/news/pizzagate-gunman-records-video-for-daughters-saying-he-standing-up-for-children/.

10 "'Pizzagate' Shooter Sentenced: What to Know About the Comet Ping Pong Conspiracies," *Fox News*, June 22, 2017, https://www.foxnews.com/us/pizzagate-shooter-sentenced-what-to-know-about-the-comet-ping-pong-conspiracies.

11 Nick Bostrom, "Are You Living in a Computer Simulation?" *Philosophical Quarterly* 53, No. 211(2003): 243-255. https://www.simulation-argument.com/simulation.pdf.

12 Robert Farley, "How Many Died as a Result of the Capitol Riot?" *Factcheck.org*, March 21, 2022, https://www.factcheck.org/2021/11/how-many-died-as-a-result-of-capitol-riot/.

13 "Sir. John A. 360 – Direct Quotes from Sir John A. Speak for Themselves," *City of Kingston*, September 6, 2019, https://getinvolved.cityofkingston.ca/sir-john-a-360/stories/direct-quotes-from-sir-john-a-these-speak-for-themselves

14   "Word of the Year," *Oxford Languages*, https://languages.oup.com/word-of-the-year/.

15   Hal Arkowitz and Scott O. Lilienfeld, "Why Science Tells Us Not to Rely on Eyewitness Accounts," *Scientific American* (January 1, 2010). https://www.scientificamerican.com/article/do-the-eyes-have-it.

16   "Education > Scientific Literacy: Countries Compared," *NationMaster*, https://www.nationmaster.com/country-info/stats/Education/Scientific-literacy.

17   *A Night in Casablanca*, directed by Archie Mayo (1946, Palm Springs, CA: Lorna Vista Productions).

ACT ONE:
A BRIEF HISTORY OF LIES

Chapter 1 – In the Beginning, There Were Lies.

18   Genesis 3:16 KJV.

19   Genesis 3:17 KJV.

20   Genesis 3:18 KJV.

21   Genesis 3:19 KJV.

22   Helen O'Neill, "Lance Armstrong's Lies Not So Different From Our Own," *Star Tribune*, January 18, 2013, https://www.startribune.com/armstrong-not-so-different-experts-on-deception-say-everyone-lies/187476051/.

23   Alex Lickerman, "Why We Lie," *Psychology Today*, March 8, 2010, https://www.psychologytoday.com/us/blog/happiness-in-world/201003/why-we-lie.

24   Dan Ariely, *The (Honest) Truth about Dishonesty: How We Lie to Everyone – Especially Ourselves* (New York, NY: Harper Collins, 2012).

25   Yuval Noah Hariri, *Homo Deus: A Brief History of Tomorrow* (New York, NY: HarperCollins, 2017).

26   "Why Do We Believe Lies?" *Bill Gates and Rashida Jones Ask Big Questions* [podcast], November 30, 2020, produced by Gates Notes, https://www.gatesnotes.com/podcast.

27   "Why Do We Believe Lies?"

28   John F. Kennedy, *Yale University Commencement Address* [speech], Yale University Commencement, New Haven, CT, June 11, 1962, https://www.americanrhetoric.com/speeches/jfkyalecommencement.htm.

29   Mark Judge, "Shelby Steele and America's 'Poetic Truth,'" *Law & Liberty*, October 23, 2020, https://lawliberty.org/shelby-steele-and-americas-poetic-truths/.

30   Judge, "Steele and America's 'Poetic Truth.'"

31   "Truth, Lies, & Uncertainty" [interactive], *Scientific American*, June 2019, https://www.scientificamerican.com/interactive/truth-lies-uncertainty1/.

32   "Truth, Lies, & Uncertainty."

33   Alex Johnson, "'Post-Truth' is Oxford Dictionaries' Word of the Year for 2016," *NBC News*, Nov 16, 2016, https://www.nbcnews.com/news/us-news/post-truth-oxford-dictionaries-word-year-2016-n685081.

34 "The Economy According to Justin Trudeau," *The Globe and Mail*, July 25, 2023, https://www.theglobeandmail.com/opinion/editorials/article-the-economy-according-to-justin-trudeau/.

35 "Economy According to Trudeau."

36 "Economy According to Trudeau."

37 Lynn Hasher, David Goldstein, and Thomas Toppino, "Frequency and the Conference of Referential Validity," *Journal of Verbal Learning and Verbal Behavior* 16, No. 1 (February 1977): 107–112.

38 Hasher, Goldstein, and Toppino, "Referential Validity."

39 Hasher, Goldstein, and Toppino, "Referential Validity."

40 Ian Maynard Begg, Ann Anas, and Suzanne Farinacci, "Dissociation of Processes in Belief: Source Recollection, Statement Familiarity, and the Illusion of Truth," *Journal of Experimental Psychology: General* 121. No. 4 (1992): 446–458.

41 F. Diane Barth, "Why We Believe Liars," *NBC News*, April 18, 2019. https://www.nbcnews.com/think/opinion/why-do-we-believe-liars-ncna993816.

Chapter 2 – Propaganda: The Good, The Bad, and The Ugly.

42 "Do Animals Lie?" *Health Diaries*, https://healthdiaries.com/animals-lie.htm.

43 H. L. Mencken, "A Carnival of Buncombe," *On Politics* (Baltimore, MD: John Hopkins University Press, 1956; 2006).

44 Phillip M. Taylor, *Munitions of the Mind* (Manchester, JK: Manchester University Press, 2003).

[45] Taylor, *Munitions.*

[46] "Sacred Congregation for the Propagation of the Faith," *History of Christian Theology*,

https://historyofchristiantheology.com/glossary/
sacred-congregation-for-the-propagation-of-the-faith/

[47] "Sacred Congregation," *History of Christian Theology.*

[48] "Congregation for the Evangelization of Peoples,"
LiquiSearch, https://www.liquisearch.com/
congregation_for_the_evangelization_of_peoples

[49] Colin Dunn, "Land Pollution Recovery: The Reclamation of Sudbury," *Greener Ideal*, November 2, 2010, https://greenerideal.
com/news/politics/
canada/8511-land-pollution-recovery-the-reclamation-of-sudbury.

[50] Oliver Darcy, "I Spent an Entire Day Watching Russia's Propaganda Network. Here's the Warped Reality I Saw Presented to Viewers," *CNN*, March 3, 2022. https://www.cnn.
com/2022/03/02/media/rt-propaganda-network/index.html.

[51] Taylor, *Munitions*: 222–224.

[52] Taylor, *Munitions*: 140.

[53] Mark Galeotti, *The Weaponization of Everything* (New Haven, CT: Yale University Press, 2022): 31.

[54] Galeotti, *Weaponization*: 332.

Chapter 3 – Lies Look Real.

[55] Denis Diderot, *Rameau's Nephew – Le Neveu de Rameau (c.1781): A Multi-Media Bilingual Edition*, ed. M. Hobson, trans. K.E.

Tunstall and C. Warnan (Cambridge, UK: Open Book Publishers, June 2016).

56   Brad Adgate, "The January 6 Hearings Are the Best Television Series of the Summer," *Forbes.com*, July 9, 2022, https://www. forbes.com/sites/bradadgate/2022/07/09/ the-january-6-hearings-are-the-best-television-series-of-the-summer/.

57   Rachel Martin and Eric Deggans, "Analyzing the Television Ratings for the First Hearing on the Jan. 6 Insurrection," *NPR*, June 6, 2022, https://www.npr.org/2022/06/13/1104529512/ analyzing-the-television-ratings-for-the-first-hearing-on-the-jan-6-insurrection.

58   " ***MEDIA ADVISORY*** TOMORROW: Rep. Matt Gaetz Leads Republican Coalition in D.C. Field Hearing on January 6th; Reacts to Trump Indictment," *Rep. Matt Gaetz Official Press Release | LegiStorm*, June 12, 2023, https://www.legistorm.com/ stormfeed/view_rss/2242242/member/3136/title/media-advisory-tomorrow-rep-matt-gaetz-leads-republican-coalition-in-dc-field-hearing-on-january-6th-reacts-to-trump-indictment.html

59   "Field Hearings: Fact Sheet on Purposes, Rules, Regulations, and Guidelines," *Congressional Research Service*, updated September 18, 2017, https://crsreports.congress.gov/product/pdf/RS/ RS20928/14,.

60   Dana Milbank, "As Trump is Arraigned, Republicans Honor the Insurrectionists," *The Washington Post*, June 16, 2023, https:// www.washingtonpost.com/opinions/2023/06/16/ house-gop-trump-indictment-reaction-jan-6/.

61 "House Conservatives on Investigations and Prosecutions for January 6 Attack on the U.S. Capitol" [video], *C-SPAN*, June 13, 2023, https://www.c-span.org/video/?528698-1/ house-conservatives-investigations-prosecutions-january-6-attack-us-capitol.

62 *Cambridge Dictionary*, s.v. "force multiplier," https://dictionary. cambridge.org/dictionary/english/force-multiplier.

63 "House Conservatives on Investigations ..." [video], *C-SPAN*.

64 "House Conservatives on Investigations ..." [video], *C-SPAN*.

65 Milbank, "As Trump is Arraigned."

66 Milbank, "As Trump is Arraigned."

67 Milbank, "As Trump is Arraigned."

68 Milbank, "As Trump is Arraigned."

69 Authority to Meet; Rule XXVI, paragraph 1, Senate Rules Affecting Committees (fas.org), A standing committee and its subcommittees are authorized to meet, November 15,2018, https://sgp.fas.org/crs/misc/98-311.pdf

70 Fakhar Naveed, "The Origin of Propaganda," *Mass Communication Talk*, October 17, 2016. https://www. masscommunicationtalk.com/the-origin-of-propaganda.html.

71 *John Ford Goes to War*, directed by Tom Thurman, written by Tom Marksbury (Lexington, KY; FBN Motion Pictures, 2002). https://www.imdb.com/title/tt0338163/

72 "Orson Welles Quotes," *BrainyQuote*, 2022, https://www. brainyquote.com/quotes/orson_welles_539042.

73 Stephen Metcalf, "How John Wayne Became a Hollow Masculine Icon," *The Atlantic*, December 2017. https://www.theatlantic.com/magazine/archive/2017/12/john-wayne-john-ford/544113/.

74 Metcalf, "John Wayne Hollow Masculine Icon."

75 Nancy Schroeder, *Wayne and Ford: The Films, the Friendship, and the Forging of an American Hero*, Deckle Edge, October 24, 2017

76 Ellyn Santiago, "READ: John Wayne's 1971 Playboy Interview Transcript," *Heavy.com*, February 19, 2019. https://heavy.com/news/2019/02/read-john-waynes-1971-playboy-interview-transcript/.

77 Samantha Ibrahim, "Sacheen Littlefeather: Raging John Wayne tried to attack me at 1973 Oscars," *The New York Post*, August 19, 2022, https://nypost.com/2022/08/19/sacheen-littlefeather-raging-john-wayne-tried-to-attack-me-at-1973-oscars/.

78 Widescreenings.com, Sacheen Littlefeather's speech on behalf of Marlon Brando at the 1973 Academy Awards, https://widescreenings.com/sacheen-littlefeather-oscar-speech.html.

79 Andrew Joseph, "The Rock on Running for President in 2020: 'I Wouldn't Rule it Out,'" *USA Today*, November 14, 2016, https://ftw.usatoday.com/2016/11/dwayne-johnson-rock-running-president-2020.

Chapter 4 – In This Theater, They Wear Masks.

80 Alexandre Koyré, *Réflexions sur le mensonge* (Paris, FR: Éditions Allia 1944; 2016).

81 Koyré, *Réflexions*: 36.

82 "AABA Statement on Race & Racism," *American Association of Biological Anthropologists (AABA)*, March 27, 2019, https:// physanth.org/about/position-statements/ aapa-statement-race-and-racism-2019/.

83 Vivian Cho, "How Science and Genetics are Reshaping the Race Debate of the 21st Century," *Harvard University*, April 2017, https://sitn.hms.harvard.edu/flash/2017/ science-genetics-reshaping-race-debate-21st-century/.

84 Abram X. Kendi, *Stamped From the Beginning* (Lebanon, IN: Bold Type Books, 2016): 23.

85 Kendi, *Stamped*: 24.

86 Kendi, *Stamped*: 24.

87 Kendi, *Stamped*: 37.

88 Kendi, *Stamped*: 38.

89 Kendi, *Stamped*: 23.

90 *Wikipedia*, s.v. "The White Man's Burden," last modified 6 September 2023, 13:01 UTC, https://en.wikipedia.org/wiki/ The_White_Man%27s_Burden#.

91 Enzo Dimatteo, "How Many Indigenous Children Died in Canada's Residential Schools?" *NOW Toronto*, June 2, 2021, https://nowtoronto.com/news/ how-many-indigenous-children-died-in-canadas-residential-schools.

92 Residential Schools, *A Chronology, Remembering the Children: an Aboriginal and Church Leaders' Tour to Prepare for Truth and Reconciliation*, http://www.rememberingthechildren.ca/history/ index.htm

93 John A. MacDonald (debate, House of Commons, Ottawa, ON, May 9, 1883).

94 Deena Robinson, "What is Greenwashing?" *Earth.org*, July 23, 2021. https://earth.org/what-is-greenwashing/.

95 Robinson, "What is Greenwashing?"

Chapter 5 – Playing to the Audience.

96 Michael Ende, *Die unendliche Geschichte (The Neverending Story)* (Stuttgart, DE: Thienemann Verlag, 1979).

97 "The History of 7-11," *7-Eleven Corporate,* http://corp.7-eleven.com/corp-BAK/history. [dead URL].

98 "Muslim Spain (711–1492)," *BBC Religions,* September 04, 2009, https://www.bbc.co.uk/religion/religions/islam/history/spain_1.shtml.

99 Erin Blakemore, "History and Culture: Who Were the Moors?" *National Geographic*, December 12, 2019,https://www.nationalgeographic.com/history/article/who-were-moors.

100 Daven Hiskey, "Did People in Medieval Times Really not Bathe?" *Today I Found Out: Feed Your Brain*, August 26, 2019, http://www.todayifoundout.com/index.php/2019/08/did-people-in-medieval-times-really-not-bathe/.

101 John Moore, "Afrikan Moors civilized Europe," *Black History.* https://blackhistory.neocities.org/moors.html.

102 Pope Eugene IV, *Bull Cantate Domino*, February 4, 1442.

103   Nazeer Ahmed, "The Atlantic Slave Trade," *History of Islam,* https://historyofislam.com/contents/onset-of-the-colonial-age/the-atlantic-slave-trade/.

104   Murray Bourne, Math of the Moors, *Interactive Mathematics,* February 7, 2007, https://www.intmath.com/blog/mathematics/math-of-the-moors-535.

105   Anne El Bey, "Bloody History Behind Thanksgiving Slaughtering Moors," *Health & Wellness* [blog], November 29, 2019, https://anneelbeycopywriter.net/bloody-history-behind-thanksgiving-slaughtering-moors/.

106   Ralph de Unamuno, "Thanksgiving or Thanks-taking," *La Presse San Diego*, November 26, 2003, https://www.laprensa-sandiego.org/archieve/november26-03/roots.htm

107   "How the Turkey Got Its Name," *Merriam-Webster,* https://www.merriam-webster.com/words-at-play/where-did-your-thanksgiving-turkey-come-from.

108   *"Lincoln and Thanksgiving," Lincoln Home National Historic Site | US National Parks Service,* https://www.nps.gov/liho/learn/historyculture/lincoln-and-thanksgiving.htm

109   Clifford N. Lazarus, "Why Many People Stubbornly Refuse to Change Their Minds," *Psychology Today,* December 24, 2018. https://www.psychologytoday.com/us/blog/think-well/201812/why-many-people-stubbornly-refuse-change-their-minds.

Chapter 6 – The Persuasive Power of Pathos.

[110] Bertrand Russell, *A History of Western Philosophy and Its Connection with Political and Social Circumstances from the Earliest Times to the Present Day* (New York, NY: Simon & Schuster, 1947).

[111] Ashley Parker and Michael Scherer, "Inside Mitch McConnell's Decades-long Effort to Block Gun Control," *The Washington Post*, May 28, 2022. https://www.washingtonpost.com/politics/2022/05/28/mcconnell-guns-mass-shootings/.

[112] Aristotle, *The" Art of Rhetoric*, Harvard University Press, Translated by John Henry Freese, 1926, E. Capps, editor *The "art" of rhetoric: Aristotle: Free Download, Borrow, and Streaming : Internet Archive*

[113] Ibid

[114] Glenn Kessler, "Trump's Repeated Claim that He Won a 'Landslide' Victory," *The Washington Post*, November 30, 2016, https://www.washingtonpost.com/news/fact-checker/wp/2016/11/30/trumps-repeated-claim-that-he-won-a-landslide-victory/.

[115] Natasha Bertrand, "Annotated: Mueller's Opening Statement," *POLITICO*, July 24, 2019. https://www.politico.com/story/2019/07/24/mueller-opening-statement-full-text-transcript-annotated-1428431.

[116] "Conway: Press Secretary gave 'Alternate Facts,'" *NBC News*, January 22, 2021, https://www.nbcnews.com/meet-the-press/video/conway-press-secretary-gave-alternative-facts-860142147643.

117　Chris Cuomo, "Let's Get After It," *CNN*, June 18, 2018, https://transcripts.cnn.com/show/CPT/date/2018-06-18/segment/01.

118　Michelle Quinn, "Trump Moves to Officially Withdraw U.S. from World Health Organization," *CBS News*, July 7, 2020, https://www.cbsnews.com/news/trump-who-world-health-organization-us-notice-of-withdrawal/.

119　Bobby Lewis (@revrrlewis), "Kellyanne Conway: 'This is COVID-19, not COVID-1 folks, and so you would think the people in charge of the World Health Organization, facts and figures, would be on top of that.'" *X*, April 15, 2020, 6:08 a.m., https://twitter.com/revrrlewis/status/1250395628305362944.

120　Lynn Hasher, David Goldstein, and Thomas Toppino, "Frequency and the Conference of Referential Validity," *Journal of Verbal Learning and Verbal Behavior* 16, No. 1 (February 1977): 107–112.

121　Muntasir Minhaz, "When is Oral Communication More Effective?" *iEdunote*. https://www.iedunote.com/effective-oral-communication

Chapter 7 – (Might as Well Face It) We're Addicted to Lies.

122　"60 Minutes News Magazine," *CBS Television*, December 13, 2015, https://www.cbsnews.com/news/60-minutes-a-new-direction-on-drugs/

123　David J.P. Phillips, "The Angel's and the Devil's Cocktail (Neuroleadership)," *David JP Phillips.com* https://www.davidjpphillips.com/keynotes/angels-and-devils/

124 Ibid.

125 "Box Office History for Die Hard Movies," *The Numbers*, https:// www.the-numbers.com/movies/franchise/ Die-Hard#tab=summary.

126 Phillips, "Angel's and Devil's Cocktail."

Chapter 8 – Villains Are Very Seductive.

127 Malcom Forbes, *The Sayings of Chairman Malcolm: The Capitalist's Handbook* (New York, NY: HarperCollins, 1978).

128 Amber Phillips, "'They're Rapists.' President's [sic] Trump Campaign Launch Speech Two years Later, Annotated: He Really Hasn't Changed Much Since" [blog post], *The Washington Post*, June 16, 2017, https://www.proquest.com/blogs-podcasts-websites/theyre-rapists-presidents-trump-campaign-launch/ docview/1910444400/.

129 Phillips, "'They're Rapists.'"

130 Phillips, "'They're Rapists.'"

131 Phillips, "'They're Rapists.'"

132 Phillips, "'They're Rapists.'"

133 *Wikipedia*, s.v. "Lindsey Graham 2016 Presidential Campaign," last modified 11 November 2022, at 16:54 UTC. https:// en.wikipedia.org/wiki/ Lindsey_Graham_2016_presidential_campaign.

134 Joe Peyronnin, "Trump: 'I Alone Can Fix It,'" *Huffington Post*, July 22, 2016, https://www.huffpost.com/entry/ trump-i-alone-can-fix-it_b_11128366.

135 *Parli: The Dictionary of Canadian Politics*, s.v. "royal jelly," https://parli.ca/royal-jelly/

136 Chris Whipple, "Ted Kennedy: The Day the Presidency Was Lost," *ABC News*, August 28, 2009. https://abcnews.go.com/Politics/TedKennedy/story?id=8436488.

Chapter 9 - Stage-Managing the Critics.

137 Taylor, *Munitions*: 147.

138 Taylor, *Munitions*: 130–131.

139 Taylor, *Munitions*: 130–131.

140 Taylor, *Munitions*: 130–131.

141 Taylor, *Munitions*: 154.

142 Taylor, *Munitions*: 155.

143 Nolan, Martin. (2005). "Orwell Meets Nixon When and Why 'the Press' Became 'the Media,'" *The International Journal of Press/Politics* 10, No. 2 (Spring 2005): 69–84. https://doi.org/10.1177/1081180X052776.

144 Caroline Graham, "'The Press, the Establishment, and Professors Are the Enemy' – Latest Archive Recordings Reveal Depth of Nixon's Paranoia," *The Daily Mail*, December 3, 2008. https://www.dailymail.co.uk/news/article-1091608/The-Press-establishment-professors-enemy--latest-archive-recordings-reveal-depth-Nixons-paranoia.html.

145 Graham, "The Press, the Establishment, and Professors ..."

146 Matt Giles, "When Richard Nixon Declared War on the Media," *Longreads*, November 8, 2018. https://longreads.

com/2018/11/08/
when-richard-nixon-declared-war-on-the-media/.

147 Taylor, *Munitions*: 147.

148 Ian Schwartz, "Trump: 'Don't Believe The Crap You See From
These People On Fake News,'" *Real Clear Politics*, July 24,
2018, https://www.realclearpolitics.com/video/2018/07/24/
trump_dont_believe_the_crap_you_see_from_these_people_on_
fake_news.html#!.

149 Charlie Spiering, "Donald Trump: Without Social Media, I
Might Not Be President," *Breitbart News*, October 21,
2017. https://www.breitbart.com/politics/2017/10/21/
donald-trump-social-media-helped-make-president/.

150 Dan Managan, "President Trump told Lesley Stahl He Bashes
Press 'To Demean You and Discredit You So ... No One Will
Believe' Negative Stories About Him," *CNBC News*, May 22,
2018. https://www.cnbc.com/2018/05/22/trump-told-lesley-
stahl-he-bashes-press-to-discredit-negative-stories.html.

151 "Russian Law Aimed at Curbing Ukraine War Criticism Casts
Chill Over Critics," *CBC.ca*, March 11, 2022. https://www.cbc.
ca/news/world/
russia-laws-ukraine-invasion-war-critics-1.6382168.

152 "Russian Law Aimed at Curbing Ukraine War Criticism..."

153 "Do Not Call Ukraine Invasion a 'War', Russia Tells Media,
Schools," *Al Jazeera News*, March 2, 2022, https://www.aljazeera.
com/news/2022/3/2/
do-not-call-ukraine-invasion-a-war-russia-tells-media-schools.

154 "156 Journalists Killed in Philippines," *Committee to Protect
Journalists*, https://cpj.org/data/killed/asia/philippines/?status=Kill

ed&motiveConfirmed%5B%5D=Confirmed&motiveUnconfirm
ed%5B%5D=Unconfirmed&type%5B%5D=Journalist
&cc_fips%5B%5D=RP&start_year=1992&end_
year=2023&group_by=location.

155 Simon Lewis, "Duterte Says Journalists in the Philippines Are 'Not Exempted From Assassination,'" *Time Magazine*, June 1, 2016, https://time.com/4353279/ duterte-philippines-journalists-assassination/.

156 Sara Fisher, "Media Wrestles With Public Trust as Coronavirus Intensifies," *Axios*, March 18, 2020, https://www.axios. com/2020/03/18/media-public-trust-coronavirus.

157 Megan Brenan, "Americans Remain Distrustful of Mass Media," *Gallup Inc.*, September 30, 2020, https://news.gallup.com/ poll/321116/americans-remain-distrustful-mass-media.aspx.

158 "Final Job Cuts Report for 2020; Over 2.3 Million, Nearly Half Due to COVID," *Challenger Covid Coverage | The Challenger Report*, January 7, 2021, https://www.challengergray.com/blog/ job-cuts-dec-2020-over-2-3-million-nearly-half-due-to-covid/.

Chapter 10 – I May Lose My Head For This.

159 Koushun Takami, *Battle Royale* (Tokyo, JA: Ohta Publishing, 1999).

160 Kim Kildong, "A New God, a New Identity, a New Japan," *The Asian Institute for Policy Studies*, June 27, 2018. http://en.asaninst. org/contents/a-new-god-a-new-identity-a-new-japan/.

161 Anthony Drago and Doublas Wellman, *Surviving Hiroshima: A Young Woman's Story* (Waynesville, NC: WriteLife Publishing, 2020).

162 "Girls Equal in British Throne Succession," *BBC News*, October 28, 2011, https://www.bbc.com/news/uk-15492607.

163 "Stephen Fry on Why a 'Preposterous' Monarchy Still Works, *CBC Television*, 2018, https://www.cbc.ca/player/play/1236941891867.

164 Grant Bailey, "EGGHEADS: Sir David Attenborough is UK's favourite intelligent celebrity – but who else makes the list?" *The Sun*, January 25, 2018, https://www.thesun.co.uk/news/5426262/sir-david-attenborough-is-uks-favourite-intelligent-celebrity-but-who-else-makes-the-list/.

Chapter 11 – I May Go to Hell For This.

165 Mark Twain, *Letters from Earth* (Toldeo, OH: EMP Press, 2013).

166 Susan Wise Bauer, *The History of the Medieval World* (New York, NY: W.W. Norton & Company, 2010): 3.

167 Bauer, *History of the Medieval World*: 7.

168 Bauer, *History of the Medieval World*: 57.

169 Bauer, *History of the Medieval World*: 57.

170 "Roman Colosseum Tour," *The Grand Colosseum History*, https://www.romecolosseumtour.com/the-grand-colosseum-history/.

171 "Discover York Minster: Timeline," *York Minster*, https://yorkminster.org/discover/timeline/.

172 "Homepage," *York Minster*, https://yorkminster.org.

173 Marshall McLuhan, "Chapter 1: The Medium is the Message," *Understanding Media: The Extensions of Man*, (New York, NY: McGraw Hill, 1964).

174 Max Roser and Esteban Ortiz-Ospina, "Literacy," *Our World in Data*, September 20, 2018, https://ourworldindata.org/literacy.

175 "The Gutenberg Bible," *Harvard Library*, https://library.harvard.edu/collections/gutenberg-bible.

176 *Wikipedia*, s.v. "Luther Bible," https://en.wikipedia.org/wiki/Luther_Bible, last revised 5 October 2023, at 12:46 UTC.

177 Robert A. Houston, "The Growth of Literacy in Western Europe from 1500 to 1800," *Brewminate: A Bold Blend of News and Ideas*, November 28, 2011, https://brewminate.com/the-growth-of-literacy-in-western-europe-from-1500-to-1800/.

178 Bill Moyers and Joseph Campbell, *The Power Of Myth* [TV series], produced by PBS Television, 1988.

Chapter 12 – Crouching Director, Hidden Producer.

179 Hannah Arendt, "Reflections: Truth and Politics," *New Yorker Magazine*, February 25, 1967.

180 David Sheddon, "Today in Media History: Edward R. Murrow Challenged the Broadcast Industry in His 1958 RTNDA Speech," *The Poytner Institute*, October 15, 2014, https://www.poynter.org/reporting-editing/2014/today-in-media-history-edward-r-murrow-challenged-the-broadcast-industry-in-his-1958-rtnda-speech/.

181 Sheddon, "Today in Media History."

182 "Total Number of Websites," *Internet Live Stat*, https://internetlivestat.com/statistics/?ty=total-number-of-websites.

183 Brian Dean, "Social Media Usage," *Backlino*, October 10, 2021, https://backlinko.com/social-media-users.

184 "Combatting COVID-19 Disinformation on Online Platforms," *Organisation for Economic Co-Operation and Development (OECD)*, July 3, 2020, https://www.oecd.org/coronavirus/policy-responses/combatting-covid-19-disinformation-on-online-platforms-d854ec48/.

185 William Turville, "Cash for Conspiracies," *Press Gazette*, June 3, 2020.

186 Brian Warner, "Alex Jones' Infowars Made A Disgusting Amount Of Money…According to Hiw Own Accidentally-Leaked Text Messages," *Celebrity Net Worth*, August 3, 2022, https://www.celebritynetworth.com/articles/celebrity/alex-jones-infowars-made-a-disgusting-amount-of-money-according-to-his-own-accidentally-leaked-text-messages/.

187 Warner, "Alex Jones' Infowars…"

188 Charles Riley, "YouTube, Apple and Facebook Remove Content from InfoWars and Alex Jones," *CNN*, August 6, 2018, https://money.cnn.com/2018/08/06/technology/facebook-infowars-alex-jones/index.html.

189 "Infowars.com - Traffic, Revenue, Competitors and Business Model," *Pipecandy.com*, https://pipecandy.com/companies/infowars-llc/ [dead URL].

190 "Number of Social Media Users in 2021/2022: Demographics and Predictions," *FinancesOnline*, https://financesonline.com/number-of-social-media-users/.

191 "Average Time Americans Spend in Religious or Spiritual Activities," *Preaching Today*, September 2010, https://www.preachingtoday.com/illustrations/2010/september/5090610.html

192 "Average Time Spent Daily on Social Media (Latest 2021 Data)," *Broadband Search*, https://www.broadbandsearch.net/blog/average-daily-time-on-social-media#post-navigation-1.

193 Batya Ungar-Sargon, *Bad News* (New York, NY: Encounter Books, 2021): 7.

194 Philip N. Howard, *Lie Machines* (New Haven, CT: Yale University Press, 2020

195 Talha Burki, "The Online Vaccine Movement in the Age of COVID-19," *The Lancet: Digital Health* 2, no. 10 (October 2020). https://www.thelancet.com/journals/landig/article/PIIS2589-7500(20)30227-2/fulltext.

196 "About Us," *Valuetainment* [YouTube Channel], https://www.youtube.com/c/VALUETAINMENT/about.

197 "Failure to Act: How Tech Giants Continue to Defy Calls to Rein in Vaccine Misinformation," *Center for Countering Digital Hate*, 2020, https://252f2edd-1c8b-49f5-9bb2-cb57bb47e4ba.filesusr.com/ugd/f4d9b9_dbc700e9063b4653a7d27f4497f3c2c2.pdf.

198 "Failure to Act."

199 "Failure to Act."

200 Alexander Zaitchik, "Meet Alex Jones," *Rolling Stone Magazine*, March 2, 2011, https://www.rollingstone.com/culture/culture-news/meet-alex-jones-175845/.

Chapter 13 – Lies Are Profitable.

201   Ryo Mac, "The Real Story Behind 'There's a Sucker Born Every Minute,'" *Medium*, July 15, 2016, https://medium.com/skeptikai/the-real-story-behind-the-quote-theres-a-sucker-born-every-minute-1db9a7220d34.

202   "VW's Former CEO to Stand Trial Over 'Dieselgate,'" techexplore.com, September 9, 2020, https://techxplore.com/news/2020-09-vw-ceo-trial-dieselgate.html.

203   Christina Neuhaus, "VW Ex-boss Denies Prior Knowledge of Pollution Cheating," *Phys.org*, January 19, 2017, https://phys.org/news/2017-01-vw-ex-boss-denies-prior-knowledge.html.

204   Christina Neuhaus, Richard Schnieder, and Tom Krisner, "VW Engineer Pleads Guilty in Emissions Case, Will Co-Operate," *CTV News*, September 9, 2016, https://www.ctvnews.ca/business/vw-engineer-pleads-guilty-in-emissions-case-will-co-operate-1.3065322.

205   Roger Parloff, "How VW Paid $25 Billion for 'Dieselgate' — and Got Off Easy," *Fortune Magazine*, February 6, 2018, https://fortune.com/2018/02/06/volkswagen-vw-emissions-scandal-penalties/.

206   Kirsten Korosec, "The First Tesla 'Range Inflation' /lawsuit Has Been Filed," *TechCrunch*, August 3, 2023, https://techcrunch.com/2023/08/03/tesla-range-inflation-lawsuit-filed/.

207   Jim Zarroli, "How Can You Tell When A CEO Is Lying?," *NPR*, October 18, 2020, https://www.npr.org/2010/10/18/130544236/how-can-you-tell-when-a-ceo-is-lying

208   Zarroli, "How Can You Tell."

209 Zarroli, "How Can You Tell."

210 Zarroli, "How Can You Tell."

211 David Larcker and Brian Tayan, "We Studied 38 Incidents of
     CEO Bad Behaviour and Measured Their Consequences,"
     Harvard Business Review, June 9, 2016. https://hbr.org/2016/06/
     we-studied-38-incidents-of-ceo-bad-behavior-and-measured-
     their-consequences.

212 *Cambridge Dictionary*, s.v. "sustainable." https://dictionary.
     cambridge.org/dictionary/english/sustainable.

213 "Living Wage Income Position Statement," *The Hershey Company*,
     2021, https://www.thehersheycompany.com/content/dam/
     hershey-corporate/documents/sustainability/HSY_Living_Wage_
     Income_Position_Statement.pdf.

214 "Cocoa," *International Institute of Tropical Agriculture
     (IITA)*. https://www.iita.org/cropsnew/cocoa/.

215 Geoffry York and Adrian Morrow, "The True Cost of Chocolate,"
     The Globe and Mail, May 12, 2023,
     https://www.theglobeandmail.com/world/
     article-chocolate-cocoa-farms-sustainable-prices/.

216 "Living Wage," *Hershey*.

217 "Sustainability Focus Area: Cocoa," The Hershey
     Company. https://www.thehersheycompany.com/en_us/home/
     sustainability/sustainability-focus-areas/cocoa.html

218 York and Morrow, "True Cost of Chocolate."

219 York and Morrow, "True Cost of Chocolate."

220 *Fairtrade International*, https://www.fairtrade.net/

221 *Fairtrade International*.

222 "2021 Cocoa Sustainability Progress Report," *Cargill,*
2022, https://www.cargill.com/sustainability/cocoa/
cocoa-sustainability-progress-report.

223 "Farmer Livelihoods | Cocoa and Chocolate," *Cargill,*
2023. https://www.cargill.com/sustainability/cocoa/
farmer-livelihoods

224 Kristy Leissle, "The Cocoa System Is Not Broken," *Doc of Choc,*
April 15, 2021, https://docofchoc.com/
cocoa-system-not-broken/

225 York and Morrow, "True Cost of Chocolate."

226 "Farm Household Income and Characteristics," *Economic Research
Service – U.S. Department of Agriculture→,* 2023, https://www.
ers.usda.gov/data-products/
farm-household-income-and-characteristics/

227 "Average farm family income in Canada from 2013 to 2018 (in
1,000 Canadian dollars)," *Statista,* 2018, https://www.statista.
com/statistics/468483/average-farm-family-income-in-canada/

228 York and Morrow, "True Cost of Chocolate."

229 Leissle, "Cocoa System Not Broken."

230 "Sustainability's Influence on Chocolate Purchase Decisions
Continues to Grow, Cargill Study Finds," *Cargill | Media Release,*
December 14, 2020, https://www.cargill.com/2020/
sustainability-influence-on-chocolate-purchase-decision

231 "Sustainability's Influence on Chocolate," *Cargill.*

232 Zarroli, *"How Can You Tell When A CEO Is Lying?"*

233 Steven Lee Myers and Sheera Frenkel, "How Disinformation
Splintered and Became More Intractable," *New York Times,*

October 20, 2022, https://www.nytimes.com/2022/10/20/
technology/disinformation-spread.html.

Chapter 14 - A Snapshot of the Theater in Action.

234 Nick Westoll, "4 Pedestrians, Including Teen, Struck and Killed
in Northwest London, Ont.: Police," *Global News*, June 6,
2021. https://globalnews.ca/news/7927021/
hyde-park-south-carriage-collision-london-ontario-police/.

235 Palak Mangat and Samantha Wright Allen, "'Brutal, Cowardly,
and Brazen Act of Violence': MPs, Leaders Demand Action After
Four Members of Muslim Family Killed in What Police Are
Treating as a Hate-Motivated Crime in London, Ont., *The Hill
Times*, June 8, 2021, https://www.hilltimes.com/
story/2021/06/08/
brutal-cowardly-and-brazen-act-of-violence-mps-leaders-demand-
action-after-four-members-of-muslim-family-killed-in-what-
police-are-treating-as-a-hate-motivated-crime-in-london-
ont/229394/.

236 Mangat and Allen, "Brutal, Cowardly, and Brazen Act of Violence."

237 Nick Paparella, "Nathaniel Veltman Case Slated to Go to Trial in
Fall 2023," *CTV News | London*, April 12, 2022, https://london.
ctvnews.ca/
hearing-and-trial-dates-set-in-nathaniel-veltman-case-1.5859150.

238 Mangat and Allen, "Brutal, Cowardly, and Brazen Act of
Violence."

239 Jeff Bennett, "Boy are we happy to see YOU at our door this
election," *Facebook*, June 8, 2021, 9:48 a.m., https://www.

facebook.com/permalink.php?story_fbid=pfbid0kn9qBGuNbEC
3aZpZFHLAEV3KoHJKRqD8VyF8CvhYhi418TpyHJgGMVR
9YwPUyMAvl&id=532941605.

240 Celina Gallardo, "Is Canada a Racist Country? One-third of
Respondents in a New Study Say Yes," *Toronto Star*, June 21,
2021. https://www.thestar.com/news/canada/2021/06/21/
is-canada-a-racist-country-one-third-of-respondents-in-a-new-
study-say-yes.html.

241 Gallardo, "Is Canada a Racist Country?"

242 Gallardo, "Is Canada a Racist Country?"

243 Mangat and Allen, "Brutal, Cowardly, and Brazen Act
of Violence."

244 "Barbaric Cultural Practices Hotline," *Parli: The Dictionary of
Canadian Politics*, https://parli.ca/barbaric-cultural-practices-
hotline/. [Dead URL]

245 "Barbaric Cultural Practices Hotline," *Parli*.

246 Stephen Harper @stephenharper), "Canada is a place of tolerance
and pluralism," *X*, June 8, 2021, 7:31 a.m., https://twitter.com/
stephenharper/status/1402257066757136389.

247 "Black Wall Street Massacre | Say Their Names" [exhibit], *Stanford
| Libraries*, https://exhibits.stanford.edu/saytheirnames/feature/
black-wall-street-massacre.

248 "Black Wall Street Massacre," *Stanford*.

249 "Black Wall Street Massacre," *Stanford*.

250 Natasha Bertrand, "The GOP is Treating Jan. 6 the Way White
Supremacists Treated the Tulsa Race Massacre," *MSNBC*, June 2,
2021, https://www.msnbc.com/opinion/

gop-treating-jan-6-way-white-supremacists-treated-tulsa-race-n1269439.

251 Bertrand, "The GOP is Treating Jan. 6…"

252 "Black Wall Street Massacre," *Stanford.*

253 Dene More, "Schools' Mission – Take the Indian Out of the Child," *The Toronto Star*, March 3, 2016, https://www.thestar.com/entertainment/books/schools-mission-take-the-indian-out-of-the-child/article_9d512ded-9e43-5002-bcde-b1afff7aeebf.html

254 Padraig Moran, "Discovery of Kamloops Remains Confirmed What They Suspected. Now Action Must Match Words, Says Survivor," *CBC Radio*, June 1, 2021, https://www.cbc.ca/radio/thecurrent/the-current-for-june-1-2021-1.6048253/discovery-of-kamloops-remains-confirmed-what-they-suspected-now-action-must-match-words-says-survivor-1.6048257.

255 Courtney Dickson and Bridgette Watson, "Remains of 215 children found buried at Former B.C. Residential School, First Nation Says," *CBC News*, May 27, 2021. https://www.cbc.ca/news/canada/british-columbia/tk-eml%C3%BAps-te-secw%C3%A9pemc-215-children-former-kamloops-indian-residential-school-1.6043778.

256 Frances D'emillio, "Pope Francis Expresses Sorrow Over Residential School Deaths But Doesn't Apologize," *Global News*, June 6, 2021. https://globalnews.ca/news/7925626/pope-francis-residential-school-deaths/.

257 Father Raymond J. de Souza, "Historically Inaccurate to Suggest Catholic Church Hasn't Apologized for Residential Schools," *National Post*, June 4, 2021. https://nationalpost.com/opinion/

raymond-j-de-souza-it-is-historically-inaccurate-to-suggest-the-catholic-church-hasnt-apologized-for-residential-schools.

258 Father Raymond J. de Souza, "Justin Trudeau Can Learn Something From The Church About Apologies," *National Post*, June 12, 2021. https://nationalpost.com/opinion/raymond-j-de-souza-justin-trudeau-can-learn-something-from-the-church-about-apologies.

259 Moran, "Discovery of Kamloops Remains."

260 Brian Giesbrecht, "Some Questions About Kamloops," *The Winnipeg Sun*, June 5, 2021.

261 Giesbrecht, "Some Questions."

262 Giesbrecht, "Some Questions."

263 "About Us," *Frontier Centre For Public Policy*, https://fcpp.org/about/.

ACT TWO: WHY WE MUST GET OUT (AND WHAT COULD HAPPEN IF WE DON'T)

Chapter 1 – We Were Warned.

264 George Orwell, *1984*. https://files.libcom.org/files/1984.pdf page 28

265 *Joint Statement of the Russian Federation and the People's Republic of China on the International Relations Entering a New Era and the Global Sustainable Development*, February 4, 2022: 3. http://www.en.kremlin.ru/supplement/5770.

266 George Orwell, "Politics and the English Language," *Horizon Journal* 13, No. 76 (1946): 252–265.

267 "Ranking of Countries by Quality of Democracy," *Democracy Matrix | University of Würzburg*, https://www.democracymatrix.com/ranking.

268 *Wikipedia*, s.v. "The Economist Democracy Index," last edited 31 August 2023, https://en.m.wikipedia.org/wiki/The_Economist_Democracy_Index

269 Dan Blumenthal, "China's Censorship, Propaganda & Disinformation," *AEI Jewish Policy Centre*, July 10, 2020, https://www.aei.org/articles/chinas-censorship-propaganda-disinformation/.

270 Blumenthal, "China's Censorship."

271 Blumenthal, "China's Censorship."

272 Katherine Gordon, "China's Fifth Poison," *Australian Institute of International Affairs*, May 2, 2014, https://www.internationalaffairs.org.au/australianoutlook/chinas-fifth-poison/.

273 *Joint Statement of the Russian Federation and the People's Republic of China* …

274 Cary Wu, "Did the Pandemic Shake Chinese Citizens' Trust in Their Government? We Surveyed Nearly 20,000 People to Find Out," *The Washinton Post*, May 5, 2021, https://www.washingtonpost.com/politics/2021/05/05/did-pandemic-shake-chinese-citizens-trust-their-government/.

275 Kaiser Kuo, "Why Do Chinese People Like Their Government?" *SupChina*, July 22, 2019, https://supchina.com/2019/07/22/why-do-chinese-people-like-their-government/.

276 Kuo, "Why Do Chinese People Like Their Government?"

277 "2019 Edelman Trust Barometer: Global Report," *Daniel J. Edelman Holdings, Inc.*, 2019, https://www.edelman.com/sites/g/files/aatuss191/files/2019-02/2019_Edelman_Trust_Barometer_Global_Report.pdf

278 "Article 1," *The Constitution of the Federation of Russia,* 1993, http://www.constitution.ru/en/10003000-02.htm

279 "Article 3," *The Constitution of the Federation of Russia,* 1993, http://www.constitution.ru/en/10003000-02.htm

280 Bob Rae, "In These Trying Times, I Look to the Works of George Orwell for Inspiration," *The Globe and Mail,* July 11, 2022, https://www.theglobeandmail.com/opinion/article-in-these-trying-times-i-look-to-the-works-of-george-orwell-for/.

281 George Orwell, "Politics and English."

282 George Orwell, "Politics and English."

283 George Orwell, "Politics and English."

Chapter 2 - News Media and Lies: A Codependent Couple.

284 Carl Sagan and Ann Druyan, *The Demon-Haunted World* (New York, NY: Random House Publishing, 1996).

285 Deanne Pittman, "Food Sales Boosts Cineplex's Profits in Third Quarter," *David McKie.com,* January 30, 2016, http://www.davidmckie.com/cineplex/.

286 Rebecca Brunch, "Wednesday Cable Ratings 1/6/21: CNN Hits All-Time Highs for Coverage of Capitol Riot, MSNBC and Fox News Also Massive, Morning Joe Jumps for Georgia Senate Coverage," *The TV Ratings Guide,* January 8, 2021, http://www.

thetvratingsguide.com/2021/01/wednesday-cable-ratings-1621-cnn-hits.html.

287 Alexandra Steigrad, "CNN Sees Ratings Dive By 90% After 2021 Coverage," *New York Post*, January 12, 2022, https://nypost.com/2022/01/12/cnn-sees-ratings-dive-by-90-from-2021-coverage/.

288 Andrey Mir, "How the Media Polarized Us," *City Journal*, Summer 2022, https://www.city-journal.org/how-the-media-polarized-us.

289 Mir, "How the Media Polarized Us."

290 Merriam-Webster, s.v. "clickbait," https://www.merriam-webster.com/dictionary/clickbait

291 David Rozado, Musa Al-Gharbi, and Jamin Halberstadt, "Prevalence of Prejudice-Denoting Words in News Media Discourse: A Chronological Analysis," *Social Science Computer Review* 41, No. 1, July 27, 2021. https://doi.org/10.1177/08944393211031452,

292 David Rozado, Musa al-Gharbi and Jamin Halberstadt, "Use of 'Sexist' and 'Racist' in the New York Times Increased Over 400% Since 2012. Why?" *The Guardian*, February 26, 2022, https://www.theguardian.com/commentisfree/2022/feb/26/media-news-article-shift-discourse-language

293 Batya Ungar-Sargon, *Bad News* (New York, NY: Encounter Books, 2021): 4.

294 Jeffrey Gottfried, Galen Stocking, et al., "Trusting the News Media in the Trump Era," *Pew Research Centre*, December 12, 2019. https://www.pewresearch.org/journalism/2019/12/12/trusting-the-news-media-in-the-trump-era/.

295 "How News Happens – A Study of the News Ecosystem of One American City," *Pew Research Centre,* January 10, 2020. https://www.pewtrusts.org/en/research-and-analysis/reports/2010/01/11/how-news-happens-a-study-of-the-news-ecosystem-of-one-american-city.

296 "How News Happens."

297 "Media Bias Chart, 10.0 Static Version," *Ad Fontes Media.* https://adfontesmedia.com/static-mbc/

298 Mir, "How the Media Polarized Us."

Chapter 3 – Silly Putty Logic.

299 Carol Tarvis, "Who's Lying, Who's Self-Justifying?" *TAM 2014,* https://www.youtube.com/watch?v=TGMi0UtvTIc.

300 Aditya Shukla, "Sense-Making: How We Make Sense Of The World & Find Meaning," *Cognition Today,* May 4, 2022. https://cognitiontoday.com/sense-making-and-meaning-making/.

301 Sally Maitlis and Marlys Christianson, "Sensemaking in Organizations: Taking Stock and Moving Forward," *The Academy of Management Annals* 8, No. 1 (June 2014): 57. https://doi.org/10.5465/19416520.2014.873177

302 Fakhar Naveed, "Definition of News," *Mass Communications Talk,* October 23, 2011. https://www.masscommunicationtalk.com/definition-of-news.html.

303 Richard Guilliatt, "A Healthy Dose of Scepticism About Belle Gibson," *The Australian,* March 13, 2015, https://www.theaustralian.com.au/opinion/a-healthy-dose-of-scepticism-about-belle-gibson/news-story/c93218d76bc623cb2d17e6384828dec.

304 "Why Truth is Not Enough," *London School of Business*, November 12, 2018, https://www.london.edu/news/ why-is-truth-not-enough-1574.

305 "Why Truth is Not Enough."

306 "History of Silly Putty," *The Crayola Company*. http://www. crayola.com/mediacenter/index.cfm?display=press_release&news_ id=164 [dead URL]

307 Charlotte Willis, "The Most Outrageous Moments From Belle Gibson's 60 Minutes Interview," *news.com.au*, June 29, 2015. https://www.news.com.au/entertainment/tv/the-most-outrageous-moments-from-belle-gibsons-60-minutes-interview/ news-story/d3f4e4d7e21f6d890cfae1411f6f29ec.

308 "Top Talk Audiences," *Talk Media*, March 2022, https://www. talkers.com/top-talk-audiences/.

309 A.J. Katz, "Monday, May 16 Scoreboard: Tucker Carlson Tonight Dominates Demo with More Than 500,000 at 8 PM," *TV Newser*, May 17, 2022, https://www.adweek.com/tvnewser/ monday-may-16-scoreboard-tucker-carlson-tonight-dominates-demo-with-more-than-500000-at-8-pm/507648/.

310 Shukla, "Sense-Making."

311 Shukla, "Sense-Making."

312 Shukla, "Sense-Making."

Chapter 4 – The Theater is Making Us Sick.

313 Nicholas O'Shaughnessy, "The Führer and the Donald: The Ghost of a Resemblance," *Brewminate: A Bold Blend of News and Ideas* (via *History News Network*), October 24, 2016, https://

brewminate.com/
the-fuhrer-and-the-donald-the-ghost-of-a-resemblance/.

314 Meredith Willson, "Ya Got Trouble" [lyrics], in *The Music Man*, Music Theatre International, 1957, https://www.lyricsondemand. com/soundtracks/m/themusicmanlyrics/yagottroublelyrics.html

315 David Smith, "Trump's Republican Convention Speech: What He Said and What He Meant," *The Guardian*, July 22, 2016, https://www.theguardian.com/us-news/ ng-interactive/2016/jul/22/ donald-trump-republican-convention-speech-transcript-annotated.

316 "Trump: I Alone Can Fix the System," *CNBC*, July 21, 2016, https://www.cnbc.com/video/2016/07/21/trump-i-alone-can-fix-the-system.html.

317 Willson, "The Music Man."

318 Willson, "The Music Man."

319 Peter Wade, Rolling Stone, June 23, 2023, Trump Tells Crowd: 'I'm Being Indicted for You' (rollingstone.com) https://www. rollingstone.com/politics/politics-news/ trump-indicted-consider-it-great-badge-of-honor-1234777874/

320 "More Than 80% of Americans Report Nation's Future Is Significant Source of Stress, Survey Says," *American Psychological Association*, June 18, 2020, https://nowtoronto.com/news/ how-many-indigenous-children-died-in-canadas-residential-schools.

321 " More Than 80% of Americans…"

322 "Stress in America: Money, Inflation, War Pile on to Nation Stuck in COVID-19 Survival Mode," *American Psychological Association*,

March 11, 2022, https://www.apa.org/news/press/releases/
stress/2022/march-2022-survival-mode.

323 "Inflation, War Push Stress to Alarming Levels at Two-Year
COVID-19 Anniversary," *American Psychological Association*,
March 10, 2022, https://www.apa.org/news/press/
releases/2022/03/inflation-war-stress

324 "The Mental Health Index™ Report | Canada, March 2021,"
Morneau Shepell. https://www.morneaushepell.com/
permafiles/93392/mental-health-index-report-canada-
march-2021.pdf.

325 Michael Lam, Carrie Lam, and Jeremy Lam, "Beware Stress: The
Silent Killer," *Dr. Lam's Blog*, 2019. https://www.drlamcoaching.
com/blog/stress-is-a-silent-killer/.

Chapter 5 – Lies Erode Trust.

326 Maria Ressa, "FULL TEXT: Maria Ressa's speech at Nobel Peace
Prize awarding," *Rappler.com*, December 10, 2021, https://www.
rappler.com/world/global-affairs/
full-text-maria-ressa-speech-nobel-peace-prize-awarding-
ceremony-2021/.

327 Kendra Cherry, "Erikson's Stages of Development," *Verywell
Mind*, August 3, 2022, https://www.verywellmind.com/
erik-eriksons-stages-of-psychosocial-development-2795740.

328 Cherry, "Erikson's Stages of Development."

329 Scott Barry Kaufman, "Who Created Maslow's Iconic Pyramid?"
Scientific American, April 23, 2019, https://blogs.

scientificamerican.com/beautiful-minds/
who-created-maslows-iconic-pyramid/.

330 "Burglary Statistics 2022 (Infographic) – How Safe is Your
Home?" *SafeAtLast*. https://safeatlast.co/blog/burglary-statistics/.

331 Kaufman, "Who Created Maslow's Pyramid?"

332 Phillip Bump, "The Evolution of the Backlash Against Affirmative
Action," *The Washington Post*, February 7, 2023. https://www.
washingtonpost.com/politics/2023/02/07/
tucker-carlson-affirmative-action/.

333 John F. Helliwel, Haifang Huang, and Shun Wang, "New
Evidence On Trust and Well-Being," *National Bureau Of
Economic Research*, July 2016. http://www.nber.org/papers/
w22450.

334 Helliwel, Huang, and Wang, "New Evidence."

335 "2023 Edelman Trust Barometer: Global Report," *Daniel J.
Edelman Holdings, Inc.*, January 2023. https://www.edelman.com/
sites/g/files/aatuss191/files/2023-01/2023%20Edelman%20
Trust%20Barometer%20Global%20Report.pdf.

336 Helliwel, Huang, and Wang, "New Evidence on Trust."

337 Sarah McCammon and Liz Baker, "Untangling Disinformation |
Disinformation Fuels Distrust At All Levels Of Government,"
NPR, March 1, 2021. https://www.npr.
org/2021/03/01/971436680/
from-the-u-s-capitol-to-local-governments-disinformation-
disrupts.

338 Kayln Kahler, "So What Did Aaron Rodgers Actually Say About
Being Vaccinated?" *Defector*, November 3, 2021. https://defector.
com/so-what-did-aaron-rodgers-actually-say-about-being-vaccinated/.

[339] Barry Wilner, "Rodgers Sought Treatments Instead of COVID-19 Vaccine," *AP News*, November 6, 2021. https://apnews.com/ article/coronavirus-pandemic-nfl-sports-health-immunizations-9484a87691720061a5cb2258a9c26078.

[340] Wilner, "Rodgers Sought Treatments."

[341] Wilner, "Rodgers Sought Treatments."

[342] Wilner, "Rodgers Sought Treatments."

[343] Nathaniel Weixel, "Joe Rogan Clarifies Vaccine Comments: 'I'm Not an Anti-vax Person,'" *The Hill*, April 29, 2021, https:// thehill.com/policy/ healthcare/551057-joe-rogan-clarifies-vaccine-comments-im-not-an-anti-vax-person/.

[344] Alex Boyd, "How Olympian Jamie Salé Became a COVID Protest Champion," *The Toronto Star*, February 5, 2023. https://www. thestar.com/news/canada/jamie-sal-was-canada-s-sweetheart-on-ice-now-the-olympian-is-championing-something-darker/article_ dbcee3e7-8fd1-53bb-befa-91aec57c4444.html.

[345] Boyd, "How Olympian Became a COVID Protest Champion."

[346] Mark Jurkowitz and Amy Mitchell, "Americans Who Got Most COVID-19 News from Trump Less Likely to be Vccinated," *Pew Research Center*, September 23, 2021, https://www.pewresearch. org/fact-tank/2021/09/23/ americans-who-relied-most-on-trump-for-covid-19-news-among-least-likely-to-be-vaccinated/.

[347] Jurkowitz and Mitchell, "Americans Who Got Most COVID-19 News…"

[348] Neena Satija and Lena H. Sun, "A Major Funder of the Anti-vaccine Movement Has Made Millions Selling Natural Health

Products," *The Washington Post*, December 20, 2019, https://
www.washingtonpost.com/investigations/2019/10/15/fdc01078-
c29c-11e9-b5e4-54aa56d5b7ce_story.html.

349 Satija and Sun, "Major Funder of the Anti-vaccine Movement …"

350 "Selz Foundation's 2017 Taxes," *The Washington Post*, June 18,
2019, https://www.washingtonpost.com/context/
selz-foundation-s-2017-taxes/025361d1-c5cf-4a51-b5bf-
ebe3b5bcf0f7/?itid=lk_inline_manual_8.

351 Lena H. Sun and Amy Brittain, "Meet the New York Couple
Donating Millions to the Anti-vax Movement," *The Washington
Post*, June 19, 2019, https://www.washingtonpost.com/national/
health-science/meet-the-new-york-couple-donating-millions-to-
the-anti-vax-movement/2019/06/18/9d791bcc-8e28-11e9-b08e-
cfd89bd36d4e_story.html.

352 Tyler Nicole Rogers, "Meet Bernard and Lisa Selz, the Couple
Bankrolling the Anti-Vax Movement," *Business Insider.com*, June
20, 2019, https://www.businessinsider.com/
bernard-lisa-selz-anti-vax-movement-millionaire-couple-2019-6.

353 Rogers, "Meet Bernard and Lisa Selz."

354 Allison R. Donahue, "Study: COVID Vaccines Saved 3M Lives
and Millions from the Hospital, But People Aren't Getting the
Booster," *Michigan Advance*, December 19, 2022. https://
michiganadvance.com/blog/
study-covid-vaccines-saved-3m-lives-and-millions-from-the-
hospital-but-people-arent-getting-the-booster/.

355 "Fault Lines," *Council of Canadian Academies*, January 26,
2023, https://www.cca-reports.ca/wp-content/uploads/2023/01/
OnePager-Fault-Lines-EN.pdf

356 "Fault Lines."

357 "Fault Lines."

358 "Fault Lines."

359 "Government and Media Fuel Cycle of Distrust, Seen as Sources of Misleading Information," *Edelman Trust Barometer 2023*, January 2023, https://www.edelman.com/sites/g/files/aatuss191/files/2023-01/2023%20Edelman%20Trust%20Barometer%20Global%20Report.pdf.

360 Helliwell, Huang, and Wang, "New Evidence On Trust."

361 Jamie Sale (@JamieSale), "World Champion + Olympic Gold medallist. Truth seeker +Freedom fighter. Canadians for Truth," *X*, Twitter https://twitter.com/JamieSale.

362 Sale, "World Champion + Olympic Gold medallist."

Chapter 6 – From Post-truth to Post-trust.

363 Derek Thompson, "Why the Age of American Progress Ended," *The Atlantic Magazine*, December 12, 2022, https://www.theatlantic.com/magazine/archive/2023/01/science-technology-vaccine-invention-history/672227/.

364 "From Merkel to Macron: These Are Some of the World's Most Educated Leaders," *Study International*, September 10, 2020. https://www.studyinternational.com/news/world-leaders-and-their-education/.

365 Ross Terrill, *Mao: A Biography* (New York, NY: Simon and Schuster, 1980): 27.

366 Steven Levitsky and Daniel Ziblatt, *How Democracies Die* (New York, NY: Broadway Books, 2018): 92.

367 Levitsky and Ziblatt, *How Democracies Die*: 3.

368 Levitsky and Ziblatt, *How Democracies Die*: 23–24.

369 Levitsky and Ziblatt, *How Democracies Die*: 76.

370 "Edelman Trust Barometer: Cycle of Distrust Threatens Actions on Global Challenges," *World Economic Forum*, January 18, 2022, https://www.weforum.org/agenda/2022/01/edelman-trust-barometer-2022-report/.

371 "Edelman Trust Barometer: Cycle of Distrust."

372 Larry Brilliant, Mark Smolinski, Lisa Danzig, and W. Ian Lipkin, "Inevitable Outbreaks: How to Stop an Age of Spillovers From Becoming an Age of Pandemics," Foreign Affairs, Jan/Feb 2023, https://www.foreignaffairs.com/world/inevitable-outbreaks-spillovers-pandemics

373 PubMed (nih.gov) Willingness to Vaccinate Against COVID-19 in the U.S.: Representative Longitudinal Evidence from April to October 2020 https://pubmed.ncbi.nlm.nih.gov/33773862/

374 Ibid.

375 Thompson, "Why the Age of American Progress Ended."

376 Thompson, "Why the Age of American Progress Ended."

377 Ravtosh Bal, "Government Science and Innovation in the New Normal: Discussion Paper, *The Institute on Governance*, November 8, 2022, https://iog.ca/publications/trust-integrity-and-science-ethics/.

378 Bal, "Government Science and Innovation."

379 "The Governance Monitor: Trust, Governance, and Governing after Election 2021," *Institute on Governance*, August 2021, https://iog.ca/trust-and-governance-after-election-2021/.

Brad Graham, *"Trust Issues: How Much Faith Do Canadians Have in Government?"* *TVO Ontario*, September 9, 2021, https://www.tvo.org/article/trust-issues-how-much-faith-do-canadians-have-in-government.

Chapter 7 – Send in the Clowns.

380 "'Post-truth' Declared Word of the Year by Oxford Dictionaries," *BBC News*, November 16, 2016, https://www.bbc.com/news/uk-37995600.

381 "'Post-truth' Declared Word of the Year."

382 Nicole Avino, "This is How to Fight Fake News at Work in a Post-trust Era," *Fast Company*, October 12, 2019, https://www.fastcompany.com/90387088/this-is-how-to-fight-fake-news-at-work-in-a-post-trust-era

383 Marjorie Taylor Greene (@mtgreenee), "We need a national divorce," *X*, February 20, 2023, 7:43 a.m., https://twitter.com/mtgreenee/status/1627665203398688768

384 Taylor Greene, "We need a national divorce."

385 Taylor Greene, "We need a national divorce."

386 Jeffery Borak, "REVIEW: In 'I'm Not a Comedian ... I'm Lenny Bruce,' The Humor is Strong, Sharp and Meaningful," *The Berkshire Eagle*, October 20, 2022. https://www.berkshireeagle.com/arts_and_culture/arts-theater/

im-not-a-comedian-im-lenny-bruce-mahaiwe/article_1fccd2ba-50a6-11ed-a2dd-cf37ed34f613.html.

387 Megan Brenan, "Americans Remain Distrustful of Mass Media," *Gallup*, September 30, 2020. https://news.gallup.com/poll/321116/americans-remain-distrustful-mass-media.aspx.

388 Brenan, "Americans Remain Distrustful."

389 Peter Houston, "2022 in Trust: Gains Made with Covid Coverage Collapse, Global Permacrisis Stokes News Avoidance," *Media Voices*, December 16, 2022, https://voices.media/2022-in-trust-gains-made-with-covid-coverage-collapse-global-permacrisis-stokes-news-avoidance/.

390 Darrell J. Bricker, RTDNA: Trust in News, *IPSO Public Affairs, RTDNA Canada*, https://www.ipsos.com/sites/default/files/ct/news/documents/2021-06/RTDNA_Trust_in_News-Report-2021-06-03-v1_0.pdf

391 Peter Houston, "2022 in Trust: Gains Made with Covid Coverage Collapse."

392 George Buchanan, *The Witty and Entertaining Exploits of George Buchanan, Who Was Commonly Called the King's Fool* (Stirling: Randall, 1814): 11.

393 "Throwback – Tucker Carlson's Epic Debate With Jon Stewart on CNN's Crossfire," *The Echo Chamber*, January 17, 2017, https://www.youtube.com/watch?v=DTXIoJn0KTs.

394 Ken Fisher, "Jon Stewart Wins, CNN Cancels Crossfire," *Ars Technica*, January 6, 2005, https://arstechnica.com/uncategorized/2005/01/4509-2/

395 Stephen Battaglio, "Tucker Carlson Departs Fox News, Pushed Out by Rupert Murdoch," *Los Angeles Times*, April 24,

2023, https://www.latimes.com/entertainment-arts/business/ story/2023-04-24/tucker-carlson-is-out-at-fox-news.

396 Mark Fisher, "Édouard Louis: 'Truth Is a Revenge Because We Live in a World of Lies,'" *The Guardian*, May 13, 2021, https:// www.theguardian.com/stage/2021/may/13/ edouard-louis-truth-is-a-revenge-because-we-live-in-a-world-of- lies.

397 "Facts and Statistics | 2021 Hate Crime Statistics," *U. S. Department of Justice*, 2022, https://www.justice.gov/hatecrimes/ hate-crime-statistics.

398 "US Sees Rise in Hate Crimes Fuelled by Racial, Ethnic Bias," *TRT World*, March 14, 2023. https://www.trtworld.com/life/ us-sees-rise-in-hate-crimes-fuelled-by-racial-ethnic-bias-66097

399 "US Sees Rise in Hate Crimes."

400 Jing Hui Wang and Greg Moreau, "Police-reported Hate Crime in Canada, 2020," *Canadian Centre for Justice and Community Safety Statistics*, March 22, 2022. https://www150.statcan.gc.ca/ n1/pub/85-002-x/2022001/article/00005-eng.htm.

401 Wang and Greg Moreau, "Police-reported Hate Crime in Canada."

402 "US Sees Rise in Hate Crimes," *TRT World*.

403 "Hatred Against Muslims 'Major Threat to Democracy': Türkiye's UN Envoy," *TRT World*, March 17, 2023. https://www.trtworld. com/americas/ hatred-against-muslims-major-threat-to-democracy- t%C3%BCrkiye-s-un-envoy-66032.

404 "Hatred Against Muslims 'Major Threat to Democracy,'" *TRT World*.

405   Michael Goodier, "Racist Hate Crimes Pass 100,000 in England and Wales for First Time," *The Guardian*, October 6, 2022. https://www.theguardian.com/uk-news/2022/oct/06/racist-hate-crimes-pass-100000-in-england-and-wales-for-first-time.

406   "US Sees Rise in Hate Crimes," *TRT World.*

Chapter 8 – The Theater Is Becoming More Dangerous.

407   "Sen. Ted Cruz: We Have an Obligation To Protect the Integrity of the Election," *Ted Cruz: U.S. Senator for Texas*, January 6, 2021, https://www.cruz.senate.gov/newsroom/press-releases/sen-cruz-we-have-an-obligation-to-protect-the-integrity-of-the-election.

408   "Cruz Says People Accusing Him of Sedition Need to 'Calm Down,'" *Republican Fighter*, January 10, 2021, https://www.republicanfighter.com/cruz-says-people-accusing-him-of-sedition-need-to-calm-down/.

409   Maureen B. Costello, "The Trump Effect: The Impact of the Presidential Campaign on our Nation's Schools," *Southern Poverty Law Centre*, 2016: 11. https://www.splcenter.org/sites/default/files/splc_the_trump_effect.pdf.

410   Ibid.

411   "Chinese Activist Yang Maodong Jailed for Six Years," *BBC News*, November 27, 2015, https://www.bbc.com/news/world-asia-china-34941406.

412   Eric Baculinao and Yuliya Talmazan, "Chinese Citizen Journalist Zhang Zhan Jailed for 'Provoking Trouble' with Wuhan Reporting," *NBC News*, December 28, 2020, https://www.

nbcnews.com/news/world/
chinese-citizen-journalist-zhang-zhan-jailed-provoking-trouble-
wuhan-reporting-n1252403.

413 "UP Assembly Passes 'Love Jihad' Legislation; 'Prohibition of
Unlawful Religious Conversion Bill' Now a Law)," *Times New
News | India News*, February 24, 2021, https://www.
timesnownews.com/india/article/
up-assembly-passes-love-jihad-legislation-prohibition-of-
unlawful-religious-conversion-bill-now-a-law/724583.

414 KloudLearn, "Never Waste a Good Crisis," *Medium.com.* April
27, 2020, https://kloudlearn.medium.com/
never-waste-a-good-crisis-8018c7d93e17.

415 Liz Szabo, "Anti-vaccine Activists Peddle Theories that Covid-19
Shots Are Deadly, Undermining Vaccination," *CNN News*,
January 25, 2021, https://www.cnn.com/2021/01/25/health/
anti-vaccine-theories-undermine-vaccination/index.html.

416 Szabo, "Anti-vaccine Activists Peddle Theories."

417 Cat Zakrzewski and Lauren Weber, "NFL Player Hamlin's
Collapse Sparks Rise in Covid Misinformation," *The Washington
Post*, January 3, 2023, https://www.washingtonpost.com/
technology/2023/01/03/covid-misinfo-damar-hamlin-collapse/.

418 Rep. Marjorie Taylor Greene (RepMTG), "Before the covid
vaccines we didn't see athletes dropping dead on the playing field
like we do now," X, January 3, 2023, 9:49 a.m., https://twitter.
com/RepMTG/status/1610302251704238080..

419 Ali Swenson, David Klepper, and Sophia Tulp, "Vaccine
Misinformation Surges on Social Media, Fox News After NFL
Player Damar Hamlin's Onscreen Heart Attack," *Fortune.org*,

January 5, 2023, https://fortune.com/2023/01/05/damar-hamlin-heart-attack-vaccine-misinformation-fox-news-tucker-carlson/.

420 Swenson, Klepper, and Tulp, "Vaccine Misinformation Surges."

421 Matthew W. Martinez, Andrew M. Tucker, O. Josh Bloom, et al., "Prevalence of Inflammatory Heart Disease Among Professional Athletes With Prior COVID-19 Infection Who Received Systematic Return-to-Play Cardiac Screening," *JAMA Cardiology* 6, No. 7 (2021): 745–752. doi:10.1001/jamacardio.2021.0565.

422 David Folkinflik and Maddy Lauria, "Fox News' Sean Hannity Admits He Knew Trump Lost 2020 election," *NPR News*, December 22, 2022, https://www.npr.org/2022/12/22/1144926308/fox-news-sean-hannity-dominion-lawsuit-trump.

423 Folkinflik and Lauria, "Fox News' Sean Hannity Admits He Knew Trump Lost."

424 Mark Joyella, "Sean Hannity Sets Ratings Record As Fox News Dominates Coverage Of Kabul Attack," *Forbes*, August 27, 2021, https://www.forbes.com/sites/markjoyella/2021/08/27/fox-news-channels-hannity-sets-ratings-record-with-5-million-viewers-thursday-night/?sh=68e0712b21d9.

Chapter 9 – Dancing with Truths.

425 Danny Clemons, "Oprah Winfrey at the Golden Globes: 'Speaking Your Truth is the Most Powerful Tool We All Have,'" *ABC7 Los Angeles*, January 7, 2018, https://abc7.com/oprah-winfrey-cecil-b-demille-award-golden-globes-globe-awards/2879380/.

426 *A Few Good Men,* directed by Rob Reiner, written by Aaron Sorkin (Beverly Hills, CA: Castlerock Entertainment, 1992). Quotation here is read by actor Jack Nicholson as Marine Colonel Nathan Jessop to actor Tom Cruise as United States Navy JAG Corps investigator and lawyer, Lieutenant Daniel Kaffee.

427 Brad Oswald, "Yes, She's Queen of all Media, But to Discovery, She's Life Itself," *Winnipeg Free Press,* January 26, 2010, https://www.winnipegfreepress.com/arts-and-life/entertainment/tv/2010/01/26/yes-shes-queen-of-all-media-but-to-discovery-shes-life-itself.

428 "Youth Risk Behavior Survey Data Summary & Trends Report: 2011-2021," *Center for Disease Control and Prevention*: 1. https://www.cdc.gov/healthyyouth/data/yrbs/pdf/YRBS_Data-Summary-Trends_Report2023_508.pdf.

429 Youth Risk Behavior Survey Data," *CDC*: 8.

430 "Free & Equal," *United Nations,* https://www.unfe.org/.

431 "Mission," *The International Organization for the Family,* https://www.profam.org/mission/.

432 "Our Team," *University of Maryland School of Medicine,* https://www.schoolmentalhealth.org/About/Our-Team/.

433 Stepanie Sy and Courtney Norris, "Teenage Girls Experiencing Record High Levels of Sadness, Violence and Trauma, CDC Says," *PBS News,* February 20, 2023. https://www.pbs.org/newshour/show/teenage-girls-experiencing-record-high-levels-of-sadness-violence-and-trauma-cdc-says.

434 IFN English, "New CDC Study Clearly Shows the Harm of the LGBT Agenda on Our Children," *International Family News,*

February 17, 2023, https://ifamnews.com/en/
new-cdc-study-clearly-shows-the-harm-of-the-lgbt-agenda-on-
our-children.

435 Michele W. Berger, "Journalist and Activist Maria Ressa on 'Facts,
Truth, Trust,'" *Penn Today | Annenberg School for Communication,
University of Pennsylvania,* November 10, 2022, https://www.asc.
upenn.edu/news-events/news/
journalist-and-activist-maria-ressa-facts-truth-trust

Chapter 10 – Woke Gets Broke.

436 Rex Murphy, "The Woke Rot at the Heart of Canada's Largest
School Board," *The National Post,* November 29, 2021. https://
nationalpost.com/opinion/
rex-murphy-the-woke-rot-at-the-heart-of-canadas-largest-school-
board.

437 Daniel Johnson, "We've Sung 'Amazing Grace' for 250 Years.
We've Only Just Begun," *Christianity Today,* September 12,
2022. https://www.christianitytoday.com/ct/2022/september-
web-only/amazing-grace-250-history-hymn-civil-rights-pop.html.

438 Johnson, "We've Sung 'Amazing Grace' for 250 Years."

439 "Amazing Grace: The Story Behind the Beloved Song" [blog
post], *Oregon Catholic Press,* January 10, 2018. https://www.ocp.
org/en-us/blog/entry/amazing-grace

440 "Amazing Grace: The Story Behind the Beloved Song."

441 *Merriam-Webster,* s.v. "woke," https://www.merriam-webster.com/
dictionary/woke

442 Natalie Morris, "How the Word 'Woke' Was Hijacked to Silence People of Colour," *Metro News UK*, March 27, 2020. https://metro.co.uk/2020/03/27/word-woke-became-tool-silence-people-colour-12426214/.

443 William Melvin Kelley, "If You're Woke You Dig It; No Mickey Mouse Can Be Expected to Follow Today's Negro Idiom Without a Hip Assist," *The New York* Timews, May 20, 1962, https://www.nytimes.com/1962/05/20/archives/if-youre-woke-you-dig-it-no-mickey-mouse-can-be-expected-to-follow.html.

444 Kathyrn Shulz, "William Melvin Kelley: The Lost Giant of American Literature," *The New Yorker*, January 22, 2018. https://www.newyorker.com/magazine/2018/01/29/the-lost-giant-of-american-literature.

445 Morris, "How 'Woke' Was Hijacked,"

446 Madeline Leesman, "Elon Musk: 'Wokeness Is Divisive, Exclusionary, and Hateful,'" *TownHall.com*, December 22, 2021. https://townhall.com/tipsheet/madelineleesman/2021/12/22/elon-musk-wokeness-is-divisive-exclusionary-and-hateful-n2600948.

447 Kate Ng, "What is the History of the Word 'Woke' and its Modern Uses?" *The Independent*, January 22, 2021, https://www.independent.co.uk/news/uk/home-news/woke-meaning-word-history-b1790787.html.

448 Matt Lavietes, "What Florida's 'Don't Say Gay' Bill Actually Says," *NBC News*, March 16, 2022, https://www.nbcnews.com/nbc-out/out-politics-and-policy/floridas-dont-say-gay-bill-actually-says-rcna19929.

449 Lavietes, "What Florida's 'Don't Say Gay' Bill Actually Says."

450 Judith Butler, "Why is the Idea of 'Gender' Provoking Backlash the World Over?" *The Guardian*, October 23, 2021, https://www.theguardian.com/us-news/commentisfree/2021/oct/23/judith-butler-gender-ideology-backlash.

451 Judith Butler, "Why is 'Gender' Provoking Backlash?"

452 "LGBTQ+ Population by Country 2023," *World Population Review*, 2023, https://worldpopulationreview.com/country-rankings/lgbtq-population-by-country.

453 "Social Acceptance of LGBTI People in 175 Countries and Locations," *Williams Institute | University of Southern California*, November 2021, https://williamsinstitute.law.ucla.edu/publications/global-acceptance-index-lgbt.

454 "Social Acceptance of LGBTI People."

455 "Judge Blocks Florida "Woke" Law, Saying it Violates the First Amendment," *CBS News*, August 19, 2022 https://www.cbsnews.com/news/florida-woke-law-blocked-by-judge-over-first-amendment-issues/

456 Ibid.

457 *Merriam-Webster*, s.v. "woke."

458 Rebecca Solnit, "We Need to Discuss the Word 'Woke,'" *The Guardian*, November 9, 2021. https://www.theguardian.com/commentisfree/2021/nov/09/woke-word-meaning-definition-progressive.

459 Thomas Chatterson Williams, "The Word 'Woke' Is More Confusing to Me Than Helpful," *The Atlantic*, March 17, 2023. https://www.theatlantic.com/ideas/archive/2023/03/wokeness-definition-social-justice-racism/673416/.

460 Alexandra Hall, "Chelsea Handler Claims She Thought Sun and Moon Were Same Thing Until She Turned 40," *Fox News*, January 19, 2023. https://www.foxnews.com/media/ chelsea-handler-claims-thought-sun-moon-same-thing-until-turned-40.

461 "Ranking of Countries by Quality of Democracy | Complete Ranking: Total Value Index 2020 (Measurement)," *Project Democracy Matrix | Julius-Maximilians-Universität Würzburg.* https://www.democracymatrix.com/ranking.

462 Summer Concepion, "Marjorie Taylor Greene Defends Calling Democrats 'Pedophiles,'" *NBC News*, April 3, 2023. https://www. nbcnews.com/politics/congress/ marjorie-taylor-greene-defends-calling-democrats-pedophiles-rcna77869.

Chapter 11 – 2024: The Theater Puts Liberal Democracy on Trial.

463 Max Fisher, The New York Times, August 19, 2022, How Democracy Is Under Threat Across the Globe https://www. nytimes.com/2022/08/19/world/democracy-threat.html)

464 "The Chocolate Industry," *International Cocoa Organization*, 2021, https://www.icco.org/chocolate-industry/

465 Patrick J. Deneen, *Regime Change: Toward a Postliberal Future* (New York, NY: Sentinel; Penguin Random House 2023): 167.

466 "National Conservatism: A Statement of Principles," *National Conservatism*, https://nationalconservatism.org/ national-conservatism-a-statement-of-principles/.

467　"ARC Launch Announcement," *The Alliance for Responsible Citizenship (ARC)*, https://www.arcforum.com/ideas/the-launch-of-arc. [Broken URL]

468　Mihai Varga and Aron Buzogány, "The Two Faces of the 'Global Right': Revolutionary Conservatives and National-Conservatives," *Association for Critical Sociology* 48, No. 6. https://doi.org/10.1177/08969205211057020

469　Phillipa Stroud, "Why we need a better story," *The Alliance for Responsible Citizenship (ARC)*, https://www.arcforum.com/ideas/why-we-need-a-better-story. [Broken URL]

470　Age of Enlightenment, Byjus Exam Prep, https://byjus.com/free-ias-prep/age-of-enlightenment-1632-1792/

471　Jordan Peterson, "My Vision for ARC," The Alliance for Responsible Citizenship (ARC). https://www.arcforum.com/ideas/my-vision-for-arc. [Broken URL]

472　Peterson, "My Vision for ARC."

473　"ARC Launch Announcement."

474　"Poilievre's Conservative Party Embracing Language of Mainstream Conspiracy Theories," *CBC News*, August 13, 2023, https://www.cbc.ca/news/politics/poilievre-world-economic-forum-rhetoric-1.6935294.

475　"Ban Ministers From Attending the World Economic Forum', Says Poilievre at Calgary Stampede," *Rebel News*, July 11, 2023, https://www.rebelnews.com/ban_ministers_from_attending_the_world_economic_forum_says_poilievre_at_calgary_stampede.

476　Jill Colvin and Linley Sanders, "Trump Enjoys Strong GOP Support After the Indictment. General Election Could Be

Different," *AP News*, August 16, 2023, https://apnews.com/article/trump-election-2024-indictments-ddfd50492dc576c0c2ca2d1afe0e4639.

477   Deneen, *Regime Change*: 167.

478   Deneen, *Regime Change*: 231.

479   Deneen, *Regime Change*: 231.

480   Yoram Hazony, "Introduction," *Conservatism Rediscovered* (Washington, DC: Regnery Publishing, 2022): xix.

481   Hazony, "Introduction," *Conservatism Rediscovered*: 390.

482   Charles King, "Review Essay, The Antiliberal Revolution, Reading the Philosophers of the New Right," *Foreign Affairs*, July/August 2023, https://www.foreignaffairs.com/reviews/antiliberal-revolution.

483   *Merriam-Webster*, s.v. "theocracy," https://www.merriam-webster.com/dictionary/theocracy

484   Adrian Vermueule, *Common Good Constitutionalism* (Cambridge, UK: Polity Press, 2022): 47.

485   Vermueule, *Common Good Constitutionalism*.

486   Vermueule, *Common Good Constitutionalism*.

487   *APA Dictionary of Psychology*, s.v. "Machiavellianism," https://dictionary.apa.org/machiavellianism

488   Conrad Swanson, "Lauren Boebert is a Christian Nationalist, Experts Say," *The Denver Post*, September 14, 2022, https://www.denverpost.com/2022/09/14/lauren-boebert-christian-nationalist-republican-colorado/.

489   Swanson, "Lauren Boebert is a Christian Nationalist."

490 Judy Woodruff, Frank Carlson, and Sarah Clune Hartman, "Iowa Republicans Discuss Role of Politics in Their Lives, Hopes for Overcoming Divisions" [video], *PBS NewsHour*, July 19, 2023, https://www.pbs.org/newshour/show/iowa-republicans-discuss-role-of-politics-in-their-lives-hopes-for-overcoming-divisions.

491 Woodruff, Carlson, and Clune Hartman, "Iowa Republicans Discuss Role of Politics in Their Lives."

492 Woodruff, Carlson, and Clune Hartman, "Iowa Republicans Discuss Role of Politics in Their Lives."

493 Greek Word Study Tool, *Tufts University*, https://www.perseus.tufts.edu/hopper/morph?l=aristoi&la=greek#lexicon

494 Deneen, *Regime Change:* 152.

495 King, "The Antiliberal Revolution."

496 King, "The Antiliberal Revolution."

497 John Paul Tasker, "Poilievre Says 'Everything Seems Broken,'" *CBC News*, January 17, 2023, https://www.cbc.ca/news/politics/poilievre-trudeau-parliament-returns-1.6728295.

498 Adrian Humphreys, "Most Canadians Agree 'Canada is Broken' — And They're Angry: Poll," *National Post*, February 6, 2023, https://nationalpost.com/news/politics/canada-is-broken-poll.

499 Dylan Robertson, "Canada Mulling 'Game Plan' if U.S. Takes Far-right, Authoritarian Shift: Joly," *CBC News*, August 17, 2023, https://www.cbc.ca/news/politics/joly-us-authoritarian-game-plan-1.6939369.

500 *Merriam-Webster*, s.v. "useful idiot," https://www.merriam-webster.com/dictionary/useful%20idiot

501   Scott Hensley, "Anger Poll: 84% Say We're Madder Than a
      Generation Ago," *NPR*, June 26. 2019, https://www.npr.org/
      sections/health-shots/2019/06/26/735757156/
      poll-americans-say-were-angrier-than-a-generation-ago

502   Noah Robertson and Patrik Jonsson, "Americans Are Angry
      About . . . Everything. Is That Bad?" *The Christian Science
      Monitor*, October 22, 2021, https://www.csmonitor.com/USA/
      Society/2021/1022/
      Americans-are-angry-about-everything.-Is-that-bad.

503   Arthur Vidro, "'An Educated Consumer is Our Best Customer,'"
      The Eagle Times, October 9, 2019, https://www.eagletimes.com/
      lifestyles/an-educated-consumer-is-our-best-customer/article_
      ffad91e8-c45a-52d1-afb4-5f446bd8c39f.html.

504   "Trust and Distrust in America | 2. The State of Personal Trust,"
      Pew Research Center, July 22, 2019, https://www.pewresearch.org/
      politics/2019/07/22/the-state-of-personal-trust/.

ACT THREE:
HOW WE CAN GET OUT (ME, YOU, AND EVERYONE)

Chapter 1 – The Solution Lies Within Us.

505   Peter Elbow, "The Uses of Binary Thinking," *Journal of Advanced
      Composition* 13, No. 1 (1993): 51–73. https://scholarworks.
      umass.edu/eng_faculty_pubs/14/

506   Elbow, "The Uses of Binary Thinking."

[507] "What Is Splitting Psychology?" *BetterHelp*, September 21, 2023, https://www.betterhelp.com/advice/psychologists/what-is-splitting-psychology/.

[508] "What Is Splitting Psychology?"

[509] Steven Lee Myers and Zolan Kanno-Youngs, "In Homeland Security, Partisan Fight Breaks Out Over Disinformation Board," *The New York Times*, May 2, 2022, https://www.nytimes.com/2022/05/02/technology/partisan-dhs-disinformation-board.html.

[510] Jill Goldenzeil, "The Disinformation Governance Board Is Dead. Here's The Right Way To Fight Disinformation," *Forbes.com*, May 18, 2022, https://www.forbes.com/sites/jillgoldenziel/2022/05/18/the-disinformation-governance-board-is-dead-heres-the-right-way-to-fight-disinformation/?sh=bf0af677a0be.

[511] Goldenzeil, "The Disinformation Governance Board Is Dead."

[512] Roger Koppl and Abigail Devereaux, "Biden Establishes a Ministry of Truth," *Wall Street Journal*, May 1, 2022, https://www.wsj.com/articles/biden-establishes-a-ministry-of-truth-disinformation-governance-board-partisan-11651432312

[513] Martin Luther King, Jr., "Out of the Long Night, *The Gospel Messenger* 107, No. 6 (February 8, 1958): 3–5. https://archive.org/details/gospelmessengerv107mors.

[514] Michael Morell, "There is a Second Sacred Wall at the CIA. Trump Disrespects that One Every Day," *The Washington Post*, January 29, 2017, https://www.washingtonpost.com/opinions/there-is-a-second-sacred-wall-at-the-cia-trump-disrespects-that-

one-every-day/2017/01/29/d1961480-e675-11e6-bf6f-
301b6b443624_story.html.

515 "Peter Drucker – Culture Eats Strategy," *Strategies for
Influence*, https://strategiesforinfluence.com/
peter-drucker-coaching-tips/.

516 Mahatma Gandhi, "General Knowledge About Health [–XXI] |
12. Accidents: Snake-Bite," *The Collected Works of Mahatma
Gandhi*, Volume XII, April 1913 to December 1914, The
Publications Division, Ministry of Information and Broadcasting,
Government of India (August 1964), https://www.
gandhiheritageportal.org/

517 "Trust and Distrust in America | State of Personal Trust,"
Pew Research.

Chapter 2 – Nurturing Our Superpowers.

518 Walt Whitman, "Walt Whitman Quotes. . . Vol. 20: Motivational
and Inspirational Life Quotes by Walt Whitman," *The Secret
Libraries* (2016), https://www.azquotes.com/
quote/313851?ref=curiosity.

519 Alex Edmans, London School of Business, *YouTube*, December 3,
2018. https://www.ted.com/talks/
alex_edmans_what_to_trust_in_a_post_truth_world

520 "Data Analytics Market Size – Global Industry, Share, Analysis,
Trends and Forecast 2022 – 2030," *Acumen Research and
Consulting*, December 2022,. https://www.
acumenresearchandconsulting.com/data-analytics-market.

521 Lynn Connaway, Donna Lanclos, and Erin Hood, "Where People Go for Information, What They Use, and Why," *EDUCAUSE Review*, December 6, 2013, https://er.educause.edu/articles/2013/12/i-always-stick-with-the-first-thing-that-comes-up-on-google---where-people-go-for-information-what-they-use-and-why.

522 Craig Medred, "Skepticism" [blog post], *Craig Medred: A Home for Readers and Thinkers*, June 1, 2020. https://craigmedred.news/2020/06/01/skepticism/.

523 Steven Grossman, "In the Words of President Ronald Reagan, 'Trust but Verify,'" *Security Week*, December 20, 2017, https://www.securityweek.com/words-president-ronald-reagan-trust-verify/.

524 "Who We Are," *Monash University*, https://www.monash.edu/about/who.

525 "What Is Critical Thinking?" *Monash University*, https://www.monash.edu/learnhq/enhance-your-thinking/critical-thinking/what-is-critical-thinking.

526 "The Benefits of Being in Two Minds," *The Conversation*, February 22, 2012, https://theconversation.com/the-benefits-of-being-in-two-minds-5388.

527 "The Benefits of Being in Two Minds."

528 " Matt Grawitch Ph.D. | About," *Psychology Today*, https://www.psychologytoday.com/us/contributors/matt-grawitch-phd.

529 Matt Grawitch, "The False Dilemma: System 1 vs. System 2," *Psychology Today*, March 3, 2021, https://www.psychologytoday.com/us/blog/a-hovercraft-full-of-eels/202103/the-false-dilemma-system-1-vs-system-2.

530 Craig Hlavaty, "When Boris Yeltsin Went Grocery Shopping in Clear Lake," *Houston Chronicle*, April 7, 2014, https://blog.chron.com/thetexican/2014/04/when-boris-yeltsin-went-grocery-shopping-in-clear-lake/.

531 Hlavaty, "When Boris Yeltsin Went Grocery Shopping."

532 Hlavaty, "When Boris Yeltsin Went Grocery Shopping."

533 *Merriam-Webster Thesaurus*, s.v. "curiosity," https://www.merriam-webster.com/thesaurus/curiosity.

534 Anthony D. Fredericks, "Why Curiosity Is Necessary for Creativity," *Psychology Today*, February 11, 2022, https://www.psychologytoday.com/ca/blog/creative-insights/202202/why-curiosity-is-necessary-creativity.

Chapter 3 – Cum Grano Salis (With a Grain of Salt).

535 James Comey, *A Higher Loyalty: Truth, Lies, and Leadership* (New York, NY: Flatiron Books, April 17, 2018), https://www.goodreads.com/work/quotes/56418004-a-higher-loyalty-truth-lies-and-leadership.

536 Cindy Tran, Daily Mail Online, Australia, February 18, 2018 Catherine Hughes reveals the 'anti-vaxxer' trolls after her baby died Riley from whooping cough https://www.dailymail.co.uk/femail/article-6719393/Catherine-Hughes-reveals-anti-vaxxer-trolls-baby-died-Riley-whooping-cough.html

537 "Corruption Watch: Catherine Hughes Quietly Appointed to Government Advisory Body," *Septic Skeptics*, February 15, 2019, https://septicskeptics.com/category/light-for-riley/.

538 Sahar Mourad, "Violence Erupts at Anti-vax Protests as Covid-deniers Descend on Cities Across Australia," *Daily Mail*, February 19, 2021, https://www.dailymail.co.uk/news/article-9280627/Anti-vax-protesters-outrageous-placards-descend-Australian-cities-days.html.

539 Isobel Asher Hamilton, "Facebook: Engagement With Anti-Vaxx Pages More Than Trebled in a Month," *BusinessInsider.com*, September 20, 2020, https://www.businessinsider.com/engagement-anti-vaxx-facebook-pages-triples-2020-9.

540 *Make Australia Healthy Again – Let's Make Our Children Healthy Once More*, 2021, https://makeaustraliahealthyagain.org/.

541 Solihin Millin, "Wake Up Australia," *YouTube*, May 30, 2020, https://www.youtube.com/watch?v=92MsSkcwkSU

542 Melissa Coade, "Reset Australia: Government Should Be Offered Anti-vaxxer Social Media Insights," *The Mandarin.com*, May 19, 2021, https://www.themandarin.com.au/157204-reset-australia-government-should-be-offered-anti-vaxxer-social-media-insights/.

543 Nicole Lyn Pesce, "Anti-vaxxer Teen Tells Congress Why He Vaccinated Himself Against His Mom's Wishes," *Market Watch*, March 6, 2019, https://www.marketwatch.com/story/these-parents-didnt-vaccinate-their-kids-so-now-the-kids-are-doing-it-themselves-2019-02-11.

544 Ethan Lindenberger, "My Parents Are Kind of Stupid and Don't Believe in Vaccines. Now that I'm 18, Where Do I Go to Get Vaccinated? Can I Get Vaccinated at My Age? [post, r/NoStupidQuestions], *Reddit*, November 16, 2018, https://www.

reddit.com/r/NoStupidQuestions/comments/9xm989/
my_parents_are_kind_of_stupid_and_dont_believe_in/.

545 Pesce, "Teen Vaccinated Himself Against Mom's Wishes."

546 Pesce, "Teen Vaccinated Himself Against Mom's Wishes."

547 Mary Ann Georgantopoulos, "An 18-Year-Old High School
Student Explained Why He Got Vaccinated Against His Mother's
Wishes In Testimony Before Congress," *BuzzFeed News*, March 5,
2019, https://www.buzzfeednews.com/article/
maryanngeorgantopoulos/teen-vaccinated-mother-anti-vaxxer.

548 Chempra McKee and Kristin Bohannon, "Exploring the Reasons
Behind Parental Refusal of Vaccines," *Journal of Pediatric
Pharmacology and Therapeutics* 21, No. 2 (March–April 2016):
104–109. doi: 10.5863/1551-6776-21.2.104

549 Pesce, "Teen Vaccinated Himself Against Mom's Wishes."

550 "Mr Bean Actor's Free Speech Video Goes Viral," *The Christian
Institute*, September 11, 2020, https://www.christian.org.uk/
news/mr-bean-actors-free-speech-video-goes-viral/.

551 Gerd Gigerenzer and Wolfgang Gaissmaier, "Heuristic Decision
Making," *Annual Review of Psychology* 62 (January 2011):451–
482. https://doi.org/10.1146/annurev-psych-120709-145346.

552 Amos Tversky and Daniel Kahneman, "Judgment Under
Uncertainty: Heuristics and Biases," *Science* 185, No. 4157
(September 27, 1974): 1124–1131.
DOI: 10.1126/science.185.4157.112.

553 John S. Hammond, Ralph L. Keeney, and Howard Raiffa, "The
Hidden Traps in Decision Making," *Harvard Business Review*
(September–October 1998). https://hbr.org/1998/09/
the-hidden-traps-in-decision-making-2.

554 Ibid.

555 Jay Richards, William Briggs, and Douglas Axe, "Stats Hold a Surprise: Lockdowns May Have Had Little Effect on COVID-19 Spread," *National Review*, October 4, 2020, https://www. nationalreview.com/2020/10/ stats-hold-a-surprise-lockdowns-may-have-had-little-effect-on-covid-19-spread/

556 "Scientific Consensus: Earth's Climate Is Warming," *NASA: Global Climate Change – Vital Signs of the Planet*, https://climate. nasa.gov/scientific-consensus/.

557 Anthony Leiserowitz, Edward Maibach, Seth Rosenthal, et al., "Climate Change in the American Mind," *Yale Program on Climate Change Communication*, December 17, 2019. https:// climatecommunication.yale.edu/publications/ climate-change-in-the-american-mind-november-2019/.

558 Sterling Burnett, "Climate Change 101: The Evidence Humans Aren't Destroying the Climate," *The Heartland Institute*, January 9, 2017, https://heartland.org/opinion/ climate-change-101-evidence-humans-arent-destroying-the-climate/

559 "More CO2 Than Ever Before In 3 Million Years, Shows Unprecedented Computer Simulation," Potsdam Institute for Climate Impact Research (PIK) March 4, 2019, https://www. pik-potsdam.de/en/news/latest-news/ more-co2-than-ever-before-in-3-million-years-shows-unprecedented-computer-simulation

560 "Evidence: How Do We Know Climate Change is Real?" *NASA: Global Climate Change – Vital Signs of the Planet*. https://climate. nasa.gov/evidence/.

561 David Coletto, "What Do Canadians Think About Climate Change and Climate Action?" *Abacus Data*, October 2021, https://abacusdata.ca/climate-change-cop26-canada/.

562 Ken Ham, *The Lie: Evolution* (Green Forest, AR: Master Books, 2008).

563 Lewis Kelly, "How to Check Your Unconscious Biases," *Folio | University of Alberta*, May 1, 2018, https://www.ualberta.ca/ folio/2018/05/how-to-check-your-unconscious-biases.html.

564 Kelly, "How to Check Your Unconscious Biases."

565 "Project Implicit," *Harvard University*, https://implicit.harvard. edu/implicit/.

566 "Bridging Perspectives, Unlocking Potential," *Intercultural Development Inventory*, 2023, https://idiinventory.com/.

567 Kelly, "Check Your Unconscious Biases."

568 Richard Feynman, "Richard Feynman's Caltech 1974 Commencement Speech" [blog post speech transcript], *Lanre Dahunsi* [blog], September 8, 2021, https://lanredahunsi.com/ richard-feynman-caltechs-1974-commencement-speech/

Chapter 4 – Well, Imagine That.

569 George Sylvester Viereck, "What Life Means to Einstein," *The Saturday Evening Post*, October 26, 1929, https://www.

saturdayeveningpost.com/wp-content/uploads/satevepost/
einstein.pdf.

570   Bill Gates. "The Best Teacher I Never Had," *YouTube*, January 27,
2016, https://www.youtube.com/watch?v=WOoJh6oYAXE

571   Richard Feynman, "The World From Another Point of view,"
YouTube, May 2, 2015, https://youtu.be/GNhlNSLQAFE?si=apA
wOTQ5INKdlB3Z.

572   Richard Feynman, "The Feynman Series: Think Like a Martian,"
YouTube, October 23, 2013, https://youtu.be/CJ8MzWncFfQ?si=
TImHXn3XK1vtNwoJ

573   Chris Hedges, *Empire of Illusion* (Toronto, ON: Vintage Canada,
2010): 101.

574   Hedges, *Empire of Illusion*.

575   "The Feynman Learning Technique," *Farnum Street (FS)*. https://
fs.blog/feynman-learning-technique/.

576   Nicole Alvino, "This is How to Fight Fake News at Work in a
Post-trust Era," *Fast Company*, August 12, 2019, https://www.
fastcompany.com/90387088/
this-is-how-to-fight-fake-news-at-work-in-a-post-trust-era.

577   Courtney G. Brooks, James M. Grimwood, and Lloyd S.
Swenson, Jr. *Chariots for Apollo: A History of Manned Lunar
Spacecraft* (Washington, DC: NASA SP-4205, 1979).
Excerpt: https://history.nasa.gov/Apollo204/chariot.html.

578   Terry Wilcutt and Tom Whitmeyer, "Apollo 1-Challenger-
Columbia Lessons Learned: Senior Management ViTW Meeting,
NASA, January 27, 2014, https://sma.nasa.gov/docs/default-
source/safety-messages/safetymessage-2014-01-27-
apollo1challengercolumbia-vits.pdf?sfvrsn=31af1ef8_6

579 Wilcutt and Whitmeyer, "Apollo 1-Challenger-Columbia Lessons Learned."

Chapter 5 – Embrace the Liar's Greatest Gift.

580 William Fear, The Critic Magazine, March 12, 2023, Orwell, Camus and truth https://thecritic.co.uk/orwell-camus-and-truth/

581 "Public Supports Both Early Voting And Requiring Photo ID to Vote," *Polling Institute | Monmouth University*, June 21, 2021, https://www.monmouth.edu/polling-institute/reports/ monmouthpoll_us_062121/.

582 Janet Adamy, "Changing U.S. Demographics Favor Democrats in Election, Report Says," *Wall Street Journal*, February 25, 2016, https://www.wsj.com/articles/ changing-u-s-demographics-favor-democrats-in-election-report- says-1456376460.

583 "1. Trends in party affiliation among demographic groups," *Pew Research Centre*, March 20, 2018, https://www.pewresearch.org/ politics/2018/03/20/1-trends-in-party-affiliation-among- demographic-groups/.

584 "1. Trends in party affiliation."

585 Jonathan Vespa, Lauren Medina, and David M. Armstrong, "Demographic Turning Points for the United States: Population Projections for 2020 to 2060," US Census Department, Revised February 2020. https://www.census.gov/content/dam/Census/ library/publications/2020/demo/p25-1144.pdf.

586 Subir Purkayastha, "Texas on the Cusp, March of Voter Suppression Laws in the US in 2021," *NewsClick*, July 22,

2021, https://www.newsclick.in/
Texas-Cusp-March-Voter-Suppression-Laws-US-2021.

[587] Adam Nagourney and Jeremy W. Peters, "How a Campaign Against Transgender Rights Mobilized Conservatives," *The New York Times*, April 17, 2023, https://www.nytimes.com/2023/04/16/us/politics/transgender-conservative-campaign.html.

[588] Nagourney and Peters, "How a Campaign Against Transgender Rights..."

[589] Kiara Alfonseca, "Map: Where Gender-Affirming Care is Being Targeted in the US," *ABC News*, April 20, 2023,https://abcnews.go.com/US/map-gender-affirming-care-targeted-us/story?id=97443087.

[590] Ivana Saric, "Trans Rights Largely Advance in Europe but Remain at Risk," *Axios*, May 17, 2023, https://www.axios.com/2023/05/17/trans-rights-europe-us.

[591] Concepion, "Marjorie Taylor Greene Defends Calling Democrats 'Pedophiles.'"

Chapter 6 – Beware the Liar's Two Greatest Powers.

[592] Goodreads.com, Quote by Malcolm Gladwell: "We have, as human beings, a storytelling proble..." (goodreads.com) https://www.goodreads.com/quotes/35767-we-have-as-human-beings-a-storytelling-problem-we-re-a#:~:text=

[593] *The Mindscape of Alan Moore*, directed by DeZ Vylenz, written by DeZ Vylenz (London, UK: Shadowsnake Films, 2003).

594 Patrick Delaney, "TIME admits 'conspiracy' of a 'cabal of powerful people' heavily influenced last election)," *LifeSite News*, February 9, 2021, https://www.lifesitenews.com/news/ time-admits-conspiracy-of-a-cabal-of-powerful-people-heavily-influenced-last-election/.

595 Delaney, "TIME admits 'conspiracy.'"

596 "Donald Trump: 'What you're seeing and what you're reading is not what's happening'" [video], *BBC News*, July 25, 2018, https:// www.bbc.com/news/av/world-us-canada-44959340.

597 Maura Zurick, "Trump Calls January 6 'A Beautiful Day,'" *Newsweek*, May 10, 2023, https://www.newsweek.com/ trump-calls-january-6-beautiful-day-1799574.

598 "Fox's Maria Bartiromo Refers to the January 6 Attack as a 'Peaceful Protest,'" *Media Matters For America*, July 11, 2021, https://www.mediamatters.org/maria-bartiromo/ foxs-maria-bartiromo-refers-january-6-attack-peaceful-protest.

599 Sites publishing this article included: Realverifiednews.com, American Gulag.org, thetruereporter.com. thewashingtoncountyauditor.com, sbynews.com, federalinquier. com, actforcanada.ca, and qanonnews.com.

Chapter 7 – A Tip Sheet for Self-defense.

600 F. Scott Fitzgerald, "Essay: The Crack-Up by F. Scott Fitzgerald" [excerpt], American Masters 16, Ep. 2 F. *Scott Fitzgerald: Winter Dreams* (August 31, 2005). https://www.pbs.org/wnet/ americanmasters/f-scott-fitzgerald-essay-the-crack-up/1028/.

601 Goodreads.com https://www.goodreads.com/ quotes/527034-the-worst-part-about-being-lied-to-is-knowing-you

602 Chris Cillizza, August 24, 2019, CNN Politics Yes, Donald Trump really believes he is 'the chosen one' https://www.cnn.com/2019/08/21/politics/donald-trump-chosen-one/index.html

603 "George Carlin – Euphemisms," *YouTube*, July 2, 2012, https://www.youtube.com/watch?v=isMm2vF4uFs.

604 André Pratte, "Under Legault, Quebec's separatists are winning by stealth," *National Post*, June 17, 2022, https://nationalpost.com/opinion/andre-pratte-under-legault-quebecs-separatists-are-winning-by-stealth.

Chapter 8 – From the Information Age to the Knowledge Age.

605 Essential CS Lewis (CCSLQ-17) Education Without Values –https://essentialcslewis.com/2016/01/09/ccslq-17-education-without-values/

606 "Ontario Preparing Students for Jobs of the Future" [news release], *Government of Ontario*, March 10, 2023, https://news.ontario.ca/en/release/1002810/ontario-preparing-students-for-jobs-of-the-future.

607 Justin Gamble, "New Report Finds Rise in Parental Rights Education Bills Has a 'Chilling Effect,'" *CNN*, August 24, 2023, https://www.cnn.com/2023/08/24/us/pen-america-parental-rights-bills-concern-reaj/index.html.

608 Maria Brand and Walter Brand, "Prussian Education Adopted by Horrace Mann," *GermanAmericanPioneers.org*, http://www.

germanamericanpioneers.org/
PrussianEducationadoptedbyHorraceMann.htm.

609 Ibid.

610 Corey A. DeAngelis and Angela Dills, "Let Mass Home Schooling Unleash Innovation," *Cato Institute*, May 21, 2020, https://www. cato.org/commentary/let-mass-home-schooling-unleash-innovation.

611 Joel Rose, "How to Break Free of Our 19th-Century Factory-Model Education System," *The Atlantic*, May 2, 2012, https:// www.theatlantic.com/business/archive/2012/05/how-to-break-free-of-our-19th-century-factory-model-education-system/256881/.

612 Wang Yong, "China's Patriotic Education: Schooling or Indoctrination?" *Bitter Winter*, July 12, 2021, https://bitterwinter. org/chinas-patriotic-education-schooling-or-indoctrination/.

613 Moriah Balingit and Laura Mecker, "Trump alleges 'left-wing indoctrination' in schools, says he will create national commission to push more 'pro-American' history," *The Washington Post*, September 18, 2020, https://www.washingtonpost.com/ education/trump-history-education/2020/09/17/f40535ec-ee2c-11ea-ab4e-581edb849379_story.html.

614 Lisa Hazeldine, "Putin is breeding a new generation of Russian militants," *The Telegraph*, August 20, 2023, https://www.msn. com/en-us/news/world/putin-is-breeding-a-new-generation-of-russian-militants/ar-AA1fwPa8.

615 Jonathan Zimmerman, "A Confederate Curriculum: How Miss Millie taught the Civil War," *Lapham's Quarterly*, November 6, 2017, https://www.laphamsquarterly.org/millie_rutherford.

616 Kenneth Neiymer, "DeSantis Says Black People Benefited From Skills Learned in Slavery," *Business Insider*, July 23, 2023, https://

www.businessinsider.com/desantis-says-black-people-benefited-from-skills-learned-in-slavery-2023-7.

[617] Jack Smith IV, March 23, 2023, Mic.com, Jordan Peterson is creating his own online university to destroy college "indoctrination cults" https://www.mic.com/articles/188569/jordan-peterson-is-creating-his-own-online-university-to-destroy-college-indoctrination-cults#:~:text=Peterson%20believes%20that%20these%20thoughts%20have%20lived%20on,departments%2C%20which%20he%20says%20have%20become%20%E2%80%9Cindoctrination%20cults.%E2%80%9D

[618] jordanbpeterson.com, Jordan Peterson's New Online University https://www.jordanbpeterson.com/podcast/jordan-petersons-new-online-university/

[619] Maxine Joselow, "Climate Deniers Ejected From Teachers Confab for Deceptive Comic," *The Washington Post*, April 11, 2023, https://www.washingtonpost.com/climate-environment/2023/04/11/co2-coalition-climate-denial/.

[620] "About AAC&U," American Association of Colleges and Universities, https://www.aacu.org/about.

[621] Carol Geary Schneider, "Keynote Address," *National Symposium on Assessment in the Humanities*, February 24, 2011. http://hdl.handle.net/2374.MIA/4508 Schneider Mp4 file

[622] Chris Hedges, *Empire of Illusion* (Toronto, ON: Vintage Canada, 2010): 103.

[623] Hedges, *Empire of Illusion*: 103.

[624] Hedges, *Empire of Illusion*: 103.

[625] Hedges, *Empire of Illusion*: 98

[626] Lady Gaga, "We need fantasy to survive because reality is too difficult," *AZ Quotes*, https://www.azquotes.com/quote/619148.

[627] Lynn Giesbrecht, "'A Lazy Thinking Problem:' [sic] U of R Professor Studying Why People Share Disinformation," *Regina Leader-Post*, July 12, 2020, https://leaderpost.com/news/local-news/a-lazy-thinking-problem-u-of-r-professor-studying-why-people-share-disinformation.

[628] Justin Gamble, "New Report Finds Rise in Parental Rights Education Bills Has a 'Chilling Effect,'" *CNN*, August 24, 2023, https://www.cnn.com/2023/08/24/us/pen-america-parental-rights-bills-concern-reaj/index.html.

Chapter 9 – The Star Wars Defense Initiative.

[629] Ana Lorena Fábrega, *The Leaning Game* (Hampshire, Great Britain, Harriman House, 2003): 5

[630] Jorge Costales, "28th Anniversary of Ronald Reagan Quoting C.S. Lewis," *2 Think Good*, March 8, 2011, https://2thinkgood.com/2011/03/08/28th-anniversary-of-ronald-reagan-quoting-cs-lewis/.

[631] "Strategic Defense Initiative (SID)," *Atomic Heritage Foundation*, July 18, 2018, https://ahf.nuclearmuseum.org/ahf/history/strategic-defense-initiative-sdi/.

[632] "Star Wars": How the Term Arose," *The New York Times*, September 25, 1985, https://www.nytimes.com/1985/09/25/world/star-wars-how-the-term-arose.html.

[633] George Lucas, "George Lucas: What Education Means to Me," *Edutopia: George Lucas Educational Foundation*, July 1, 2003, https://www.edutopia.org/foreword-george-lucas..

[634] John Kelly, "Director James Cameron Works with NASA on Future Mars Mission," *Space.com*, February 9, 2005, https://www.space.com/783-director-james-cameron-works-nasa-future-mars-mission.html.

[635] Amy Erin Borovoy, "Big Thinkers: Howard Gardner on Multiple Intelligences," *Edutopia: George Lucas Educational Foundation*, April 1, 2009,. https://www.edutopia.org/multiple-intelligences-howard-gardner-video.

[636] Borovoy, "Big Thinkers: Howard Gardner on Multiple Intelligences."

[637] Borovoy, "Big Thinkers: Howard Gardner on Multiple Intelligences."

[638] Jennifer Cutraro, "How Creativity Powers Science," *Science News Explores*, May 24, 2012, https://www.snexplores.org/article/how-creativity-powers-science.

Chapter 10 – The School Bus Proposition.

[639] Alan Maley and Tamas Kiss, *Creativity and English Language Teaching*, (Charles E. Merrill Publisher, 2018): 50.

[640] Tomas Chamorro-Premuzic, "Working With Creatives: A Short Guide For Everyone Else," *Fast Company*, October 20, 2017, https://www.fastcompany.com/40484057/creative-people-are-hard-to-work-with-heres-what-to-do-about-it.

[641] James C. Kaufman, "The Four C Model of Creativity," *Walden University*. https://www.waldenu.edu/online-masters-programs/ms-in-education/resource/the-four-c-model-of-creativity.

[642] Robina Shaheen, "Creativity and Education," *Creative Education* 1, No. 3: 166–169. https://doi.org/10.4236/ce.2010.13026.

[643] Shaheen, "Creativity and Education."

644 Shaheen, "Creativity and Education."

645 Shaheen, "Creativity and Education."

646 A. Maley, T. Kiss, *Creativity and English Language Teaching*, 2018, Chapter 3 page 62

647 James C. Kaufman and Robert J. Sternberg, eds., *The Cambridge Handbook of Creativity* (Cambridge, UK: Cambridge University Press, 2010): 252. https://doi.org/10.1017/CBO9780511763205.

648 Kaufman and Sternberg *The Cambridge Handbook of Creativity*.

649 Tomas Chamorro-Premuzic, "The Dark Side of Creativity," *Harvard Business Review*, November 25, 2015, https://hbr.org/2015/11/the-dark-side-of-creativity.

F. Gino & D. Ariely. "The Dark Side of Creativity: Original Thinkers Can Be More Dishonest," *Journal of Personality and Social Psychology* 102, No. 3(2012), 445–459. https://doi.org/10.1037/a0026406

650 Edward de Bono, *The Use of Lateral Thinking* (New York, NY: Penguin Books, 1967).

Chapter 11 - Bus Drivers Needed.

651 Anthony Pratkanis, *Good Propaganda or Propaganda for Good*, published in *Propaganda and American Democracy*, edited by Nancy Snow, Louisiana State University Press, 2014, p. 37

652 "Homeschooling Statistics in 2023 (Latest U.S. Data)," *Parenting Mode*, October 2, 2023,https://parentingmode.com/homeschooling/.

653 Joseph Woodard, "Growth in the Homeschooled Population," *Canadian Centre for Home Education (CCHE)*, https://cche.ca/growth-in-the-homeschooled-population/.

654 Emma Brown and Peter Jamison, "Christian Home-schooler Michael Farris Made Parental Rights a GOP Issue," *The Washington Post*, August 29, 2023, https://www.washingtonpost.com/education/2023/08/29/michael-farris-homeschoolers-parents-rights-ziklag/.

655 Brown and Jamison, "Christian Home-schooler Made Parental Rights a GOP Issue."

656 Brown and Jamison, "Christian Home-schooler Made Parental Rights a GOP Issue."

657 Brown and Jamison, "Christian Home-schooler Made Parental Rights a GOP Issue."

Chapter 13 – Ich bin ein Berliner (I am a Berliner)

658 Farhaan Ladhani, "Keynote Address," *Meeting of the National Security Transparency Advisory Group (NS-TAG)*, January 26, 2022, https://www.canada.ca/en/services/defence/nationalsecurity/national-security-transparency-commitment/national-security-transparency-advisory-group/summary-report-meeting-january-2022.html.

659 "June 25, 1963: 'Ich bin ein Berliner' Speech," *Presidential Speeches | John F. Kennedy Presidency*, https://millercenter.org/the-presidency/presidential-speeches/june-26-1963-ich-bin-ein-berliner-speech.

660 "Budget 2023: A Made-In-Canada Plan," *Government of Canada*, 2023, https://www.budget.canada.ca/2023/pdf/budget-gdql-egdqv-2023-en.pdf.

661 "Canadians Don't Understand Political System: Survey," *CTV News*, December 14, 2008, https://www.ctvnews.ca/canadians-don-t-understand-political-system-survey-1.351539.

662 "Canadians Don't Understand Political System."

663 "Canadians Don't Understand Political System."

664 "New Annenberg Survey Asks: 'How Well Do Americans Understand the Constitution?'" *Annenberg Public Policy Center, University of Pennsylvania*, September 16, 2011, https://www.annenbergpublicpolicycenter.org/new-annenberg-survey-asks-how-well-do-americans-understand-the-constitution/.

665 "'How Well Do Americans Understand the Constitution?'"

666 "Civics and Citizenship" (revised 2022), *Ministry of Education, Government of Ontario*, https://www.dcp.edu.gov.on.ca/en/curriculum/canadian-and-world-studies/courses/chv2o. Note this course includes learning on the mechanisms of government, Indigenous governance systems and structures, the historical foundations of the rights and freedoms we enjoy in Canada, ways in which government policy affects individuals' lives and the economy, and ways for students to serve their communities.

667 Dan Myers, "Has McDonald's Really Sold 'Billions and Billions' of Burgers?" *Yahoo! Life*, May 20, 2016, https://www.yahoo.com/lifestyle/mcdonald-really-sold-billions-billions-201626926.html.

668 "Feynman Learning Technique."

669 Geoff Zochodne, "Majority of New Hydro One board Will Go To Major Shareholders," *Financial Post*, July 12, 2018, https://

financialpost.com/news/fp-street/
majority-of-new-hydro-one-board-will-go-to-major-shareholders.

670 Patrick White, "Why Pope Francis faces calls to revoke the
     Doctrine of Discovery," *The Globe and Mail*, July 22,
     2022, https://www.theglobeandmail.com/canada/
     article-pope-visit-doctrine-of-discovery/.

671 "Joint Statement of the Dicasteries for Culture and Education
     and for Promoting Integral Human Development on the
     'Doctrine of Discovery,'" *The Vatican*, March 3, 2023, https://
     press.vatican.va/content/salastampa/en/bollettino/
     pubblico/2023/03/30/230330b.html.

672 "Joint Statement of the Dicasteries for Culture and Education."

673 "Joint Statement of the Dicasteries for Culture and Education."

674 James Conca, "Finland Breaks Ground On World's First Deep
     Geologic Nuclear Waste Repository," *Forbes*, May 31,
     2021, https://www.forbes.com/sites/jamesconca/2021/05/31/
     finland-breaks-ground-on-its-deep-geologic-nuclear-waste-
     repository/?sh=16c81776103f.

675 Laurie Swami, "NWMO response to the Globe and Mail,"
     Township of Ignace, March 2021, https://www.ignace.ca/images/
     NWMO_Respond_to_Globe_and_Mail_Article.pdf.

676 Swami, "NWMO response to the Globe and Mail."

677 *Merriam-Webster*, s.v. "best practice," https://www.merriam-
     webster.com/dictionary/best%20practice

678 Goodreads.com Quote by Albert Einstein: "Learn from yesterday,
     live for today and hope f..."https://www.goodreads.com/
     quotes/9093409-learn-from-yesterday-live-for-today-and-hope-
     for-tomorrow